5th Workshop on South and Southeast Asian NLP

(WSSANLP 2014)

AA005270

Held at COLING 2014

Dublin, Ireland
23 August 2014

ISBN: 978-1-63439-223-5

Printed from e-media with permission by:

Curran Associates, Inc.
57 Morehouse Lane
Red Hook, NY 12571

Some format issues inherent in the e-media version may also appear in this print version.

Printed by Curran Associates, Inc. (2014)

For permission requests, please contact the Association for Computational Linguistics at the address below.

Association for Computational Linguistics
209 N. Eighth Street
Stroudsburg, Pennsylvania 18360

Phone: 1-570-476-8006
Fax: 1-570-476-0860

acl@aclweb.org

Additional copies of this publication are available from:

Curran Associates, Inc.
57 Morehouse Lane
Red Hook, NY 12571 USA
Phone: 845-758-0400
Fax: 845-758-2634
Email: curran@proceedings.com
Web: www.proceedings.com

Preface

Welcome to the 5th Workshop on South and Southeast Asian Natural Language Processing (WSSANLP - 2014), a collocated event at the 25th International Conference on Computational Linguistics (COLING 2014) , 23 - 29 August, 2014.

South and Southeast Asia comprise of the countries, Afghanistan, Bangladesh, Bhutan, India, Maldives, Nepal, Pakistan and Sri Lanka. Southeast Asia, on the other hand, consists of Brunei, Burma, Cambodia, East Timor, Indonesia, Laos, Malaysia, Philippines, Singapore, Thailand and Vietnam.

This area is the home to thousands of languages that belong to different language families like Indo-Aryan, Indo-Iranian, Dravidian, Sino-Tibetan, Austro-Asiatic, Kradai, Hmong-Mien, etc. In terms of population, South Asian and Southeast Asia represent 35 percent of the total population of the world which means as much as 2.5 billion speakers. Some of the languages of these regions have a large number of native speakers: Hindi (5th largest according to number of its native speakers), Bengali (6th), Punjabi (12th), Tamil(18th), Urdu (20th), etc.

As internet and electronic devices including PCs and hand held devices including mobile phones have spread far and wide in the region, it has become imperative to develop language technology for these languages. It is important for economic development as well as for social and individual progress.

A characteristic of these languages is that they are under-resourced. The words of these languages show rich variations in morphology. Moreover they are often heavily agglutinated and synthetic, making segmentation an important issue. The intellectual motivation for this workshop comes from the need to explore ways of harnessing the morphology of these languages for higher level processing. The task of morphology, however, in South and Southeast Asian Languages is intimately linked with segmentation for these languages.

The goal of WSSANLP is:

• Providing a platform to linguistic and NLP communities for sharing and discussing ideas and work on South and Southeast Asian languages and combining efforts.
• Development of useful and high quality computational resources for under resourced South and Southeast Asian languages.

We are delighted to present to you this volume of proceedings of the 5th Workshop on South and Southeast Asian Natural Language Processing. We have received total 18 submission in the categories of long paper and short paper. On the basis of our review process, we have competitively selected 7 long (regular) papers for oral presentations and 7 short papers for poster presentations.

We look forward to an invigorating workshop.

Christian Boitet (Chair WSSANLP-2014),
University of Grenoble I, France

M.G. Abbas Malik (Co-Chair WSSANLP-2014),
Faculty of Computing and Information Technology (North Jeddah Branch),
King Abdulaziz University, Saudi Arabia

The Fifth Workshop on South and Southeast Asian Natural Language processing WSSANLP-2014

WSSANLP Organizers

Workshop Chair

Christian Boitet, University of Grenoble I, France

Workshop Co-Chairs

M. G. Abbas Malik, King Abdulaziz University, Saudi Arabia

Organizing Committee

Amitava Das, University of North Texas, USA

Sadaf Abdul Rauf, Fatima Jinnah Women University, Pakistan

WSSANLP Invited Speaker

Vincent Berment, INaLCO, Paris, France (Lecturer)
LIG/GÉTALP, Grenoble, France (Associated Researcher)
Taranis Software, Paris, France (Director)

Program Committee

Sadaf Abdul Rauf, Fatima Jinnah Women University, Pakistan
Naveed Afzal, King Abdulaziz University, Saudi Arabia
Aasim Ali, University of the Punjab, Pakistan
M. Waqas Anwar, COMSATS Institute of Information Technology, Pakistan
Bal Krishna Bal, Kathmandu University, Nepal
Sivaji Bandyopadhyay, Jadavpur University, India
Vincent Berment, GETALP-LIG / INALCO, France
Laurent Besacier, GETALP-LIG, Université de Grenoble, France
Pushpak Bhattacharyya, IIT Bombay, India
Hervé Blanchon, GETALP-LIG, Université de Grenoble, France
Christian Boitet, GETALP-LIG, Université de Grenoble, France
Erik Cambria, National University of Singapore, Singapore
Eric Castelli, International Research Center MICA, Vietnam
Sandipan Dandapat, IIT Guwahati, India
Amitava Das, University of North Texas, USA
Alexander Gelbukh, Center for Computing Research, CIC, Mexico
Choochart Haruechaiyasak, NECTEC, Thailand
Sarmad Hussain, Al-Khawarizmi Institute of Computer Science, University of Engineering and

Technology, Pakistan
Aravind K. Joshi, University of Pennsylvania, USA
Abid Khan, University of Peshawar, Pakistan
Malhar Kulkarni, Indian Institute of Technology Bombay, India
Amba Kulkarni, Department of Sanskrit Studies, University of Hyderabad, India
A. Kumaran, Microsoft Research, India
Gurpreet Singh Lehal, Punjabi University, Patiala, India
M. G. Abbas Malik, King Abdulaziz University, Saudi Arabia
Bali Ranaivo-Malançon, University Malaysia Sarawak, Malaysia
Fuji Ren, University of Tokushima, Japan
Hammam Riza, Agency for the Assessment and Application of Technology (BPPT), Indonesia
Paolo Rosso, Universitat Politècnica de València, Spain
Huda Sarfraz, Beacon house National University, Pakistan
Dipti Mishra Sharma, IIIT Hyderabad, India
Sunil Sivadas, Institute for Infocomm Research, Singapore
L. Sobha, AU-KBC Research Centre, India
Virach Sornlertlamvanich, TCL, National Institute of Information and Communication Technology, Thailand
Sriram Venkatapathy, Xerox Research Center Europe, France
Eric Wehrli, University of Geneva, Switzerland

Table of Contents

WSSANLP 2014 Program

Saturday August 23, 2014

(8:45 - 9:00) Openning Session

(9:00 - 10:15) Invited Talk

\+ by Vincent Berment

(10:15 - 10:45) Coffee Break

Session Regular Papers 1: (10:45 - 12:30) WSSANLP Session 1

10:45 *Towards Identifying Hindi/Urdu Noun Templates in Support of a Large-Scale LFG Grammar*
Sebastian Sulger and Ashwini Vaidya

11:10 *Konkanverter - A Finite State Transducer based Statistical Machine Transliteration Engine for Konkani Language*
Vinodh Rajan

11:35 *Integrating Dictionaries into an Unsupervised Model for Myanmar Word Segmentation*
Ye Kyaw Thu, Andrew Finch, Eichiro SUMITA and Yoshinori Sagisaka

12:00 *A Framework for Learning Morphology using Suffix Association Matrix*
Shilpa Desai, Jyoti Pawar and Pushpak Bhattacharyya

(12:30 - 14:00) Lunch break

Saturday August 23, 2014 (continued)

(17:00 - 17:15) Closing Remarks

Towards Identifying Hindi/Urdu Noun Templates in Support of a Large-Scale LFG Grammar

Sebastian Sulger
Department of Linguistics
University of Konstanz
Germany
sebastian.sulger@uni-konstanz.de

Ashwini Vaidya
University of Colorado
Boulder, CO
80309 USA
vaidyaa@colorado.edu

Abstract

Complex predicates (CPs) are a highly productive predicational phenomenon in Hindi and Urdu and present a challenge for deep syntactic parsing. For CPs, a combination of a noun and light verb express a single event. The combinatorial preferences of nouns with one (or more) light verb is useful for predicting an instance of a CP. In this paper, we present a semi-automatic method to obtain noun groups based on their co-occurrences with light verbs. These noun groups represent the likelihood of a particular noun-verb combination in a large corpus. Finally, in order to encode this in an LFG grammar, we propose linking nouns with templates that describe preferable combinations with light verbs.

1 Introduction

A problem that crops up repeatedly in shallow and deep syntactic parsing approaches to South Asian languages like Urdu and Hindi[1] is the proper treatment of complex predicates (CPs). In CPs, combinations of more than one element are used to express an event (e.g., *memory* + *do* = *remember*). In Urdu/Hindi, only about 700 simple verbs exist (Humayoun, 2006); the remaining verbal inventory consists of CPs. CPs are encountered frequently in general language use, as well as in newspaper corpora. Thus, any NLP application, whether shallow or deep, whether its goal be parsing, generation, question-answering or the construction of lexical resources like WordNet (Bhattacharyya, 2010) encounters CPs sooner rather than later.

There is a range of different elements that may combine with verbs to form a CP: verbs, nouns, prepositions, adjectives all occur in CPs. The constraints and productive mechanisms in verb-verb CPs are comparatively well-understood (e.g, see Hook (1974), Butt (1995), Butt (2010) and references therein). The domain of noun-verb CPs (N-V CPs) is less well understood, the standard theoretical reference being Mohanan (1994). It is only recently that researchers have tried to come up with linguistic generalizations regarding N-V CPs, some by using manual methods and linguistic introspection (Ahmed and Butt, 2011), others using a combination of manual and statistical methods (Butt et al., 2012).

Ahmed and Butt (2011) have suggested that the combinatory possibilities of N-V combinations are in part governed by the lexical semantic compatibility of the noun with the verb. Similar observations have been made for English (Barrett and Davis, 2003; North, 2005). If this is true, then lexical resources such as WordNet could be augmented with semantic specifications or feature information that can then be used to determine dynamically whether a given N-V combination is licit or not.

Knowledge about this kind of lexical-semantic information is essential in computational grammars. For example,lexicon entries and templates are required to define predicational classes. Implementing such a grammar for a language that makes heavy use of CPs calls for two requirements. First, the lexical items taking part in CP formation need to be present in the lexicon of the grammar; and second, the grammar needs to be engineered in a way that represents the correct linguistic generalizations. Any ap-

[1]Urdu is an Indo-Aryan language spoken primarily in Pakistan and parts of India, as well as in the South Asian diaspora. It is structurally almost identical to Hindi, although the lexicon and orthography differs considerably.

Proceedings of the 5th Workshop on South and Southeast Asian NLP, 25th International Conference on Computational Linguistics, pages 1–10,
Dublin, Ireland, August 23-29 2014.

proach that is short of either of these requirements will result either in loss in coverage or overgeneration of the grammar.

The Hindi/Urdu ParGram Grammar forms part of a larger international research effort, the ParGram (Parallel Grammars) project (Butt et al., 1999; Butt et al., 2002; Butt and King, 2007). All of the grammars in the ParGram project are couched within the LFG framework and are implemented using the development platform XLE (Crouch et al., 2012). The grammars are developed manually and not via learning methods, which allows for a theoretically sound analysis that is also efficient from a computational point of view. The Hindi/Urdu ParGram Grammar aims at covering both Hindi and Urdu, which is a design decision that suggests itself due to the many structural conformities of the two languages (Butt et al., 2002). One weakness of the grammar is its currently relatively small lexicon, compared to other ParGram grammars. Adding to the lexicon is a critical step in extending the grammar coverage. This is even more true for N-V CPs due to the high frequency of such constructions in running text. Thus, we see the Hindi/Urdu ParGram Grammar as an ideal test bed for developing a lexical resource of Hindi nouns.

This paper is a first step in terms of constructing such a lexical resource for Hindi nouns. Following up on previous work, we assume that there are distinct groups of nouns; nouns that are part of a certain group tend to co-occur with the same light verb(s) and differ in their usage from members of other groups. Contrary to what has been done before, though, we do not dive into available corpora blindly to identify the groupings. Instead, we make use of a manually annotated treebank for Hindi, the Hindi and Urdu Treebank (HUTB, Bhatt et al. (2009)). Thus, we construct a *seed list* of nouns known to partake in CP formation in the HUTB. Since the HUTB is limited in its coverage, we then turn to a large Hindi corpus collected specifically for the present study and use clustering algorithms to put the nouns in the seed list into groups, based on light verb co-occurrence.[2]

Our aim is to arrive at a broad notion of noun similarity. If we can find groups of nouns that behave alike with respect to their light verbs, these groups can be included in an application such as the Hindi/Urdu ParGram Grammar to boost coverage as well as precision. Note that this notion of noun similarity is not the same as semantic classes in the sense of Levin (1993); however, it can serve as input for future research into semantic noun classification.

2 N-V Complex Predicates in Hindi and Urdu

As mentioned above, CPs are an important means of forming verbal predication in Hindi and Urdu. There is no single way of forming CPs; it is possible to find V-V CPs (Butt, 1995), ADJ-V combinations, P-V CPs (Raza, 2011) and N-V CPs (Mohanan, 1994) (see Ahmed et al. (2012) for some examples of each CP type.). In the present paper, we focus on identifying patterns of N-V CP formation. Here, the noun contributes the main predicational content. The verb in such constructions is usually called a light verb (Mohanan, 1994; Butt, 2003). The term represents the fact that these verbs are semantically bleached and specify additional information about the predication, such as whether the predicate has an agentive, telic or stative flavor. The light verb also determines the case marking on the subject, controls agreement patterns and contributes tense and aspect information. This is illustrated in (1).

(1) a. nadya=ne kɑhani yad k-i
Nadya.F.Sg=Erg story.F.Sg memory.F.Sg do-Perf.F.Sg
'Nadya remembered a/the story (agentively).' (lit. 'Nadya did memory of a/the story.')

b. nadya=ko kɑhani yad hɛ
Nadya.F.Sg=Dat story.F.Sg memory.F.Sg be.Pres.3.Sg
'Nadya remembers/knows a/the story.' (lit. 'At Nadya is memory of a/the story.')

[2] Note that despite the many structural conformities between Hindi and Urdu, the main difference between the two languages is in the lexicon; Modern Standard Hindi vocabulary is based on Sanskrit, while Urdu draws from a Persio-Arabic lexicon. This means that in principle, the methodology presented in this paper applied to Hindi needs to be applied to both languages separately. The equivalent Urdu study is pending future work and currently faces two major obstacles. First, the Urdu portion of the HUTB has not yet been released. Second, there is a major shortage of Urdu resources, with comparatively small corpora becoming available only recently (Urooj et al., 2012). Readily available Urdu sources (e.g., Wikipedia) are of minor quality.

c. nadya=ko kahani yad a-yi
Nadya.F.Sg=Dat story.F.Sg memory.F.Sg come-Perf.F.Sg
'Nadya remembered a/the story.' (lit. 'The memory of a/the story came to Nadya.')

In all of the examples in (1), it is evident that the noun and the verb form a single predicational element. The object *kahani* 'story' is thematically licensed by the noun *yad* 'memory', but it is not realized as a genitive, as would be typical for arguments of nouns (and as in the English literal translations). Rather, *kahani* 'story' functions as the syntactic object of the joint predication (see Mohanan (1994) for details on the argument structure and agreement patterns).

3 Previous Work

A recent study on the semantic classes of Persian N-V CPs using distributional vector-space methods has shown that verb vectors are a very useful indicator of noun similarity (Taslimipoor et al., 2012). The reported results are significantly better using the light verb dimension; Taslimipoor et al. (2012) state that this affirms their original intuition that a verb-based vector space model can better capture similarities across CPs. This finding is in agreement with our intuition that features based on light verbs best capture generalizations about N-V CPs.

There have been two studies on noun similarity based on co-occurrence of noun and light verb. Ahmed and Butt (2011) look at the light verbs *kar* 'do', *ho* 'be', *hu-* 'become' and identify three classes of nouns based on co-occurrence patters. The first consists of psychological nouns that occur with all three light verbs. The examples shown in (1) represent the class that is compatible with all of the light verbs surveyed. Other CP classes may only be compatible with a subset of light verbs. The second and third classes consist of nouns that are classified as more or less agentive in nature- based on their capacity to form CPs with *hu-* 'become'. For example, the noun *tamir* 'construction' is only compatible with the light verb *kar* 'do' but disallows *hu-* 'become'.

(2) a. bılal=ne makan tamir kı-ya
Bilal.M.Sg=Erg house.M.Sg construction.F.Sg do-Perf.M.Sg
'Bilal built a/the house.'

b. *bılal=ko makan tamir hɛ/hu-a
Bilal.M.Sg=Dat house.M.Sg construction.F.Sg be.Pres.3.Sg/be.Part-Perf.M.Sg
'Bilal built a/the house.'

In a follow-up study, Butt et al. (2012) attempted to identify Urdu N-V CPs automatically. After filtering out the irrelevant combinations, they found that most nouns were either psychological nouns (and occurred with all three light verbs) or nouns that were highly agentive and disallowed *hu-* 'become'. However, one of the drawbacks of their method was the use of an untagged corpus, which required extensive filtering in order to separate the light and non-light instances of these verbs.

We will draw upon the results of these two studies to motivate this present work. The classes identified by Ahmed and Butt (2011) seem promising, but the corpus work was done manually, and the total size of their data set is limited to 45 nouns. This can hardly serve as input to the development of a large-scale noun lexicon for a grammar. In constructing a lexical resource, we thus take a different route in that we try to expand the search space by using an external, manually-crafted resource and a larger set of light verbs to come up with more substantial noun groups.[3] In addition, we circumvent the problems faced in Butt et al. (2012)'s paper by filtering the list of nominal predicates in advance and by making use of a tagged corpus.

[3]One might argue that there are other features, beyond the light verbs, that one could use in identifying noun classes/groups, e.g., additional arguments licensed, case marking, etc. The reason why we (and other researchers before us) limit ourselves to the light verb occurrences is that Hindi and Urdu make rampant use of pro-drop (Kachru, 2006; Schmidt, 1999; Mohanan, 1994), which means that often, not all arguments are present in a sentence. Thus, the only reliable source of information about the noun is in fact the light verb, since this is the only obligatory element aside from the noun itself.

4 Methodology

In order to build a lexical resource of semantically similar nouns, we first need to identify whether these occur as part of a N-V CP. As we want to improve upon previous work, our aim was to include a large number of nouns. The Hindi portion of the Hindi and Urdu Treebank (Bhatt et al., 2009) includes N-V CPs that have been manually tagged with the dependency label POF (which stands for "part of"). The diagnostic criteria used for identifying CPs in the treebank is based on native speaker intuition. The POF label is used for adjectives and adverbs as well as nouns. We extracted only POF cases that were nouns only. This gave us an initial list of candidate nouns that were further filtered for spelling variations and annotation errors. After this stage, we had a list of 1207 nouns, which we will refer to as our *seed list*. The seed list consists of nouns that are a part of N-V CPs in the treebank.

Our aim was to include nouns that had at least 50 or more occurrences in order to ensure that we were looking at the most well-attested noun and light verb co-occurrences. For this task, the Hindi Treebank corpus (400,000 words) by itself would not be sufficient. For instance, if we applied our cutoff of 50 occurrences to the instances in the treebank, we would be left with only 20 nouns, which would not give us any meaningful groups. Therefore, we chose to use a larger corpus (including the treebank) in order to give us co-occurrence patterns for a noun from the seedlist. At the same time, we did not look at co-occurrence patterns with *any* verb. Instead, we chose a list of the most frequent light verbs from the treebank. This list is given below:

(3) *ho* 'be', *kar* 'do', *de* 'give', *le* 'take', *rakh* 'put', *lag* 'attach', *a* 'come'

Given the seed list and a short list of light verbs, our next step was the extraction of co-occurrences from a larger corpus.

4.1 Extracting Co-occurrences from a Large Corpus

In order to obtain a larger corpus, we scraped two large online sources of Hindi: the BBC Hindi website[4] as well as the Hindi Wikipedia.[5] Along with the Hindi Treebank, this corpus contains about 21 million tokens (BBC Hindi: $\sim$7 million, Hindi Wikipedia: $\sim$10 million, Hindi Treebank $\sim$4 million); by including the Wikipedia part, the resulting corpus extends beyond the newspaper domain. In a second step, the corpus was automatically POS tagged using the tagger described in Reddy and Sharoff (2011).

We were interested in extracting co-occurrences that had the following pattern: *seed list item + light verb*. A match would only occur if one of the light verbs occurred directly to the right of the noun (i.e., an item tagged as NN by the POS tagger). Our method therefore did not take into account any N-V CPs that were syntactically flexible, i.e., when the noun and the light verb did not occur next to each other. Those cases where the noun may be scrambled away from the light verb (e.g., topicalization of the noun) are not numerous and occur rarely in the Hindi Treebank (only about 1% of the time).[6]

4.2 Clustering & Evaluation

In the next step, a clustering algorithm was applied to the data. This was done using the clustering tool described in Lamprecht et al. (2013). At the moment, the tool features two clustering algorithms: the k-means algorithm (MacQueen, 1967) as well as the Greedy Variance Minimization (GVM) algorithm.[7] We made use of an automatic method using Hindi WordNet (Bhattacharyya, 2010) to choose the best partition value. We followed the technique described in Van de Cruys (2006), which uses WordNet relations to arrive at the most semantically coherent clusters. We define semantic coherence as the similarity between items in a cluster, based on an overlap between their WordNet relations. Specifically, for each $k = 2-10$, we iterated through the automatically generated clusters and performed the following steps:

1. Using WordNet, we extracted synonyms, hypernyms and hyponyms for every word in a cluster.

[4] http://www.bbc.co.uk/hindi

[5] http://dumps.wikimedia.org/hiwiki

[6] Mohanan (1994) even goes so far as to call the topicalization of nouns in N-V CPs ungrammatical.

[7] http://code.google.com/p/tomgibara/

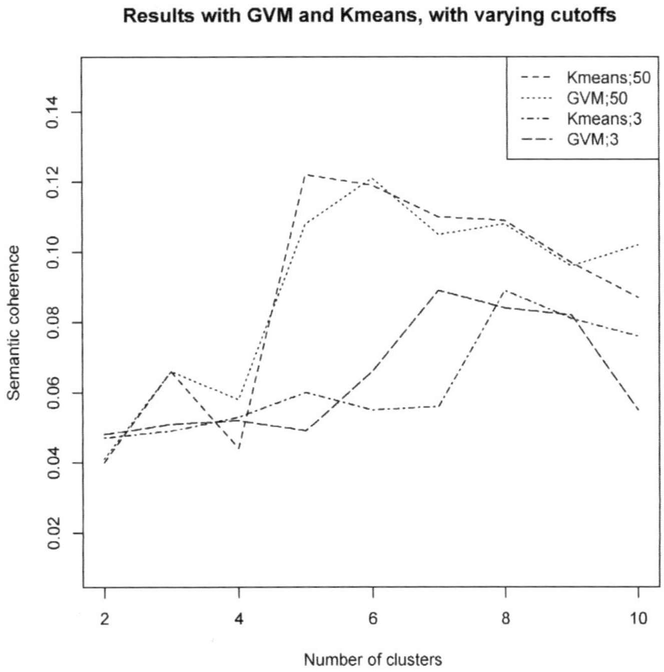

Figure 1: Choosing the best value for k. k-means with a frequency cutoff of 50 gives us the most semantically coherent clusters for $k = 5$

2. A word that had the most semantic relations with every word in the cluster was chosen as its centroid.
3. The co-hyponyms i.e., the hyponyms of the hypernyms for this centroid were extracted from WordNet (along with its synonyms, hypernyms and hyponyms).
4. In order to calculate precision for each cluster, we counted the number of words in that cluster that overlapped with the words in the centroid's relations.

We averaged the precision across all clusters for every k value. We found that precision for each cluster gradually improved until we got the most semantically coherent partitions for $k = 5$ using k-means, for 522 nouns occurring with a frequency of 50 and above. Table 1 shows the values for k using our WordNet evaluation method, for $k = 5 - 9$.

	Frequency = 3		**Frequency = 50**	
Size of k	**GVM**	**k-means**	**GVM**	**k-means**
5	0.049	0.060	0.107	0.122
6	0.066	0.055	0.121	0.119
7	0.089	0.056	0.104	0.110
8	0.084	0.089	0.108	0.109
9	0.082	0.081	0.095	0.097

Table 1: Semantic coherence values for $k = 5 - 9$ for clustering algorithms GVM and k-means

In Figure 1, we have plotted the semantic coherence values against the number of clusters to show the best results. The k-means algorithm performed only slightly better than GVM, and after $k = 5$, the semantic coherence of the clusters declined again. As a point of comparison, we also plotted k-means and GVM results for nouns that occurred more than 3 times in the data (i.e., using a far smaller cutoff). In this configuration, the best results are achieved for a higher k value (i.e., between 7 or 8), but we rejected this on the basis of a better semantic coherence value for k-means with a cutoff of 50.

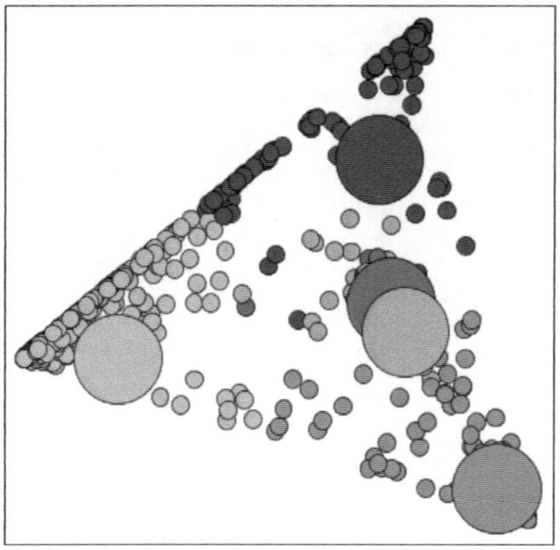

Figure 2: Visualization for $k = 5$ clusters

5 Analysis

Lamprecht et al. (2013)'s tool is useful for visual cluster inspection; e.g., the tool created the visual clustering in Figure 2 using the k-means algorithm with $k = 5$. The visualization enables the user to inspect the data points and derive initial generalizations. For example, Figure 2 shows a visualization with colored circles that encode membership within a cluster. The larger circles represent cluster centroids. The visualization enables us to see three most frequently occurring light verbs, viz. *kar* 'do', *ho* 'be' and *de* 'give', represented by light green, dark blue and pink respectively. Many nouns alternate with 'do' and 'be', hence there is a visible continuum between the light green and dark blue data points. The two clusters in the centre show a dark green cluster, consisting of only a handful of nouns that alternate with the light verbs *rakh* 'keep', *lag* 'attach' and *a* 'come'. The light blue cluster on the other hand is larger and is dominated by the light verb *le* 'take'.

In order to further interpret the results of our study, we also referred to a secondary result from our WordNet evaluation. While extracting the extent of overlap of the semantic relations, we also extracted the 'semantic' centroids i.e. words that had the most semantic relations with every other word in the cluster (see Section 4.2). For our best result of $k = 5$, these centroids also revealed semantic similarities in the five clusters that we found. For instance, dynamic events that are inanimate and abstract and take an agentive argument will lend themselves to combinations with *kar* 'do'. Similarly, events that include the semantic property of 'transfer' will occur with *de* 'give' (although there is ostensibly an overlap here, as these events invariably also require agentive arguments). The light verb *ho* 'be' occurs often with nouns that denote mental states, resulting in an experiencer subject — but this group also includes nouns that alternate with *kar*. Less frequently occurring light verbs, especially *rakh* 'keep', *lag* 'to attach' and *a* 'come' show fewer alternations, as they do not occur in combination with all nouns and are grouped together in this result. These light verbs often form N-V CPs with a more idiosyncratic meaning, in fact Davison (2005) has argued that some of these light verbs may form 'incorporation idioms' (rather than true N-V CPs).

The average figures of N-V CP co-occurrences for a certain cluster inform us about the likelihood of a certain group of nouns to co-occur with a certain light verb. For instance, this noun grouping shows a high likelihood of occurrence with *kar* 'do' and *le* 'take', but not very likely at all with *lag* 'attach'. We take this distribution to reflect a difference in the syntactic behavior of the nouns: While the productive patterns indicate CP formation, the less productive patterns do not represent CPs at all. This is a finding in line with Butt et al. (2012), who ended up deleting many low-frequency patterns which turned out to be non-CP combinations. Similar tendencies can be derived for the five groups of nouns derived from our clustering experiment above. This information is useful for a task like lexicon development for a computational grammar. The following section therefore explores the possibility of encoding noun group information in a computational Lexical Functional Grammar.

6 Noun Groups in Hindi/Urdu Grammar Development

Our experiments show that nouns appear with several different distributions, often with one dominant light verb, but also with the possibility of occurring with one or two other light verbs. The clusters do not represent absolute certainties about N-V CPs, but report *tendencies* of occurrences; e.g., the relative frequencies of the cluster centroid for the noun group dominated by *de* 'give' is shown below.

(4) *de* 'give' 0.75, *kar* 'do' 0.08, *le* 'take' 0.06, *ho* 'be' 0.06, *a* 'come' 0.02, *rakh* 'keep' 0.02, *lag* 'attach' 0.01

In this section, we discuss the integration of our Hindi noun groupings into the grammar via the construction of templates that can be augmented to model the relevant linguistic generalizations in terms of constraints inspired by optimality theory (OT, Prince and Smolensky (2004)). A serious evaluation of the effect on the grammar of adding in this lexical resource is planned for future work.

6.1 Templates in XLE

In XLE, grammar writers can define templates in a special section of the grammar that can be called from the lexicon. Templates allow generalizations to be captured and, if necessary, changes to be made only once, namely to the template itself (Butt et al., 1999; Dalrymple et al., 2004). Consider the template in (5), which models intransitive verbs in English; these are represented in LFG terms as predicates that apply to a single grammatical function, a subject. The lexical entry in (6) for the English intransitive verb *laugh* calls up the `INTRANS` template; the argument supplied to the template is substituted for the `P`(redicate) value inside the template definition.

(5)
```
INTRANS(P) = (^ PRED) = '_P<(^ SUBJ)>'
@NOPASS.
```

(6)
```
laugh V @(INTRANS laugh).
```

In ParGram grammars, the lexicons are generally organized so that each verb subcategorization frame corresponds to a different template. Similarly, templates can be defined to encode a given set of generalizations about how certain groups of nouns combine with different light verbs. Consider the N-V CPs in (7). The noun *ıshara* 'signal' forms part of the cluster dominated by *de* 'give' (i.e., the cluster with the frequencies shown in (4)) and thus occurs most frequently with *de* 'give' as well as *kar* 'do'.

(7) a. nadya=ne bılal=ko ıshara dı-ya
Nadya.F.Sg=Erg Bilal.M.Sg=Dat signal.M.Sg give-Perf.M.Sg
'Nadya signaled Bilal.' (lit. 'Nadya gave a signal to Bilal.')

b. nadya=ne bılal=ko ıshara kı-ya
Nadya.F.Sg=Erg Bilal.M.Sg=Acc signal.M.Sg do-Perf.M.Sg
'Nadya signaled Bilal.' (lit. 'Nadya made a signal towards Bilal.')

The lexical entry of the noun *ıshara* 'signal' is given in (8).[8] The entry points to the template `NVGROUP2` which is defined as in (9). This version of the template constrains the verbal type of the overall predication to be a CP either with the light verb *de* 'give' or with the light verb *kar* 'do', or to not be a CP at all. Thus, only light verb options with relative frequencies equaling or above 0.08 (i.e., 8%) are accepted, an arbitrary threshold.

[8]The transliteration scheme employed in the Hindi/Urdu ParGram Grammar is described in Malik et al. (2010).

(8) `iSArA NOUN-S XLE (^ PRED) = 'iSArA<(^ OBJ)>'`

```
                        @NVGROUP2.
```

(9)
```
NVGROUP2 = { (^ VTYPE COMPLEX-PRED-FORM) =c dE
            |(^ VTYPE COMPLEX-PRED-FORM) =c kar
            | ~ (^ VTYPE COMPLEX-PRED-FORM)}
```

6.2 Preferred CPs

The template in (9), however, misses out on the fact that for all the groups identified, there are N-V combinations that are more productive (and thus more likely to be CP constructions) than other combinations (which are more likely to be non-CP constructions, e.g., plain objects). In XLE, grammar developers can model statistical generalizations using special marks that were inspired by Optimality Theory (Prince and Smolensky, 2004). On top of the classical constraint system of existing LFG grammars, a separate projection, o-structure, determines a preference ranking on the set of analyses for a given input sentence. A relative ranking is specified for the constraints that appear in the o-projection, and this ranking serves to determine the winner among the competing candidates. The constraints are also referred to as OT marks and are overlaid on the existing grammar (Frank et al., 1998).

OT marks can be added in the appropriate place in the grammar to punish or prefer a certain analysis. For example, (10) states that `Mark1` is a member of the optimality projection. The order of preference of a sequence of OT marks can be specified in the configuration section of the grammar; an example preference ordering is given in (11). Here, the list given in `OPTIMALITYORDER` shows the relative importance of the marks. In this case `Mark5` is the most important, and `Mark1` is the least important. Marks that have a `+` in front of them are preference marks. The more preference marks that an analysis has, the better. All other marks are dispreference marks (the fewer, the better).

(10) `... Mark1 $ o::* ...`

(11) `OPTIMALITYORDER Mark5 Mark4 Mark3 +Mark2 +Mark1.`

Given the relative ordering of light verb tendencies in our noun groups, we can augment the templates with OT marks that represent such tendencies. The noun template in (9) is changed in two ways. First, *all* the light verbs are included; second, each disjunct is extended by two OT marks that represent the statistical likelihood of this particular combination forming a CP or not.[9] The ordering of the marks is shown in (13), where the mark `cp-dispref` is most severely punished, and the mark `+cp-pref` is most strongly preferred. With an ordering like this, a CP analysis for (7a) is preferred, while a compositional analysis is dispreferred by XLE; the inverse will apply to *ıshara lag*, which is not a CP.

(12)
```
NVGROUP2 = { { (^ VTYPE COMPLEX-PRED-FORM) =c dE
              cp-pref $ ::*
              | ~ (^ VTYPE COMPLEX-PRED-FORM)
              non-cp-dispref $ ::* }
              ...
              |(^ VTYPE COMPLEX-PRED-FORM) =c lag}.
              cp-dispref $ o::*
              | ~ (^ VTYPE COMPLEX-PRED-FORM)
              non-cp-pref $ ::* } }.
```

(13) `OPTIMALITYORDER cp-dispref non-cp-dispref +cp-pref +non-cp-pref.`

[9]For space reasons, only the disjuncts for *de* 'give' as well as *lag* 'attach' are shown.

7 Conclusion

We have discussed a corpus study of Hindi/Urdu N-V CPs that makes use of a novel methodology in terms of a noun seed list and an evaluation based on WordNet. We found that the k-means algorithm with $k = 5$ and a frequency cutoff of 50 gave us the best result in terms of semantic coherence of the resulting clusters. We are optimistic that the resulting noun groups can be used in different NLP settings and have presented one such setting, the Hindi/Urdu ParGram Grammar, where lexical information about nouns and their combinatory possibilities in CPs are vital for grammar extension.

Acknowledgements

We would like to thank the DAAD (Deutscher Akademischer Austausch Dienst) for sponsoring Ashwini Vaidya's research stay at the University of Konstanz and Dr Miriam Butt for hosting her. We are also thankful to Dr Miriam Butt, Dr Martha Palmer and Christian Rohrdantz for their feedback on this paper. Any errors that remain are our own.

References

Tafseer Ahmed and Miriam Butt. 2011. Discovering Semantic Classes for Urdu N-V Complex Predicates. In *Proceedings of the International Conference on Computational Semantics (IWCS 2011)*.

Tafseer Ahmed, Miriam Butt, Annette Hautli, and Sebastian Sulger. 2012. A Reference Dependency Bank for Analyzing Complex Predicates. In Nicoletta Calzolari, Khalid Choukri, Thierry Declerck, Mehmet Uğur Doğan, Bente Maegaard, Joseph Mariani, Jan Odijk, and Stelios Piperidis, editors, *Proceedings of the Eight International Conference on Language Resources and Evaluation (LREC'12)*. European Language Resources Association (ELRA), May.

Leslie Barrett and Anthony R Davis. 2003. Diagnostics for determining compatibility in English support-verb-nominalization pairs. In *Proceedings of the 4th international conference on Computational Linguistics and Intelligent text processing (CICLing 03)*.

Rajesh Bhatt, Bhuvana Narasimhan, Martha Palmer, Owen Rambow, Dipti Sharma, and Fei Xia. 2009. A Multi-Representational and Multi-Layered Treebank for Hindi/Urdu. In *Proceedings of the Third Linguistic Annotation Workshop*, pages 186–189, Suntec, Singapore, August. Association for Computational Linguistics.

Pushpak Bhattacharyya. 2010. IndoWordNet. In *Proceedings of the Seventh Conference on International Language Resources and Evaluation (LREC'10)*, pages 3785–3792.

Miriam Butt and Tracy Holloway King. 2007. Urdu in a Parallel Grammar Development Environment. *Language Resources and Evaluation: Special Issue on Asian Language Processing: State of the Art Resources and Processing*, 41.

Miriam Butt, Tracy Holloway King, María-Eugenia Niño, and Frédérique Segond. 1999. *A Grammar Writer's Cookbook*. CSLI Publications.

Miriam Butt, Helge Dyvik, Tracy Holloway King, Hiroshi Masuichi, and Christian Rohrer. 2002. The Parallel Grammar Project. In *Proceedings of the COLING-2002 Workshop on Grammar Engineering and Evaluation*, pages 1–7.

Miriam Butt, Tina Bögel, Annette Hautli, Sebastian Sulger, and Tafseer Ahmed. 2012. Identifying Urdu Complex Predication via Bigram Extraction. In *In Proceedings of COLING 2012, Technical Papers*, pages 409 – 424, Mumbai, India.

Miriam Butt. 1995. *The Structure of Complex Predicates in Urdu*. CSLI Publications.

Miriam Butt. 2003. The Light Verb Jungle. *Harvard Working Papers in Linguistics*, 9.

Miriam Butt. 2010. The Light Verb Jungle: Still Hacking Away. In Mengistu Amberber, Brett Baker, and Mark Harvey, editors, *Complex Predicates in Cross-Linguistic Perspective*. Cambridge University Press.

Dick Crouch, Mary Dalrymple, Ronald M. Kaplan, Tracy Holloway King, John T. Maxwell III, and Paula Newman, 2012. *XLE Documentation*. Palo Alto Research Center.

Mary Dalrymple, Ronald M. Kaplan, and Tracy Holloway King. 2004. Linguistic Generalizations over Descriptions. In Miriam Butt and Tracy Holloway King, editors, *Proceedings of the LFG04 Conference*. CSLI Publications.

Alice Davison. 2005. Phrasal predicates: How N combines with V in Hindi/Urdu. In Tanmoy Bhattacharya, editor, *Yearbook of South Asian Languages and Linguistics*, pages 83–116. Mouton de Gruyter.

Anette Frank, Tracy Holloway King, Jonas Kuhn, and John T. Maxwell III. 1998. Optimality Theory Style Constraint Ranking in Large-scale LFG Grammars. In *Proceedings of the LFG98 Conference*. CSLI Publications.

Peter Hook. 1974. *The Compound Verb in Hindi*. Center for South and Southeast Asian Studies, University of Michigan.

Muhammad Humayoun. 2006. Urdu Morphology, Orthography and Lexicon Extraction. Master's thesis, Department of Computing Science, Chalmers University of Technology.

Yamuna Kachru. 2006. *Hindi*. John Benjamins.

Andreas Lamprecht, Annette Hautli, Christian Rohrdantz, and Tina Bögel. 2013. A Visual Analytics System for Cluster Exploration. In *Proceedings of the 51st Annual Meeting of the Association for Computational Linguistics: System Demonstrations*, pages 109–114, Sofia, Bulgaria, August. Association for Computational Linguistics.

Beth Levin. 1993. *English Verb Classes and Alternations. A Preliminary Investigation*. The University of Chicago Press.

James B. MacQueen. 1967. Some Methods for Classification and Analysis of Multivariate Observations. In *Proceedings of 5th Berkeley Symposium on Mathematical Statistics and Probability*, pages 281–297. University of California Press.

Muhammad Kamran Malik, Tafseer Ahmed, Sebastian Sulger, Tina Bögel, Atif Gulzar, Ghulam Raza, Sarmad Hussain, and Miriam Butt. 2010. Transliterating Urdu for a Broad-Coverage Urdu/Hindi LFG Grammar. In *Proceedings of the Seventh Conference on International Language Resources and Evaluation (LREC 2010)*.

Tara Mohanan. 1994. *Argument Structure in Hindi*. CSLI Publications.

Ryan North. 2005. *Computational Measures of the Acceptability of Light Verb Constructions*. Ph.D. thesis, University of Toronto.

Alan Prince and Paul Smolensky. 2004. *Optimality Theory: Constraint Interaction in Generative Grammar*. Blackwell Publishing.

Ghulam Raza. 2011. *Subcategorization Acquisition and Classes of Predication in Urdu*. Ph.D. thesis, University of Konstanz.

Siva Reddy and Serge Sharoff. 2011. Cross Language POS Taggers (and other Tools) for Indian Languages: An Experiment with Kannada using Telugu Resources. In *Proceedings of the Fifth International Workshop On Cross Lingual Information Access*, pages 11–19, Chiang Mai, Thailand, November. Asian Federation of Natural Language Processing.

Ruth Laila Schmidt. 1999. *Urdu: An Essential Grammar*. Routledge.

Shiva Taslimipoor, Afsaneh Fazly, and Ali Hamzeh. 2012. Using Noun Similarity to Adapt an Acceptability Measure for Persian Light Verb Constructions. In Nicoletta Calzolari (Conference Chair), Khalid Choukri, Thierry Declerck, Mehmet Uğur Doğan, Bente Maegaard, Joseph Mariani, Jan Odijk, and Stelios Piperidis, editors, *Proceedings of the Eighth International Conference on Language Resources and Evaluation (LREC'12)*, Istanbul, Turkey, may. European Language Resources Association (ELRA).

S. Urooj, F. Jabeen, F. Adeeba, R. Parveen., and S. Hussain. 2012. Urdu Digest Corpus. In *Proceedings of the Conference on Language and Technology 2012*, Lahore, Pakistan.

Tim Van de Cruys. 2006. Semantic Clustering in Dutch. In *Proceedings of the Sixteenth Computational Linguistics in Netherlands (CLIN)*, pages 17–32.

Konkanverter - A Finite State Transducer based Statistical Machine Transliteration Engine for Konkani Language

Vinodh Rajan
School of Computer Science
University of St Andrews
Scotland, UK
vrs3@st-andrews.ac.uk

Abstract

We have developed a finite state transducer based transliteration engine called *Konkanverter* that performs statistical machine transliteration between three different scripts used to write the Konkani language. The statistical machine transliteration system consists of cascading finite state transducers combining both rule-based and statistical approaches. Based on the limited availability of parallel corpora, this cascading approach is found to perform significantly better than a pure rule-based approach or pure statistical approach.

1 Introduction

Konkani is an Indian language spoken by approximately 2.5 million people (Gov. of India, 2001), mainly in the Indian state of Goa. It also has a substantial amount of linguistic minority population living in neighboring states of Karnataka and Kerala. In Goa, Konkani uses the Devanagari script and the Roman script (locally known as *Romi*). In Karnataka and Kerala, the dominant regional scripts, Kannada and Malayalam, are being used to write the language. Muslim sections of the Konkani population are also known to use a Perso-Arabic based alphabet. This polygraphic scenario is unique to Konkani in contemporary Indian linguistic milieu.

Among these different orthographies, Devanagari, Kannada and the Roman script are the mainstream orthographic systems. For all practical purposes, Konkani can therefore be considered to possess synchronic trigraphia. There are several important features that differentiate these orthographies. Consonants of Indic scripts carry an inherent schwa, which is unmarked, while other vowel combinations with a consonant are represented as combining signs. However, absence of schwa in a consonant is marked by explicit orthographic consonantal clusters or using a special sign called a *Virāma*. All orthographies other than Devanagari universally show explicit schwa deletion. Devanagari and Kannada distinguish vowel lengths, but their distribution and representation are very idiosyncratic to each orthography. In contrast to the Indic scripts, *Romi* does not differentiate vowel length at all. Most importantly, the *Romi* orthography does not distinguish schwa from vowel *o*. Both are represented using the same grapheme *o*. Several Indic graphemic combinations are also rendered as vowel digraphs or trigraphs in *Romi*. As a result, many Indic sequences are merged in *Romi* orthography. Table 1 lists some sample words in various orthographies.

Synchronic trigraphia is a major issue of political contention inside the community, each group favoring the usage of a particular script as the official orthography. Different orthographic communities exist in isolation with minimal interaction and with its own literary tradition, as very few people are fluent in multiple orthographies. A statistical machine transliteration engine with reasonable accuracy would greatly enable cohesion and interaction among the greater linguistic community. Facilitating the usage of multiple scripts would also encourage more linguistic diversity among the community.

Proceedings of the 5th Workshop on South and Southeast Asian NLP, 25th International Conference on Computational Linguistics, pages 11–19, Dublin, Ireland, August 23-29 2014.

Devanagari	*Kannada*	*Romi*
देवनागरी dēvanāgarī	ದೇವ್ನಾಗರಿ dēvnāgari	devnagri
झटको jhaṭakō	ಝಟ್ಕೊ jhaṭko	zhottko
दिवंचे divaṃcē	ದಿಂವ್ಚೆ diṃvce	dinvche
देवादयेन dēvādayēna	ದೆವಾದಯೆನ್ devādayen	devadoien
सत्तेवयल्या sattēvayalyā	ಸತ್ತೆವಯ್ಲ್ಯಾ sattevaylyā	sat'tevoilea

Table 1: Sample *Konkani* words in various orthographies

2 Related Work

Machine transliteration frequently occurs within machine translation when either named entities or out of vocabulary (OOV) words are encountered. Machine transliteration is also useful for cross-language information retrieval (CLIR). Consequently, a significant amount of work has been done in this field (Arbabi et al., 1994; Knight and Graehl, 1998). Machine transliteration can generally be classified as rule-based or statistical depending on the approach.

Rule-based transliteration is typically performed through hand-crafted rules and is usually graphemic in nature. Within Indic transliteration, there have been several attempts on rule-based approaches. Malik et al (2008) implemented a Hindi-Urdu transliteration system with finite-state transducers using a universal intermediate transcription (UIT). It was based on the graphemic equivalence between Perso-Arabic script and Devanagari script. Similarly, Kishorjit (2011) developed a rule-based transliteration system also based on direct graphemic correspondence between Meetei Mayek and Bengali script.

On the other hand, statistical machine transliteration systems typically use procedures familiar from statistical machine translation, including character alignments and subsequent training on the aligned data. Jia et al (2009) also developed a noisy channel model for the English-Chinese language pair using Moses, an SMT tool. Malik et al (2013) evaluated 28 different kinds of statistical models for Hindi-Urdu machine transliteration using GIZA++ and Moses. Similarly, Chinnakotla et al (2009) used the same tools for three language pairs - English-Hindi, English-Tamil and English-Kannada, focusing on fine-tuning the character sequence model (CSM). Singh (2012) evaluated both rule-based and statistical methods for bidirectional Bengali script and Meetei Mayek transliteration. A hybrid approach combining FSM based techniques with a statistical word language model with better performance was proposed by Malik et al (2009).

3 Initial Attempts

Konkani, being a minor language did not have any parallel corpora that could have been harnessed for statistical machine transliteration. The World Konkani Center, Mangalore had attempted to manually mine transliteration rules by studying the three orthographies and analyzing the differences. They also developed schwa deletion and schwa insertion rules for the orthographies, modeled on Hindi schwa deletion rules. For the initial machine transliteration system, we refined and improved upon these rules and implemented a rule-based transliteration system. In the absence of corpora, we iterated the rule-based system in an ardent attempt to improve accuracy. However, the performance of the transliteration engine was not very satisfactory and could not be improved beyond a certain limit. The performance of this rule-based engine is discussed in section 5.

Even though significant effort had to be spent towards the creation of a parallel corpus, it was finally decided to incorporate statistical models to improve accuracy. A monolingual untagged text corpus was obtained for Konkani in Devanagari script. In liaison with linguistic experts, we manually constructed a substantially sized corpus, despite several practical difficulties. Table 2 lists the word count of parallel word lists in each orthographic pair. This corpus will be released into the public domain, after some revisions and proof-checking. Currently it is available on

Orthography	*Word Count*
Devanagari - Kannada	23 187
Devanagari - Romi	38 550
Kannada - Romi	14 396

Table 2: Word count of parallel corpora

request.

We initially contemplated using an interlingua-like approach by choosing Devanagari as the intermediate script, thus reducing the need for a dedicated Kannada-Romi transliteration module and parallel corpus. However, we were skeptical of the error propagation that might occur if the conversion to the intermediate script itself is not very accurate.

4 Architecture

The implementation of the framework has been done entirely using OpenFst (Allauzen et al., 2007). Thrax (Tai et al., 2011) was used to define context-dependent rewrite rules and compile those rules into finite-state transducers compatible with Openfst. Thrax was also used to define finite state acceptors. We found Thrax to be particularly robust and flexible in generating various FSTs. Character alignments were performed using Phonetisaurus (Novak et al., 2011). N-gram models were created with the OpenGrm Ngram library (Roark et al., 2012), which also generates the models as FSTs.

Below, we describe the detailed architecture for each transliteration pair.

4.1 Devanagari to Kannada

Input text was first converted into an intermediate romanized encoding, where schwa is explicitly denoted. This also results in converting the script from syllabic to alphabetic form. This eases defining rules to a considerable extent, since independent vowels and dependent vowel signs need not be dealt with separately. We have used a customized encoding which only uses monographs and hence maintains a direct grapheme-to-grapheme correspondence with Indic scripts. However, to increase readability standardized Indic romanization scheme ISO 15919 has been used instead for presentation in this paper.

Before proceeding with schwa deletion rules, let us define the necessary sets. Let $\mathcal{V}$ stand for the class of vowels, $\mathcal{C}$ for the class of consonants, $\mathcal{C}_{nj}$ be a list of consonants that cannot occur as a second element of a triconsonantal cluster and $\mathcal{D}$ for the dependent signs *Chandrabindu*, *Anusvara* and *Visarga*. The morphemic boundary is denoted by $\mathcal{M}$. The beginning of string and end of string is denoted by s_i and s_f respectively. $\mathcal{E}$ denotes a null character with Σ denoting the entire alphabet.

Let $\mathcal{S}$ be an orthographic syllable, while $\mathcal{S}_{-a}$ is the set of syllables that do not contain schwa. $\mathcal{S}_{nj}$ is the set of syllables that do not start with $\mathcal{C}_{nj}$, while $\mathcal{S}_{nj-a}$ is the set that excludes the syllables with schwa. Using regular expressions, these are defined as:

$$\mathcal{S} \leftarrow \mathcal{C}*\mathcal{V}\mathcal{D}? \quad , \quad \mathcal{S}_{-a} \leftarrow \mathcal{C}*(\mathcal{V}-a)\mathcal{D}? \quad , \quad \mathcal{S}_{nj} \leftarrow \mathcal{C}_{nj}?\mathcal{C}\mathcal{V}\mathcal{D}? \quad , \quad \mathcal{S}_{nj-a} \leftarrow \mathcal{C}_{nj}?\mathcal{C}(\mathcal{V}-a)\mathcal{D}?$$

The initial word boundary $\mathcal{B}_i$ and final word boundary $\mathcal{B}_f$ are: $\mathcal{B}_i \leftarrow \mathcal{M}|s_i$ and $\mathcal{B}_f \leftarrow \mathcal{M}|s_f$.

The general schwa deletion rules have been given below as context dependent rewrite rules. These rules are expressed in the form $\phi \rightarrow \psi/\lambda\_\_\rho$. Here, ϕ is replaced by ψ whenever it is preceded by λ and succeeded by ρ, λ and ρ being the left and right contexts respectively. The rules below are listed with a corresponding sample case. These rules were compiled as finite-state transducers (Narasimhan et al., 2004)

We have produced a list of possible suffixes and prefixes from the collected corpus. Let $\mathcal{P}_{re}$ denote the set of prefixes and $\mathcal{S}_{uf}$ the set of prefixes. We then mark the morphemic boundary

$\mathcal{M}$ as:

$$\mathcal{B}_m = \mathcal{E} \rightarrow \mathcal{M}/\mathcal{P}_{re}\_\_\_\mathcal{S}_{uf}$$

The schwa deletion rules can be effectively summarized as follows.

$$\mathcal{W}_f = a \rightarrow \mathcal{E}/(\mathcal{B}_i\mathcal{S} + \mathcal{C}+)\_\_\_\mathcal{B}_f \quad | \quad \text{āsāta} \rightarrow \text{āsāt}$$
$$\mathcal{W}_3 = a \rightarrow \mathcal{E}/(\mathcal{B}_i\mathcal{S}\mathcal{C})\_\_\_(\mathcal{S}_{-a}\mathcal{B}_f) \quad | \quad \text{āṃvaḍō} \rightarrow \text{āṃvḍō}$$
$$\mathcal{W}_{3vy} = a \rightarrow \mathcal{E}/(\mathcal{B}_i\mathcal{S}(y|v))\_\_\_(\mathcal{S}\mathcal{B}_f) \quad | \quad \text{payasa} \rightarrow \text{pays}$$
$$\mathcal{W}_4 = a \rightarrow \mathcal{E}/(\mathcal{B}_i\mathcal{S}\mathcal{C})\_\_\_(\mathcal{S}_{nj}\mathcal{S}\mathcal{B}_f) \quad | \quad \text{āḍakātī} \rightarrow \text{āḍkātī}$$
$$\mathcal{W}_{4y} = a \rightarrow \mathcal{E}/(\mathcal{B}_i\mathcal{S}\mathcal{S}y)\_\_\_(\mathcal{S}_{nj}\mathcal{B}_f) \quad | \quad \text{ulayatāṃ} \rightarrow \text{ulāytāṃ}$$
$$\mathcal{W}_{4_3} = a \rightarrow \mathcal{E}/(\mathcal{B}_i\mathcal{S}\mathcal{S}_{-a}\mathcal{C})\_\_\_(\mathcal{S}_{nj}\mathcal{B}_f) \quad | \quad \text{vicāratā} \rightarrow \text{vicārtā}$$
$$\mathcal{W}_{P2} = a \rightarrow \mathcal{E}/(\mathcal{B}_i\mathcal{S}\mathcal{C})\_\_\_(\mathcal{S}_{nj}\mathcal{S}\mathcal{S} + \mathcal{B}_f) \quad | \quad \text{vācatakūca} \rightarrow \text{vāctakūc}$$
$$\mathcal{W}_{Pl} = a \rightarrow \mathcal{E}/(\mathcal{B}_i\mathcal{S}\mathcal{S}(y|l|v))\_\_\_(\mathcal{S}_{nj}\mathcal{S}\mathcal{S} + \mathcal{B}_f) \quad | \quad \text{vājayatālō} \rightarrow \text{vājaytālō}$$
$$\mathcal{W}_{P3} = a \rightarrow \mathcal{E}/(\mathcal{B}_i\mathcal{S}_{-a}\mathcal{S})\_\_\_(\mathcal{S}_{nj}\mathcal{S}\mathcal{S} + \mathcal{B}_f) \quad | \quad \text{juvānapana} \rightarrow \text{juvānpan}$$
$$\mathcal{W}_{tri} = a \rightarrow \mathcal{E}/(\mathcal{S}\mathcal{C})\_\_\_\mathcal{S}_{nj} \quad | \quad \text{gōyāṃtalyā} \rightarrow \text{gōyāṃtlyā}$$
$$\mathcal{W}_{grm} = a \rightarrow \mathcal{E}/(\mathcal{B}_i\mathcal{S}\mathcal{S}\mathcal{S} + (w|y))\_\_\_l\mathcal{V}\mathcal{D}?) \quad | \quad \text{gōyāṃtalē} \rightarrow \text{gōyāṃtlē}$$

Let $\mathcal{B}_r$ denote the removal of morphemic boundaries. The overall schwa deletion can be constructed by composing all of the above transducers:

$$\mathcal{W}_d = \mathcal{B}_m \circ \mathcal{W}_3 \circ \mathcal{W}_{3vy} \circ \mathcal{W}_{4y} \circ \mathcal{W}_{4_3} \circ \mathcal{W}_{P2} \circ \mathcal{W}_{Pl} \circ \mathcal{W}_{P3} \circ \mathcal{W}_{tri} \circ \mathcal{W}_{grm} \circ \mathcal{W}_f \circ \mathcal{B}_r$$

Devanagari has two additional vowels ऍ *ĕ* and ऑ *ŏ*, and two special conjunct characters ऱ्य *ṛy* and ऱ्ह *ṛh*. They were directly mapped to the Kannada characters ಎ *e*, ಒ *o*, ಯಱ *ry* and ಹಱ *rh* respectively. Let this mapping be $\mathcal{R}_{vc}$.

In Kannada, *i* and *u* are used at word endings, where *ī* and *ū* are found in Devanagari.

$$\mathcal{R}_i = \bar{i} \rightarrow i/(\mathcal{C} + \_\_\_\mathcal{D}?\mathcal{B}_f \quad | \quad \text{satī} \rightarrow \text{sati}$$
$$\mathcal{R}_u = \bar{u} \rightarrow u/(\mathcal{C} + \_\_\_\mathcal{D}?\mathcal{B}_f \quad | \quad \text{vastū} \rightarrow \text{vastu}$$

The Devanagari sequence *vaṃk* corresponds to *ṃvk* in Kannada, let this be $\mathcal{R}_{vmk}$ The overall rule-based transduction is:

$$\mathcal{R}_{kn} = \mathcal{W}_d \circ \mathcal{R}_{vc} \circ \mathcal{R}_i \circ \mathcal{R}_u \circ \mathcal{R}_{vmk}$$

The precedence for the rule-based compositions were decided based on emperical observations.

The input word $\mathcal{I}$ is composed with the overall rule-based transducer. The second (output) projection of this transducer is used for later operations.

$$\mathcal{R}_{knp} = \pi_2(\mathcal{R}_{kn} \circ \mathcal{I})$$

When either *ī* or *ū* appears before a final schwa-consonant, with or without a preceding *r* or *ṃ*, it can retain its length or become short. Also, *ē* and *ō*, which usually transform into short vowels *e* and *o*, are retained in case of loan words. Additional arcs were added to the transducer $\mathcal{R}_{knp}$ to reflect this. The new transducer $\mathcal{R}_{knm}$ contains multiple paths for a given input.

We then created a lexical acceptor $\mathcal{A}_{Lkn}$ from the Kannada words in the corpus. For a given lattice, this removes all non-lexical entries.

$$\mathcal{T}_{knl} = \mathcal{R}_{knm} \circ \mathcal{A}_{Lkn}$$

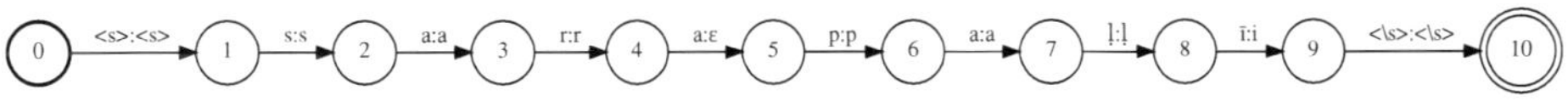

Figure 1: Transducer $\mathcal{R}_{kn}$ for the Devanagari input सरपळी *sarapaḷī*

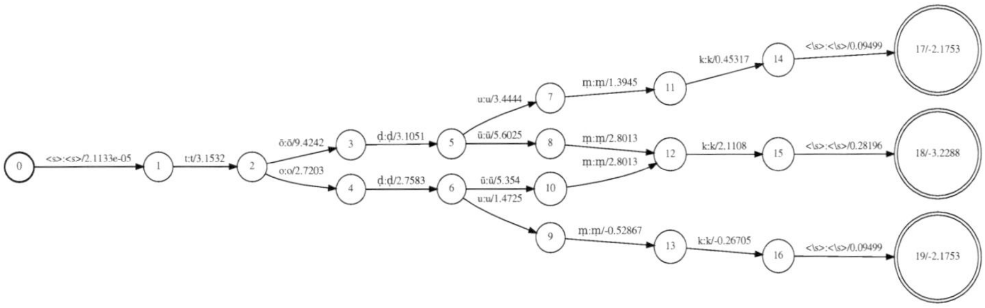

Figure 2: Weighted Transducer $\mathcal{T}_{dv2kn}$ for the Devanagari input तोड्डूंक *tōḍūṃka*. Weights indicate negative log n-gram probabilities

In case none of the outputs are present in the lexicon, or if multiple paths are lexically valid (in case of several standard variants), we proceed to choose the best path by utilizing n-gram probabilities. An n-gram word model $\mathcal{N}_{kn}$ was generated based on the list of Kannada words in the corpus.

If $\mathcal{T}_{knl}$ is null then,

$$\mathcal{T}_{dv2kn} = \mathcal{R}_{knm} \circ \mathcal{N}_{kn}$$

Else,

$$\mathcal{T}_{dv2kn} = \mathcal{T}_{knl} \circ \mathcal{N}_{kn}$$

$\mathcal{T}_{dv2kn}$ is the final transducer that transliterates Devanagari to Kannada. The best path was chosen from the lattice as the most probable transliteration.

4.2 Kannada to Devanagari

Kannada to Devanagari transliteration is more complex than Devanagari to Kannada. Since Kannada orthography shows explicit schwa deletion, schwa needs to be inserted in this case.

First, we inverted the schwa deletion transducer $\mathcal{W}_d$, effectively making it perform schwa insertion. However, reversing the schwa deletion results in multiple alternate paths, all of which are theoretically viable. In order to prune the lattice, a cluster acceptor $\mathcal{A}_{Cdv}$ was created. $\mathcal{A}_{Cdv}$ rejects all paths that contain non-standard consonantal clusters for the Devanagari orthography. This list of non-standard clusters was manually created by analyzing the Devanagari corpus.

For example, the word ಚಿಕ್ಟುನ್ ciktun could hypothetically have resulted from schwa deletion of चिकटून cikaṭūna or चिक्टून ciktūna (ignoring additional hypotheses for word-internal *u*) . However, the cluster क्ट kṭ is a non-standard ligature and is highly unlikely to appear in Devanagari orthography. The acceptor would prune any path that would result in the cluster kṭ. Similarly, the word ವಸ್ತು vastu could have resulted from वसतू vasatū or वस्तू vastū. But स्त st being a standard consonantal cluster, both are equally plausible. In this case, a lexicon lookup or n-gram model is necessary to choose the most probable output.

Similarly, inverting $\mathcal{R}_{kn}$ also results in multiple alternate paths for *i* and *u* among others.

Since Devanagari only uses long ē and ō, let $\mathcal{R}_{eo}$ be the transducer that replaces the short vowels *e* and *o* with the corresponding long vowels.

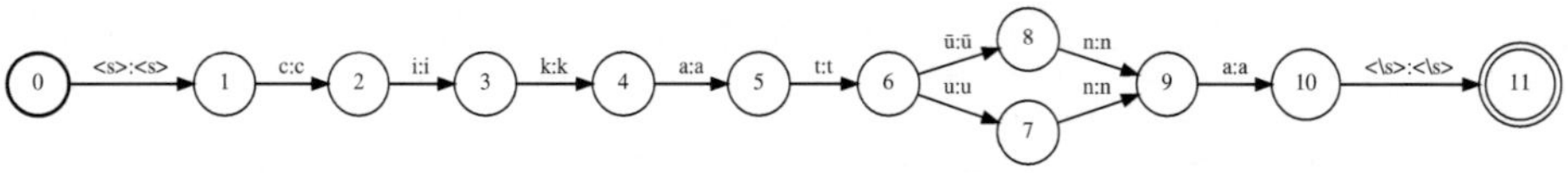

Figure 3: Transducer $\mathcal{R}_{dv}$ for the Kannada input ಚಿಕ್ಟುನ್ *cikṭun*

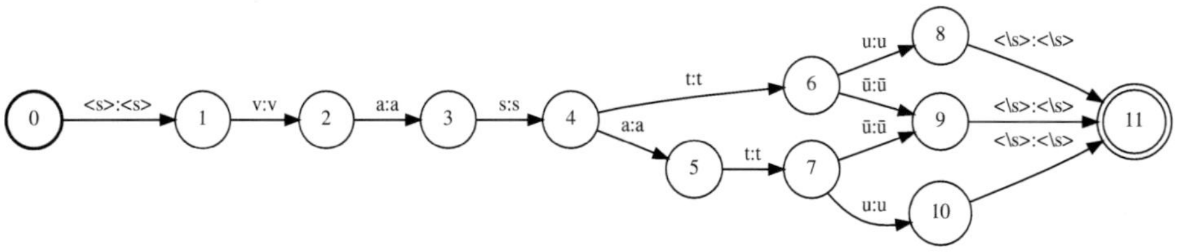

Figure 4: Transducer $\mathcal{R}_{dv}$ for the Kannada input ವಸ್ತು *vastu*

The final rule-based transducer $\mathcal{R}_{dv}$ is,

$$\mathcal{R}_{dv} = \mathcal{R}_{kn}^{-1} \circ (\mathcal{W}_d^{-1} \circ \mathcal{A}_{Cdv}) \circ \mathcal{R}_{eo}$$

In case of non-standard input such as words which already have a schwa in a position where none is possible, the composition fails. In this case we have a rule-based Schwa insertion transducer $\mathcal{W}_{ir}$ that inserts an additional arc that inserts schwa to non-standard consonantal clusters. In this case,

$$\mathcal{R}_{dv} = \mathcal{R}_{kn}^{-1} \circ \mathcal{W}_{ir} \circ \mathcal{R}_{eo}$$

Similar to $\mathcal{T}_{dv2kn}$, the Kannada to Devanagari transducer $\mathcal{T}_{kn2dv}$ is formed with a Devanagari lexical acceptor and if needed, a corresponding Devanagari n-gram word model.

$$\mathcal{T}_{kn2dv} = (\pi_2(\mathcal{R}_{dv} \circ \mathcal{I}) \circ \mathcal{A}_{Ldv}) \circ \mathcal{N}_{dv} \qquad or$$
$$\mathcal{T}_{kn2dv} = \pi_2(\mathcal{R}_{dv} \circ \mathcal{I}) \circ \mathcal{N}_{dv}$$

4.3 Kannada to Romi

As in previous transliterations, we romanized the input. Since Romi and Kannada share different graphemic sets, we proceed with performing a character alignment with a Kannada-Romi parallel wordlist. Romanizing the input very marginally improves the character alignment process, since both input and output are then alphabetic scripts (as compared to syllabic to alphabetic alignment). We initially experimented with tools such as GIZA++, but found Phonetisaurus produced better alignments compared to other tools as it uses many-to-many alignments developed specifically for grapheme to phoneme systems (Jiampojamarn et al., 2007).

A sample alignment sequence from Phonetisaurus is given below:

meḷillem̩ | mellil'lem → m}m e}e ḷ}l|l i}i l}l|' l}l e}e m̩}m
gaḍyem̩tlyān | gaddientlean → g}g ā}a ḍ}d|d y}i e}e m̩}n t}t l}l y}e ā}a n}n
bhāratāsārkyā | bharotasarkea → bh}b|h ā}a r}r a}o t}t ā}a s}s ā}a r}r k}k y}e ā}a
bhiyeli | bhieli → bh}b|h i|y}i e}e l}l i}i

Where } denotes individual character alignment, | between characters indicates grapheme chunks, and ḍ}d|d implies that the source grapheme «ḍ» is mapped to the target graphemic chunk «dd».

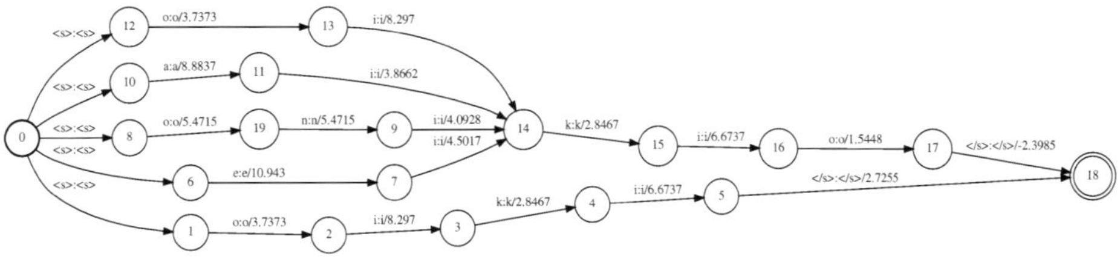

Figure 5: 5 best paths of $\mathcal{L}_p$ for Kannada input ಐಕ್ಯ *aiky*

This alignment lattice was then used to create a joint sequence n-gram model (Galescu and Allen, 2002) $\mathcal{N}_{knrm}$. This is then composed with the input word $\mathcal{I}$, whose output projection we use. We also modify the resulting transducer by removing edges with grapheme chunks and replacing it with succeeding edges with the individual graphemes of the chunk. This is necessary for later operations.

Some graphemic sequences such as geminate vowel graphemes *aa*, *ii* etc. do not occur in the orthography. We construct a transducer $\mathcal{A}_{rm}$, which accepts only paths with standard graphemic sequences. Thus effectively creating a pruned lattice $\mathcal{L}_p$.

$$\mathcal{L}_p = \pi_2(\mathcal{I} \circ N_{knrm}) \circ \mathcal{A}_{rm}$$

We created a Romi lexical acceptor $\mathcal{A}_{Lrm}$ which is composed with $\mathcal{L}_p$. If all the paths are non-lexical, we select the cheapest path from $\mathcal{L}_p$.

$$\mathcal{T}_{kn2rm} = \mathcal{L}_p \circ \mathcal{A}_{Lrm} \quad or \quad \mathcal{T}_{knr2rm} = shortest(\mathcal{L}_p)$$

4.4 Romi to Kannada

We produced a similar set of transducers as in Kannada → Romi. The lattice pruner here rejects non-standard Indic forms like digraphic vowel sequences. We generated a new joint sequence n-gram model by swapping the original training data and retraining it. We initially attempted to invert $\mathcal{N}_{knrm}$, to avoid re-training, but the accuracy was found to be 18% lower than a retrained model.

$$\mathcal{L}_p = \pi_2(\mathcal{I} \circ N_{rmkn}) \circ \mathcal{A}_{ind}$$
$$\mathcal{T}_{kn2rm} = \mathcal{L}_p \circ \mathcal{A}_{Lkn} \quad or \quad \mathcal{T}_{kn2rm} = shortest(\mathcal{L}_p)$$

4.5 Devanagari to Romi

We performed an initial schwa deletion on the input using $\mathcal{W}_d$. We found that schwa-deleted input improves the joint sequence n-gram model. Schwa deletion being a grammatical process, removing one of the underlying uncertainties effectively improves the performance. As a result of this, the joint sequence n-gram model performs better with preprocessed input.

Following Schwa deletion, a similar process to that described in section 4.3 is performed, to generate the transducer $\mathcal{T}_{dv2rm}$.

$$\mathcal{L}_p = \pi_2((\mathcal{W}_d \circ \mathcal{I}) \circ N_{dvrm}) \circ \mathcal{A}_{rm}$$
$$\mathcal{T}_{dv2rm} = \mathcal{L}_p \circ \mathcal{A}_{Lrm} \quad or \quad \mathcal{T}_{dv2rm} = shortest(\mathcal{L}_p)$$

4.6 Romi to Devanagari

We performed a rule-based schwa insertion on the input here. However, we did not see any substantial improvement in the performance in terms of accuracy, as compared to the raw input. However, we retained the preprocessing, to take advantage of even the marginal improvement. Also, the preprocessing model could be improved in the future. We performed a similar set of

Script Pair	*Rules-bases System*	*Statistical System*	*Cascading System*
Devanagari - Kannada	83.9%	84.59%	90.383%
Kannada - Devanagari	79.49%	90.16%	96.66%
Devanagari - Romi	74.88%	78.02%	95.39%
Romi - Devanagari	54.02%	74.04%	83.41%
Kannada - Romi	81.29%	87.63%	96.12%
Romi - Kannada	68.01%	82.21%	97.87%

Table 3: Accuracy of three different systems

transductions as in section 4.4.

$$\mathcal{L}_p = \pi_2((\mathcal{W}_{ir} \circ \mathcal{I}) \circ N_{rmdv}) \circ \mathcal{A}_{ind}$$
$$\mathcal{T}_{rm2dv} = \mathcal{L}_p \circ \mathcal{A}_{Ldv} \quad or \quad \mathcal{T}_{rm2dv} = shortest(\mathcal{L}_p)$$

5 Evaluation

For the procedures involving statistical methods, we split the corpus with 90% being used for training and the remaining 10% for testing. The accuracy results for the orthographies are reported in table 3. For the rule-based system, the initial system developed was used for the evaluation. For the pure statistical approach, we used Phonetisaurus's in-built g2p system. The cascading system was that discussed in this paper.

As expected, the initial rule-based system has the least accurate performance. Although it is theoretically possible to mine all rules that can apply to a system, in practice the rule-mining process is highly inefficient and user-dependent. The statistical system performs better than the rule-based system. The mediocre performance of the statistical system can be mainly attributed to the limited corpora that we possess. Konkani being an inflectional language, the effective number of unique words in the corpus is considerably lower than the absolute word count. The hybrid system performs best when compared to others.

Of all the transliteration pairs, Romi to Devanagari appears to have the lowest accuracy of all the three systems. Compared to other transliteration pairs, Romi to Devanagari is the most complex system as it involves both schwa insertion and disambiguation of confounded graphemic sequences. The poor performance of the hybrid system can be attributed to the fact that we had used a rule-based schwa insertion as a part of preprocessing. While this system worked well for an Indic system such as Kannada, it turned out to be not very efficient for Romi, where consonantal sequences are rendered as vowel digraphs or trigraphs.

6 Conclusion

We have developed a finite state transducer based transliteration engine called *Konkanverter* which performs statistical machine transliteration between three different scripts used to write the Konkani language. We have explained the detailed architecture of this statistical machine transliteration system, which consists of cascading finite state transducers combining both rule-based and statistical approaches. The transliteration engine was evaluated and its performance was reported. This cascading approach is found to perform significantly better than a pure rule-based approach or pure statistical approach.

Acknowledgements

This work was supported by the World Institute of Konkani Language (WIKL) part of the World Konkani Centre, Mangalore, India. The author would also personally like to thank Mr Gurudath Bantwalkar, Asst Director of WIKL for all his linguistic expertise regarding the Konkani language.

References

Cyril Allauzen, Michael Riley, Johan Schalkwyk, Wojciech Skut, and Mehryar Mohri. 2007. OpenFst: A general and efficient weighted finite-state transducer library. In *Proceedings of the Ninth International Conference on Implementation and Application of Automata, (CIAA 2007)*, volume 4783 of *Lecture Notes in Computer Science*, pages 11–23. Springer. `http://www.openfst.org`.

Mansur Arbabi, Scott M Fischthal, Vincent C Cheng, and Elizabeth Bart. 1994. Algorithms for Arabic name transliteration. *IBM Journal of research and Development*, 38(2):183–194.

Manoj Kumar Chinnakotla and Om P Damani. 2009. Experiences with English-Hindi, English-Tamil and English-Kannada transliteration tasks at news 2009. In *Proceedings of the 2009 Named Entities Workshop: Shared Task on Transliteration*, pages 44–47. Association for Computational Linguistics.

Lucian Galescu and James F Allen. 2002. Pronunciation of proper names with a joint n-gram model for bi-directional grapheme-to-phoneme conversion. In *INTERSPEECH*.

Ministry of Home affairs Gov. of India. 2001. Abstract of speakers' strength of languages and mother tongues – 2001. `http://www.censusindia.gov.in/Census_Data_2001/Census_Data_Online/Language/Statement1.aspx`. Accessed: 2014-05-30.

Yuxiang Jia, Danqing Zhu, and Shiwen Yu. 2009. A noisy channel model for grapheme-based machine transliteration. In *Proceedings of the 2009 Named Entities Workshop: Shared Task on Transliteration*, pages 88–91. Association for Computational Linguistics.

Sittichai Jiampojamarn, Grzegorz Kondrak, and Tarek Sherif. 2007. Applying many-to-many alignments and hidden markov models to letter-to-phoneme conversion. In *HLT-NAACL*, volume 7, pages 372–379.

N Kishorjit. 2011. Manipuri transliteration from Bengali script to Meitei Mayek: A rule based approach, c. singh et al.(eds.): Icisil 2011, ccis vol. 139, part 2.

Kevin Knight and Jonathan Graehl. 1998. Machine transliteration. *Computational Linguistics*, 24(4):599–612.

M. G. Abbas Malik, Christian Boitet, and Pushpak Bhattacharyya. 2008. Hindi Urdu machine transliteration using finite-state transducers. In *Proceedings of the 22nd International Conference on Computational Linguistics-Volume 1*, pages 537–544. Association for Computational Linguistics.

M. G. Abbas Malik, Laurent Besacier, Christian Boitet, and Pushpak Bhattacharyya. 2009. A hybrid model for Urdu Hindi transliteration. In *Proceedings of the 2009 Named Entities Workshop: Shared Task on Transliteration*, pages 177–185. Association for Computational Linguistics.

M. G. Abbas Malik, Christian Boitet, Laurent Besacier, and Pushpak Bhattcharyya. 2013. Urdu Hindi machine transliteration using SMT. In *the Proceedings of the 4th Workshop on South and Southeast Asian Natural Language Processing, International Joint Conference on Natural Language Processing*, pages 43—57.

Bhuvana Narasimhan, Richard Sproat, and George Kiraz. 2004. Schwa-deletion in Hindi text-to-speech synthesis. *International Journal of Speech Technology*, 7(4):319–333.

Josef Novak, Dong Yang, Nobuaki Minematsu, and Keikichi Hirose. 2011. Initial evaluations of an open source WFST-based phoneticizer. *The University of Tokyo, Tokyo Institute of Technology*.

Brian Roark, Richard Sproat, Cyril Allauzen, Michael Riley, Jeffrey Sorensen, and Terry Tai. 2012. The OpenGrm open-source finite-state grammar software libraries. In *Proceedings of the ACL 2012 System Demonstrations*, pages 61–66, Jeju Island, Korea, July. Association for Computational Linguistics.

Thoudam Doren Singh. 2012. Bidirectional bengali script and meetei mayek transliteration of web based manipuri news corpus. In *the Proceedings of the 3rd Workshop on South and Southeast Asian Natural Language Processing (SANLP) of COLING*, pages 181–189.

Terry Tai, Wojciech Skut, and Richard Sproat. 2011. Thrax: An open source grammar compiler built on openfst. ASRU.

Integrating Dictionaries into an Unsupervised Model for Myanmar Word Segmentation

Ye Kyaw Thu
NICT
Keihanna Science City
Kyoto, Japan
yekyawthu@nict.go.jp

Andrew Finch
NICT
Keihanna Science City
Kyoto, Japan
andrew.finch@nict.go.jp

Eiichiro Sumita
NICT
Keihanna Science City
Kyoto, Japan
eiichiro.sumita@nict.go.jp

Yoshinori Sagisaka
GITI/Speech Science Research Lab.
Waseda Univerity
Tokyo, Japan
ysagisaka@gmail.com

Abstract

This paper addresses the problem of word segmentation for low resource languages, with the main focus being on Myanmar language. In our proposed method, we focus on exploiting limited amounts of dictionary resource, in an attempt to improve the segmentation quality of an unsupervised word segmenter. Three models are proposed. In the first, a set of dictionaries (separate dictionaries for different classes of words) are directly introduced into the generative model. In the second, a language model was built from the dictionaries, and the n-gram model was inserted into the generative model. This model was expected to model words that did not occur in the training data. The third model was a combination of the previous two models. We evaluated our approach on a corpus of manually annotated data. Our results show that the proposed methods are able to improve over a fully unsupervised baseline system. The best of our systems improved the F-score from 0.48 to 0.66. In addition to segmenting the data, one proposed method is also able to partially label the segmented corpus with POS tags. We found that these labels were approximately 66% accurate.

1 Introduction

In many natural language processing applications, for example machine translation, parsing and tagging, it is essential to have text that is segmented into sequences of tokens (these tokens usually represent 'words'). In many languages, including the Myanmar language (alternatively called the Burmese language), Japanese, and Chinese, words are not necessarily delimited by white space in running text. However, in some low-resource languages (Myanmar being one) broad-coverage word segmentation tools are scarce, and there are two common approaches to dealing with this issue. The first is to apply unsupervised word segmentation tools to a body of monolingual text in order to induce a segmentation. The second is to use a dictionary of words in the language together with a set of heuristics to identify word boundaries in text.

Myanmar language can be accurately segmented into a sequence of syllables using finite state automata (examples being (Berment, 2004; Thu et al., 2013a)). However, words composed of single or multiple syllables are not usually separated by white space. Although spaces are sometimes used for separating phrases for easier reading, it is not strictly necessary, and these spaces are rarely used in short sentences. There are no clear rules for using spaces in Myanmar language, and thus spaces may (or may not) be inserted between words, phrases, and even between a root word and its affixes. Myanmar language is a resource-poor language and large corpora, lexical resources, and grammatical dictionaries are not yet widely available. For this reason, using corpus-based machine learning techniques to develop word segmentation tools is a challenging task.

Proceedings of the 5th Workshop on South and Southeast Asian NLP, 25th International Conference on Computational Linguistics, pages 20–27, Dublin, Ireland, August 23-29 2014.

2 Related Work

In this section, we will briefly introduce some proposed word segmentation methods with an emphasis on the schemes that have been applied to Myanmar.

Many word segmentation methods have been proposed especially for the Thai, Khmer, Lao, Chinese and Japanese languages. These methods can be roughly classified into dictionary-based (Sornlertlamvanich, 1993; Srithirath and Seresangtakul, 2013) and statistical methods (Wu and Tseng, 1993; Maosong et al., 1998; Papageorgiou and P., 1994; Mochihashi et al., 2009; Jyun-Shen et al., 1991). In dictionary-based methods, only words that are stored in the dictionary can be identified and the performance depends to a large degree upon the coverage of the dictionary. New words appear constantly and thus, increasing size of the dictionary is a not a solution to the out of vocabulary word (OOV) problem. On the other hand, although statistical approaches can identify unknown words by utilizing probabilistic or cost-based scoring mechanisms, they also suffer from some drawbacks. The main issues are: they require large amounts of data; the processing time required; and the difficulty in incorporating linguistic knowledge effectively into the segmentation process (Teahan et al., 2000). For low-resource languages such as Myanmar, there is no freely available corpus and dictionary based or rule based methods are being used as a temporary solution.

If we only focus on Myanmar language word segmentation, as far as the authors are aware there have been only two published methodologies, and one study. Both of the proposed methodologies operate according using a process of syllable breaking followed by Maximum Matching; the differences in the approaches come from the manner in which the segmentation boundary decision is made. In (Thet et al., 2008) statistical information is used (based on bigram information), whereas (Htay and Murthy, 2008) utilize a word list extracted from a monolingual Myanmar corpus.

In a related study (Thu et al., 2013a), various Myanmar word segmentation approaches including character segmentation, syllable segmentation, human lexical/phrasal segmentation, unsupervised and semi-supervised word segmentation, were investigated. They reported that the highest quality machine translation was attained either without word segmentation using simply sequences of syllables, or by a process of Maximum Matching with a monolingual dictionary. In this study the effectiveness of approaches unsupervised word segmentation using latticelm (with 3-gram to 7-gram language models) and supervised word segmentation using KyTea was evaluated, however, none of the approaches was able to match the performance of the simpler syllable/Maximum Matching techniques.

In (Pei et al., 2013) an unsupervised Bayesian word segmentation scheme was augmented by using a dictionary of words. These words were obtained from segmenting the data using another unsupervised word segmenter. The probability distribution over these words was calculated from occurrence counts, and this distribution was interpolated into the base measure.

3 Methodology

3.1 Baseline Non-parametric Bayesian Segmentation Model

The baseline system, and the model that forms the basis for all of the models is a non-parametric Bayesian unsupervised word segmenter similar to that proposed in (Goldwater et al., 2009). The major differences being the sampling strategy and the base measure. The principles behind this segmenter are described below.

Intuitively, the model has two basic components: a model for generating an outcome that has already been generated at least once before, and a second model that assigns a probability to an outcome that has not yet been produced. Ideally, to encourage the re-use of model parameters, the probability of generating a novel segment should be considerably lower then the probability of generating a previously observed segment. This is a characteristic of the Dirichlet process model we use and furthermore, the model has a preference to generate new segments early on in the process, but is much less likely to do so later on. In this way, as the cache becomes more and more reliable and complete, so the model prefers to use it rather than generate novel segments. The probability distribution over these segments (including an infinite number of unseen segments) can be learned directly from unlabeled data by Bayesian inference of the hidden segmentation of the corpus.

The underlying stochastic process for the generation of a corpus composed of segments s_k is usually written in the following from:

$$G|_{\alpha,G_0} \sim DP(\alpha, G_0)$$
$$\mathbf{s}_k|G \sim G \tag{1}$$

G is a discrete probability distribution over the all segments according to a *Dirichlet process prior* with *base measure* G_0 and concentration parameter α. The concentration parameter $\alpha > 0$ controls the variance of G; intuitively, the larger α is, the more similar G_0 will be to G.

3.1.1 The Base Measure

For the base measure G_0 that controls the generation of novel sequence-pairs, we use a spelling model that assigns probability to new segments according to the following distribution:

$$\begin{aligned} G_0(\mathbf{s}) &= p(|\mathbf{s}|)p(\mathbf{s}||\mathbf{s}|) \\ &= \frac{\lambda^{|\mathbf{s}|}}{|\mathbf{s}|!}e^{-\lambda|V|^{-|\mathbf{s}|}} \end{aligned} \tag{2}$$

where $|\mathbf{s}|$ is the number of tokens in the segment; $|V|$ and is the token set size; and λ is the expected length of the segments.

According to this model, the segment length is chosen from a Poisson distribution, and then the elements of the segment itself is generated given the length. Note that this model is able to assign a probability to arbitrary sequences of tokens drawn from the set of tokens V (in this paper V is the set of all Myanmar syllables). The motivation for using a base measure of this form, is to overcome issues with overfitting when training the model; other base measures are possible for example the enhancement proposed in Section 3.4.

3.1.2 The Generative Model

The generative model is given in Equation 3 below. The equation assignes a probability to the kth segment $\mathbf{s}_k$ in a derivation of the corpus, given all of the other segments in the history so far $\mathbf{s}_{-k}$. Here $-k$ is read as: "up to but not including k".

$$p(\mathbf{s}_k|\mathbf{s}_{-k}) = \frac{N(\mathbf{s}_k) + \alpha G_0(\mathbf{s}_k)}{N + \alpha} \tag{3}$$

In this equation, N is the total number of segments generated so far, $N(\mathbf{s}_k)$ is the number of times the segment $\mathbf{s}_k$ has occurred in the history. G_0 and α are the base measure and concentration parameter as before.

3.1.3 Bayesian Inference

We used a blocked version of a Gibbs sampler for training. In (Goldwater et al., 2006) they report issues with mixing in the sampler that were overcome using annealing. In (Mochihashi et al., 2009) this issue was overcome by using a blocked sampler together with a dynamic programming approach. Our algorithm is an extension of application the forward filtering backward sampling (FFBS) algorithm (Scott, 2002) to the problem of word segmentation presented in (Mochihashi et al., 2009). We extend their approach to handle the joint segmentation and alignment of character sequences. We refer the reader to (Mochihashi et al., 2009) for a complete description of the FFBS process. In essence the process uses a forward variable at each node in the segmentation graph to store the probability of reaching the node from the source node of the graph. These forward variables are calculated efficiently in a single forward pass through the graph, from source node to sink node (forward filtering). During backward sampling, a single path through the segmentation graph is sampled in accordance with its probability. This sampling process uses the forward variables calculated in the forward filtering step.

In each iteration of the training process, each entry in the training corpus was sampled without replacement; its segmentation was removed and the models were updated to reflect this. Then a new segmentation for the sequence was chosen using the FFBS process, and the models were updated with the counts from this new segmentation. The two hyperparameters, the Dirichlet concentration parameter α, and the Poisson rate parameter λ were set by slice sampling using vague priors (a Gamma prior in the case of α and the Jeffreys prior was used for λ). The token set size V used in the base measure was set to the number of types in the training corpus, and $V = 3363$.

3.2 Dictionary Augmented Model

The dictionary augmented model is in essence the same model as proposed by (Thu et al., 2013b), but a different dictionary was used. Their method integrates dictionary-based word segmentation (similar to the maximum matching approaches used successfully in (Thet et al., 2008; Htay and Murthy, 2008; Thu et al., 2013a)) into a fully unsupervised Bayesian word segmentation scheme.

Dictionary-based word segmentation has the advantage of being able to exploit human knowledge about the sequences of characters in the language that are used to form words. This approach is simple and has proven to be a very effective technique in previous studies. Problems arise due to the coverage of the dictionary. The dictionary may not be able to cover the running text well, for example in the case of low-resource languages the dictionary might be small, or in the case of named entities, even though a comprehensive dictionary of common words may exist, it is likely to fall far short of covering all of the words that can occur in the language.

Unsupervised word segmentation techniques, have high coverage. They are able to learn how to segment by discovering patterns in the text that recur. The weakness of these approaches is that they have no explicit knowledge of how words are formed in the language, and the sequences they discover from text may simply be sequences in text that frequently occur and may bear no relationship to actual words in the language. As such these units, although they are useful in the context of the generative model used to discover them, may not be appropriate for use in an application that might benefit from these segments being words in the language. We believe that machine translation is one such application.

This method gives the unsupervised method a means of exploiting a dictionary of words in its training process, by allowing the integrated method to use the dictionary to segment text when appropriate, and otherwise use its unsupervised models to handle the segmentation. To do this a separate dictionary generation process is integrated into the generative model of the unsupervised segmenter to create a semi-supervised segmenter that segments using a single unified generative model.

3.3 Dictionary Set Augmented Model

In this model, the a set of subsets of the dictionary were extracted based on the part-of-speech labels contained in the dictionary (Lwin, 1993). This set of subsets was not a partition of the original dictionary since some of the types in the dictionary were ambiguous causing some overlap of the subsets. In the previous model, during the generative process a decision was made, with a certain probability learned from the data, as to whether the segment would be generated from the unsupervised sub-model or the dictionary sub-model. In this model, the decision to generate from the dictionary model is refined into a number of decisions to generate from a number of subsets of the dictionary, each with its own probability. These probabilities were re-estimated from the sampled segmentation of the corpus at the end of each iteration of the training (in a similar manner to the dictionary augmented model). A diagram showing the generative process is shown in Figure 1.

3.4 Language Model Augmented Model

In (Theeramunkong and Usanavasin, 2001) dictionary approaches were deliberately avoided in order to address issues with unknown words. Instead a decision tree model for segmentation was proposed. Our approach although different in character (since a generative model is used), shares the insight that knowledge of how words are constructed is key to segmentation when dictionary information is absent.

In this model we used the dictionary resource, but in a more indirect manner. We use a language model to capture the notion of exactly what constitutes a segment. To do this words in the dictionary were first segmented into syllables. Then, a language model was trained on this segmented dictionary. This model will assign high probabilities to the words it has been trained on, and therefore in some sense is able to capture the spirit of the dictionary-based methods described previously. However, it will also have learned something about the way Myanmar words are composed from syllables, and can be expected to assign a higher probability to unknown words that resemble the words it has been trained on, than to sequences of syllables that are not consistent with its training data.

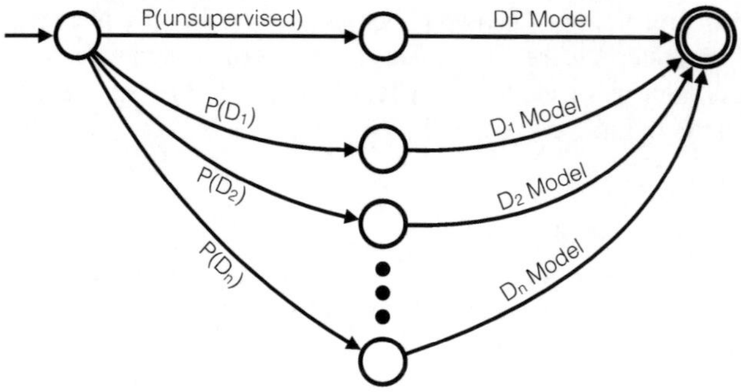

Figure 1: Generative process with multiple dictionaries competing to generate the data alongside an unsupervised Dirichlet process model.

This model can be naturally introduced directly into the Dirichlet process model as a component of the base measure. Equation 2 decomposes into two terms:

1. A Poisson probability mass function: $\frac{\lambda^{|\mathbf{s}|}}{|\mathbf{s}|!}e^{-\lambda}$

2. A uniform distribution over the vocabulary: $\frac{1}{|V|^{|\mathbf{s}|}}$.

The first term above models the choice of length for the segment. The second term models the choice of syllables that comprise the segment is in essence a unigram language model that provides little information about segments are constructed, and serves simply to discourage the formation of long segments that would lead to overfitting. We directly replace the part of the base measure with our more informative language model built from the dictionary.

4 Experiments

4.1 Overview

In the experimental section we aim to analyze two aspects of the performance of the proposed segmentation approaches. Firstly their segmentation quality and secondly for those approaches that are capable of partially labeling the corpus, the accuracy of the labeling.

4.2 Corpora

For all our experiments we used a 160K-sentence subset of the Basic Travel Expression (BTEC) corpus (Kikui et al., 2003), for the Myanmar language. This corpus was segmented using an accurate rule-based approach into individual syllables, and this segmentation was used as the base segmentation in all our experiments.

In addition a test corpus was made by sampling 150-sentences randomly from the corpus. This corpus was then segmented by hand and the segments were annotated manually using the set of POS tags that our system was capable of annotating, together with an 'UNK' tag to annotate segments that fell out of this scope. The test sentences were included in the data used for the training of the Bayesian models. These sentences were treated in the same manner the rest of the data in that they were initially syllable segmented. At the end of the training, the test sentences together with the segmentation assigned by the training, were extracted from the corpus, and their segmentation/labeling was evaluated with reference to the human annotation.

4.3 Segmentation Performance

We used the Edit Distance of the Word Separator (EDWS) to evaluate the segmentation performance of the models. This technique yields precision, recall and F-score statistics from the edit operations required to transform one segmented sequence into another by means of the insertion, deletion and substitution of segmentation boundaries. In this measure the substitution operator corresponds to an identity substitution and therefore indicates a correct segment boundary. Insertions correspond to segmentation boundaries in

Method	Precision	Recall	F-score	Sub	Ins	Del
Unsupervised	82.27	33.82	0.48	348	681	75
Maximum Matching	78.39	99.42	0.88	1023	6	282
Dictionary	89.67	57.34	0.70	590	439	68
Dictionary Set	89.46	51.99	0.66	535	494	63
Language Model (LM)	88.15	31.10	0.46	320	709	43
Dictionary Set + LM	91.27	49.76	0.64	512	517	49

Table 1: Segmentation Performance.

the segmented output that do not correspond to any segmentation boundary in the reference. Deletions correspond to segmentation boundaries in the reference that do not correspond to any segmentation boundary in the segmented output. Precision recall and F-score are calculated as follows using the Chinese Word Segmentation Evaluation Tookit (Joy, 2004):

$$\text{precision} = \frac{\text{\#substitutions}}{\text{\#segment boundaries in output}}$$

$$\text{recall} = \frac{\text{\#substitutions}}{\text{\#segment boundaries in reference}}$$

$$\text{F-score} = \frac{2 * \text{precision} * \text{recall}}{\text{precision} + \text{recall}}$$

Table 1 shows the segmentation performance all of the systems. In terms of precision we see an improvement when the additional models are added to the baseline unsupervised model. The maximum matching strategy has the lowest precision but the highest recall, this is due to the over-generation of segmentation boundaries in regions where no dictionary matches are possible. In these regions the reference segmentation boundaries are always annotated (since the model defaults to syllable segmentation in these regions), but at the expense of precision. This is reflected in the relatively low numbers of insertions (6), and the relatively high number of deletions (282). As expected the dictionary set approach gave similar performance to the Dictionary approach. The language model approach produced a respectable level of precision, but a low value for recall. When integrated into the dictionary-based models however, it was able to increase precision.

4.4 Labeling Accuracy

We evaluated the accuracy of the labeling on two methods: the first method used only a set of dictionaries (as described in Section 3.3). This method was able to label with an accuracy of 64.53%. The second method consisted of the same technique, but with the addition of the language model trained on the syllable segmented dictionaries (as described in Section 3.4). We found that the dictionary-based language model was able to improved the labeling accuracy 1.2% to 65.73%.

5 Examples and Analysis

Figure 2 shows an example an unsupervised segmentation with a typical error. Frequent words are often attached to neighboring words to form erroneous compound segments. In this example, taken from real output of the segmenter, the word 'De' (this) has been attached to the word 'SarOuk' (book), and similar the words in the phrase 'KaBeMharLe' (where is it) have all been segmented as a single segment (which occurs frequently in the corpus).

In Figure 3, a typical segmentation from the maximum matcher is shown. In this example the word 'BarThar' (language) occurs in the dictionary but the word 'JaPan' (Japan) does not. The maximum matcher defaults to segmenting the word for Japan into its component syllables, whereas the unsupervised segmenter with dictionary has attempted an unsupervised segmentation on this part of the string. The word 'Japan' occurs sufficiently frequently in the BTEC corpus that the segmenter has been able to

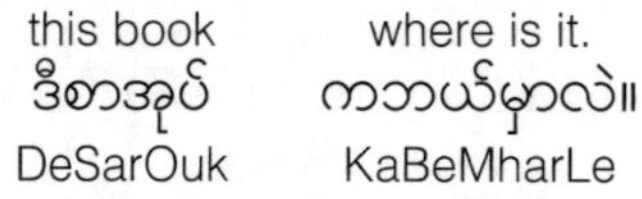

Figure 2: An unsupervised segmentation.

learn the word during training and has thereby managed to successfully segment the word in the output. The word for language was segmented by means of the embedded dictionary model.

Figure 4 shows an example of the partial labeling produced from the model that used a set of dictionaries in combination with a dictionary-based language model in the base measure. Due to the small amount of resources available, substantial parts of the sequence are unable to be labeled (and are annotated with the 'U' tag in the figure, indicating that they were segmented by the unsupervised component of the model). The remainder of the words are annotated with POS tags corresponding to the dictionary they were generated from.

Figure 3: A segmentation from maximum matching.

Figure 4: A partially labeled segmentation.

6 Conclusion

In this paper we have proposed and investigated the effectiveness of several methods intended to exploit limited quantities of dictionary resources available for low resource languages. Our results show that by integrating a dictionary directly into an unsupervised word segmenter we were able to improve both precision and recall. We found that attempting to model word formation using a language model on its own was ineffective compared with the approaches that directly used a dictionary. However, this language model proved useful when used in conjunction with the direct dictionary-based models, where it served to assist the modeling of words that were not in the dictionary. In future work we intend to develop the dictionary set approach by extending it to introduce basic knowledge of the morphological structure of the language directly into the model.

References

Vincent Berment. 2004. Sylla and gmsword: applications to myanmar languages computerization. In *Burma Studies Conference*.

Sharon Goldwater, Thomas L. Griffiths, and Mark Johnson. 2006. Contextual dependencies in unsupervised word segmentation. In *ACL-44: Proceedings of the 21st International Conference on Computational Linguistics and the 44th annual meeting of the Association for Computational Linguistics*, pages 673–680, Morristown, NJ, USA. Association for Computational Linguistics.

Sharon Goldwater, Thomas L Griffiths, and Mark Johnson. 2009. A bayesian framework for word segmentation: Exploring the effects of context. *Cognition*, 112(1):21–54.

Hla Hla Htay and Kavi Narayana Murthy. 2008. Myanmar word segmentation using syllable level longest matching. In *IJCNLP*, pages 41–48.

Joy, 2004. *Chinese Word Segmentation Evaluation Toolkit.*

Chang Jyun-Shen, Chi-Dah Chen, and Shun-Der Chen. 1991. Chinese word segmentation through constraint satisfaction and statistical optimization. In *Proceedings of ROC Computational Linguistics Conference*, pages 147–165.

G. Kikui, E. Sumita, T. Takezawa, and S. Yamamoto. 2003. Creating corpora for speech-to-speech translation. In *Proceedings of EUROSPEECH-03*, pages 381–384.

San Lwin. 1993. *Myanmar - English Dictionary*. Department of the Myanmar Language Commission, Ministry of Education, Union of Myanmar.

Sun Maosong, Shen Dayang, and Benjamin K. Tsou. 1998. Chinese word segmentation without using lexicon and hand-crafted training data. In *Proceedings of the 17th international conference on Computational linguistics - Volume 2*, COLING '98, pages 1265–1271, Stroudsburg, PA, USA. Association for Computational Linguistics.

Daichi Mochihashi, Takeshi Yamada, and Naonori Ueda. 2009. Bayesian unsupervised word segmentation with nested pitman-yor language modeling. In *ACL-IJCNLP '09: Proceedings of the Joint Conference of the 47th Annual Meeting of the ACL and the 4th International Joint Conference on Natural Language Processing of the AFNLP: Volume 1*, pages 100–108, Morristown, NJ, USA. Association for Computational Linguistics.

Papageorgiou and Constantine P. 1994. Japanese word segmentation by hidden markov model. In *Proceedings of the workshop on Human Language Technology*, HLT '94, pages 283–288, Stroudsburg, PA, USA. Association for Computational Linguistics.

Wenzhe Pei, Dongxu Han, and Baobao Chang. 2013. A refined hdp-based model for unsupervised chinese word segmentation. In Maosong Sun, Min Zhang, Dekang Lin, and Haifeng Wang, editors, *Chinese Computational Linguistics and Natural Language Processing Based on Naturally Annotated Big Data*, volume 8202 of *Lecture Notes in Computer Science*, pages 44–51. Springer Berlin Heidelberg.

Steven L Scott. 2002. Bayesian methods for hidden markov models : Recursive computing in the 21st century. *Journal of the American Statistical Association*, 97(457):337–351.

Virach Sornlertlamvanich. 1993. Word segmentation for thai in machine translation system. *Machine Translation, National Electronics and Computer Technology Center, Bangkok*, pages 50–56.

A Srithirath and P. Seresangtakul. 2013. A hybrid approach to lao word segmentation using longest syllable level matching with named entities recognition. In *Electrical Engineering/Electronics, Computer, Telecommunications and Information Technology (ECTI-CON), 2013 10th International Conference on*, pages 1–5, May.

W. J. Teahan, Rodger McNab, Yingying Wen, and Ian H. Witten. 2000. A compression-based algorithm for chinese word segmentation. *Comput. Linguist.*, 26(3):375–393, September.

Thanaruk Theeramunkong and Sasiporn Usanavasin. 2001. Non-dictionary-based thai word segmentation using decision trees. In *In Proceedings of the First International Conference on Human Language Technology Research.*

Tun Thura Thet, Jin-Cheon Na, and Wunna Ko Ko. 2008. Word segmentation for the myanmar language. *J. Information Science*, 34(5):688–704.

Ye Kyaw Thu, Andrew Finch, Yoshinori Sagisaka, and Eiichiro Sumita. 2013a. A study of myanmar word segmentation schemes for statistical machine translation. *Proceeding of the 11th International Conference on Computer Applications*, pages 167–179.

Ye Kyaw Thu, Andrew Finch, Eiichiro Sumita, and Yoshinori Sagisaka. 2013b. Unsupervised and semi-supervised myanmar word segmentation approaches for statistical machine translation.

Zinmin Wu and Gwyneth Tseng. 1993. Chinese text segmentation for text retrieval: Achievements and problems. *Journal of the American Society for Information Science*, 44(5):532–542.

A Framework for Learning Morphology using Suffix Association Matrix

Shilpa Desai
Department of Computer Science and Technology
Goa University, Goa, India
sndesai@gmail.com

Jyoti Pawar
Department of Computer Science and Technology
Goa University, Goa, India
jyotidpawar@gmail.com

Pushpak Bhattacharyya
Department of Computer Science and Engineering
IIT, Powai, Mumbai India
pb@cse.iitb.ac.in

Abstract

Unsupervised learning of morphology is used for automatic affix identification, morphological segmentation of words and generating paradigms which give a list of all affixes that can be combined with a list of stems. Various unsupervised approaches are used to segment words into stem and suffix. Most unsupervised methods used to learn morphology assume that suffixes occur frequently in a corpus. We have observed that for morphologically rich Indian Languages like Konkani, 31 percent of suffixes are not frequent. In this paper we report our framework for Unsupervised Morphology Learner which works for less frequent suffixes. Less frequent suffixes can be identified using p-similar technique which has been used for suffix identification, but cannot be used for segmentation of short stem words. Using proposed Suffix Association Matrix, our Unsupervised Morphology Learner can also do segmentation of short stem words correctly. We tested our framework to learn derivational morphology for English and two Indian languages, namely Hindi and Konkani. Compared to other similar techniques used for segmentation, there was an improvement in the precision and recall.

1 Introduction

Learning morphology by a machine is crucial for tasks like stemming, machine translation etc. Rule based affix stripping approach, semi-supervised, unsupervised learning of morphology and finite state approach as some of the well known methods used to learn morphology by a machine. Rule based affix stripping approaches (Lovins, 1968; Porter, 1980; Paice, 1990; Loftsson, 2008; Maung et. al, 2008) depend heavily on linguistic input and require a lot of human effort, especially for morphologically rich languages. Pure unsupervised approaches learn morphology from a corpus (Freitag, 2005; Goldsmith, 2001; Hammarström, 2011). The accuracy of pure unsupervised methods is relatively low. Semi-supervised approaches use minimal linguistic input and unsupervised methods to automate morphology learning process (Forsberg, 2007; Lindén, 2008; Chan, 2008; Dreyer, 2011). Semi-supervised approaches perform better than pure unsupervised approaches. Finite state approaches (Koskenniemi, 1983; Beesley & Kartunnen, 2003) represent morphology using finite state machines. Finite state approaches require linguistic input in the form of paradigm identification. Unsupervised and semi-supervised methods can provide input to build finite state based morphology systems reducing the time taken to build such systems.

In this paper we report the framework for an Unsupervised Morphology Learner. Most unsupervised segmentation techniques (Freitag, 2005; Goldsmith, 2001; Hammarström, 2011) which learn morphology from a corpus assume that suffixes are frequent in a corpus. We observed that for morphologically rich Indian languages like Hindi and Konkani, the assumption that suffixes are frequent does not hold true. These languages are morphologically rich and 31 percent of verb suffixes are not frequent in the corpus. Thus, we choose not to make any such assumption about the frequency of suffix occurrence in our unsupervised learning of morphology. One promising methodology for unsupervised segmentation which does not make any suffix frequency assumptions is p-similar

Proceedings of the 5th Workshop on South and Southeast Asian NLP, 25th International Conference on Computational Linguistics, pages 28–36, Dublin, Ireland, August 23-29 2014.

technique for morpheme segmentation first proposed by Gaussier (1999). Researchers have used this method for suffix identification and not for segmentation (Gaussier, 1999; Sharma, 2006). We extended this less studied technique to segment words by introducing the concept of suffix association matrix, thus giving us an unsupervised method which correctly identifies suffixes irrespective of their frequency of occurrence in the corpus and also segments short stem words. To the best of our knowledge, most reported work which uses p-similar technique for suffix identification (Gaussier, 1999; Sharma, 2006) enforce a restriction on stem-length that it should be at least five. This restriction works well for suffix identification but not for segmentation. For Indian languages like Hindi and Konkani, we observed that the restriction leads to an inability to segment many words with short stem-length. Especially many verb stems in Indian languages have stem-length less than five. To overcome this shortcoming, we have proposed an Unsupervised Morphology Learner (UML) framework.

We implemented UML framework for derivational morphology and tested our method for English language and two Indian languages namely Konkani and Hindi. The rest of the paper is organized as follows; section 2 is on related work. Section 3 provides the terminology used in the paper. The motivation for this work is presented in section 4. Unsupervised Morphology Learner (UML) framework is presented in section 5. Experimental results are discussed in section 6 and finally we conclude the paper in section 7.

2 Related Work

Unsupervised learning of morphology is done at different levels, namely, affix list identification, segmenting word into stem and affix, and generating a list of paradigms i.e. a list of all stems with information of the suffixes that each stem combines with (Hammarström, 2011). In his survey paper, Hammarström (2011) summarizes work related to unsupervised morphology. Most recent work in morphology learning is semi-supervised. Such methods use a small set of example paradigms as input to train the system and classify unseen words into paradigms or learn new paradigms (Lindén, 2009; Dreyer, 2011).

A popular pure unsupervised morphology technique was first proposed by Goldsmith (2001) which does not assume any linguistic input. Goldsmith (2001) introduced a set of heuristics that develops a probabilistic morphological grammar, and used Minimum Description Length (MDL) as a tool to evaluate it. The technique used for affix and paradigm identification was based on affix occurrence frequency. Several different authors have appreciated MDL as the motivation for segmentation. Some authors (Gelbukh et. al., 2004; Bacchin, 2005) have used random segmentation and picked the best segmentation to minimize size or find splits where constituent morphemes occur in multiple splits.

Our work is inspired by a less studied p-similar technique proposed by Gaussier (1999). p-similar techniques have been used for suffix identification rather than segmentation in most related unsupervised morphology learners (Sharma, 2006). Here the restriction on stem-length first proposed by Gaussier is upheld. Sharma's (2006) work deals with neutral suffix only and does not capture non-neutral suffixes. These studies are limited to suffix identification and do not generate paradigms.

3 Terminology Used

Let L be a language with alphabet set $\sum$.

$W= \{w| w \subset \sum^*\}$ be set of valid words in language L.

Let $d: W \rightarrow W$ denote a derivation function where $d(w_x)=w_y$ iff words w_x and w_y are derivationally related to each other in L.

Let $w_x s_y$ denote concatenation of strings w_x and s_y where $w_x, s_y \in \sum^*$.

Let S_N be set of neutral derivational suffixes.

$S_N = \{s|w_2=w_1 s \text{ and } w_2,w_1 \in W \text{ and } d(w_1)=w_2 \text{ and } s \in \sum^*\}$

For example, when s=er, w_1=farm and w_2=farmer

Let S_B be set of non-neutral derivational suffixes.

$S_B = \{s_x,s_y|ws_x=ws_y \text{ and } d(ws_x)=ws_y \text{ and } w, s_x, s_y \in \sum^* \text{ and } w \notin W\}$

For example, when s_x=ify, s_y=ity and w=quant suffixes *ify, ity* are non neutral suffixes.

4 Motivation

Primarily, frequency based suffix identification techniques (Goldsmith, 2001; Hammarström, 2011) commonly used in recent times, fail to identify suffixes with low frequency. We explored suffix identification techniques which could identify suffixes irrespective of frequency of occurrence in the corpus. We chose one such method p-similar technique. However p-similar technique (Gaussier, 1999) cannot be used directly for segmentation as it results in a high number of false positives. Hence we proposed a suffix association matrix to avoid the false positives. According to p-similar technique, given two words x, y ∈ W, if ∃ b_1 such that $x=b_1s_1$ and $y=b_1s_2$ where $b_1, s_1, s_2 \in \sum^+$, then b_1 is a stem and s_1, s_2 are suffixes, provided they satisfy the following conditions:

a. A suffix is valid only when it occurs with at least two different stems
b. A stem is valid when it occurs with at least two identified suffixes
c. Stem length should be five or more

The third condition on stem length was introduced to improve the precision of the suffix list generated. However the aim was to only generate a suffix list and not segment word into stem + suffix. We probed the possibility of applying this effective p-similar technique to segment words. We faced the following issues when trying to use p-similar technique for segmentation:

- The technique failed for short-stem length words because of the restriction placed on stem-length. Example words with stem like *walk*, *talk* are not segmented.
- When words like addiction, addictive, aggression and aggressive are part of the input, suffixes identified are *"on"* and *"ve"* in place of *"ion"* and *"ive"*. This problem is called over-stemming.
- When words like *cannon, cannot, America, American, agent, agency* are part of the input, *"n"* and *"t"* are identified as suffix. Although *"n"* and *"t"* are valid suffix for some words, *cannon=canno+n* and *cannot=canno+t* are wrong segmentation.

We realize that the candidate stem-suffix pair b_i+s_i identified using the p-similar technique falls under one of the following cases:

Case 1: b_i is a valid stem and s_i is a valid suffix for stem b_i. For example, *mistake+NULL*, *mistake+n* are valid. Suffixes *NULL* and *n* are valid for stem *mistake*.

Case 2: b_i is an invalid stem and s_i is a invalid suffix. Example *addicti+on* and *addicti+ve* and *aggressi+on* and *aggressi+ve* are invalid; *addict+ion* and *addict+ive* and *aggress+ion* and *aggress+ive* are valid.

Case 3: b_i is a valid stem and s_i is a invalid suffix for stem b_i. For example *year+n* is invalid. Suffix *n* is invalid for stem *year* while suffix *NULL* and *ly* are valid for stem year.

Case 4: b_i is an invalid stem for any suffix and s_i is valid for some other stem. Example *canno+n* and *canno+t* are invalid pairs; *absen-ce* and *absen-t* and valid; *mistake+NULL* and *mistake+n* are valid.

To overcome the problems faced in cases 2, 3 and 4 we have proposed the following framework

5 Unsupervised Morphology Learner Framework

UML can be used to learn derivational morphology or inflectional morphology. When the input given is a lexicon, the framework will learn derivational morphology. If a corpus is used as input it will learn both derivational and inflectional morphology and not distinguish between the two. We have tested our framework with lexicon as input to learn derivational morphology. The framework for the proposed UML is shown below in Figure 1. UML has five modules. It uses a lexicon resource or a corpus as input. It generates three final resources and two intermediate resources which are enhanced into the final resources.

The resource used as input could be:

- Lexicon L: It is list of dictionary words found in the language. This resource is generated from a WordNet of a language used to learn derivational morphology or
- Corpus C: A collection of un-annotated text used to learn both inflectional and derivational morphology.

The intermediate resource generated:

- *Candidate Stem-Suffix List*: It is the initial list of stems and suffixes identified for an input language using the p-similar technique. It consists of two sets namely set of suffix S_{suffix} and set of stem S_{stem}. Sample entries in these set for English language are S_{suffix} = *{ er, ic, ly, ness, ment, …}* and S_{stem}= *{adorn, attack,….}*
- *Initial Paradigms:* This is a list of all stems with information of which suffixes combine with which stems in the input lexicon L or Corpus. Sample entry in *Initial Paradigms List* is *ic.y= academ + allerg + geometr + homeopath + horrif + letharg + majest + prehistor + specif + strateg* where *"ic"* and *"y"* are suffixes which combine with the stems like *adadem.*

The final resources generated:

- *Stem-Suffix List:* This resource is generated from the *Candidate Stem-Suffix List* resource by pruning invalid suffixes. It is a useful resource as it gives the stems of words from a lexicon which could later be used for identifying stems in a corpus for stemming inflectional words.
- *Suffix-Association Matrix:* This resource helps us identify for how many instances a suffix s_1 has occurred with a suffix s_2 in the Lexicon/Corpus. It is a crucial resource in eliminating the shortcoming of p-similar technique to morphologically segment words with short stem length as well as overcome chance association of suffix found.
- *Morphology Paradigms:* This resource contains paradigms extracted from the words found in the input lexicon/corpus. It is a refined version of *Initial Paradigm* resource.

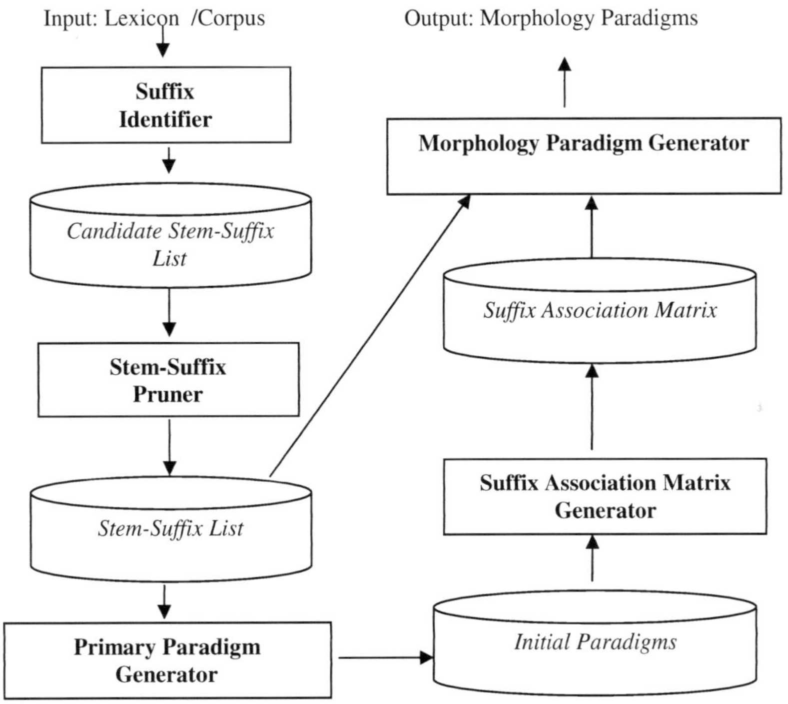

Figure 1: Unsupervised Morphology Learner (UML) Framework

UML comprises of five main modules, a brief description and algorithm for each of the module is given below:

Module 1 - Suffix Identifier

Description: Identifies the Candidate suffixes using p-similar technique. It generates a temporary resource namely *Candidate Stem-Suffix List*. For every word in the corpus, it checks if there is another word with a common stem, adds common stem to stem list and rest to suffix list, provided that a stem occurs with more than one suffix and a suffix occurs with more than one stem.

Input: Lexicon of the language L (or raw un-annotated corpus for inflectional morphology C)
Output: *Candidate Stem-Suffix List* resource
Algorithm:

For each input word $p \in L$,
find $q, r, s \in L$, such that $\exists\, b_1, b_2, b_3$
where $p=b_1s_1$, $q=b_1s_2$, $r=b_2s_1$, $s= b_2s_3$ where $b_1, b_2, b_3, s_1, s_2, s_3 \in \sum^*$.
Add b_1 to set of stems S_{stem},
Add s_1 to set of suffixes S_{suffix},
EndFor

Module 2 - Stem-suffix pruner:
Description: This module applies heuristic $\mathbf{H_1}$ stated below. $\mathbf{H_1}$ is framed to correct the stem-suffix list to fix the problem of over-stemming.
$\mathbf{H_1}$: Given suffix s_i for stem b_i if $\exists\, a \in \sum^*$ such that $as_i \in S_{suffix}$ and $b_ja=b_i$ and $b_j \in S_{stem}$ where S_{stem} is set of stems and S_{suffix} is set of suffixes then replace b_i by b_j and s_i by as_i
Input: *Candidate Stem-Suffix List* resource
Output: *Stem-Suffix List* resource
Algorithm:

For each suffix s_1 from suffix list,
If $\exists\, a \in \sum^*$ such that $as_1 \in S_{suffix}$ and $b_2a=b_1$ and $b_1, b_2 \in S_{stem}$ then
replace b_1 by b_2 and s_1 by as_1.
EndIf
EndFor

Module 3 - Primary Paradigm Generator:
Description: Using *Stem-Suffix List* this module generates the *Initial Paradigms* list. A paradigm is composed of suffixes that go together for a list of stems in the input lexicon/corpus.
Input: *Stem-Suffix List* resource
Output: *Initial Paradigms* resource
Algorithm:

For each input word $p \in L$, if $p=b_1s_1$ where $b_1 \in S_{stem}$ and $s_1 \in S_{suffix}$.
Set paradigm-string= s_1.
For every $q \in L$ such that $q= b_1s_2$ where $b_1 \in S_{stem}$ and $s_2 \in S_{suffix}$,
Set paradigm-string = paradigm-string.s_2.
Add paradigm-string to $S_{paradigm}$, set of paradigm.
EndFor
EndFor
For each paradigm-string $p_1 \in S_{paradigm}$ where p_1 ="$s_{x1}.s_{x2} \ldots s_{xn}=b_1$"
and $s_{x1}, s_{x2}, \ldots, s_{xn} \in S_{suffix}$ and $b_1 \in S_{stem}$
Set collapse-paradigm-string = $s_{x1}.s_{x2} \ldots s_{xn}=b_1$
If $\exists$ paradigm-string $p_2 \in S_{paradigm}$ such that p_2 =" $s_{x1}.s_{x2} \ldots s_{xn}=b_2$" and $b_2 \in S_{stem}$
Set collapse-paradigm-string = collapse-paradigm-string + b_2
Add collapse-paradigm-string to $S_{initial\text{-}paradigm}$, set of Initial Paradigms
EndIf
EndFor

Module 4- Suffix Association Matrix Generator:
Description: From the *Initial Paradigms*, this module computes the *Suffix Association Matrix* resource. Suffix association matrix is a square matrix where each row and column corresponds to a suffix in suffix list. An entry in this matrix gives how many times a particular suffix occurs with another suffix in the *Initial Paradigms* resource.
Input: *Initial Paradigms* resource
Output: *Suffix Association Matrix* resource

Algorithm:

Let M be suffix association matrix which is $| S_{suffix}| * | S_{suffix}|$. If $S_{suffix} = \{s_1, s_2, ...s_p\}$ M has dimension p X p.

Initialize M=0;

For each paradigm-string $p_1 \in S_{initial\text{-}paradigm}$ where p_1 ="$s_{x1}.s_{x2} \ldots s_{xn}=b_1+ b_2+ b_3+\ldots+ b_m$"

For i= 1 to n

For j= i+1 to n

$M[s_{xi}][s_{xj}]= M[s_{xi}][s_{xj}] + m$; where $s_{xi} = s_q$ and $s_{xi} = s_r$ and $1<= q, r <=p$

EndFor

EndFor

EndFor

Module 5 - Morphology Paradigm Generator:

Description: Using *Stem-Suffix List* and Suffix Association Matrix this module generates *Morphology Paradigms List* resource. It is a pruned version of *Initial Paradigms* resource which uses Suffix Association matrix to remove less likely suffix combination in *Initial Paradigms*

Input: *Stem-Suffix List* resource

Output: *Initial Paradigms* resource

Algorithm:

For each input word $p \in L$, if $p=b_1s_1$ where $b_1\in S_{stem}$ and $s_1\in S_{suffix}$.

Set paradigm-string= s_1.

For every $q \in L$ such that $q= b_1s_2$ where $b_1\in S_{stem}$ and $s_2 \in S_{suffix}$,

If $M[s_1][s_2]$ > threshold value

Set paradigm-string = paradigm-string.s_2.

Add paradigm-string to $S_{paradigm}$, set of paradigm.

EndIf

EndFor

EndFor

For each paradigm-string $p_1 \in S_{paradigm}$ where p_1 ="$s_{x1}.s_{x2} \ldots s_{xn}=b_1$"

and $s_{x1}, s_{x2}, \ldots, s_{xn}\in S_{suffix}$ and $b_1\in S_{stem}$

Set collapse-paradigm-string = $s_{x1}.s_{x2} \ldots s_{xn}=b_1$

If $\exists$ paradigm-string $p_2\in S_{paradigm}$ such that p_2 =" $s_{x1}.s_{x2} \ldots s_{xn} =b_2$" and $b_2\in S_{stem}$

Set collapse-paradigm-string = collapse-paradigm-string + b_2

Add collapse-paradigm-string to $S_{initial\text{-}paradigm}$, set of Initial_Paradigms

EndIf

EndFor

5.1 Significance of Suffix Association Matrix

Suffix association matrix is a measure of how many times a particular suffix is associated with another suffix in the input resource. It is an important contribution as it provides us an alternate way to prune invalid stem-suffix pairs identified, rather than a restriction on the stem-length. Suffixes which are associated with each other more frequently are more likely to provide a correct paradigm than those where we find only a few chance instances of suffix associations.
Figure 2 illustrates an instance of suffix association matrix for the English language

	NULL	er	ing	ly
NULL	-	46	225	129
er	46	-	22	15
ing	225	22	-	0
ly	129	15	0	-

Figure 2: Instance of Suffix Association Matrix

This matrix helps handle valid stem with invalid suffix case. For instance wrong segmentation of the word *"bother"* as *"both+er"*. From the Suffix Association Matrix we check with which suffixes *er* is commonly associated. We then make a list of words with stem *"both"* and other suffix which commonly associate with suffix *"er"* like suffix *"ing"* We search a corpus for existence of such words like *"bothing"*. Thus rejecting the segmentation *bother=both+er*. This matrix also provides a solution to invalid stem with valid suffix. For instance *canno+n* and *canno+t* are invalid segmentations although the suffix *"n"* and *"t"* are valid in some other context. In such a rare association of a suffix *"n"* and *"t"* the corresponding entry in the suffix association matrix is found to be very low. We ran our algorithm for various values of threshold and found five as an optimal value. Any suffix association below five were pruned as chance associations.

5.2 Significance of heuristic H_1

This heuristic is used to handle the problem of over-stemming that occurs in p-similar technique. For example the p-similar technique identifies both *"ion"* and *"on"* as suffix. While segmenting a word like *"addiction"* we need to decide if *"addicti+on"* or *"addict+ion"* is correct. H_1 helps us in correctly segmenting the word as *"addict+ion"*.

5.3 Limitations of UML

UML is restricted to identify concatenative morphology paradigms only. Presently it identifies suffixes only and does not support irregular morphology wherein the stem undergoes a change before suffixation.

6 Experimental Results

The implementation of UML is done in Java. After applying our method, the paradigms obtained were compared to the paradigms obtained using p-similar method with minimum stem-size five. The precision was computed as ratio of number of words correctly segmented to total number of words segmented. Recall is computed as ratio of number of words correctly segmented to number of words in given input which could be segmented. The results have been tabulated in Table 1 below.

Method	Number of Paradigms	Recall	Precision	F-Score
Language : *English*				
Data Set: English lexicon with 21813 entries was obtained from the English WordNet[1]				
p-similar with stems size >5	**1163**	**0.85**	**0.93**	**0.89**
UML for derivational morphology	**413**	**0.92**	**0.93**	**0.92**
Language : *Hindi*				
Data Set: Hindi lexicon with 23807 entries was extracted from the Hindi WordNet[2]				
p-similar with stems size >5	**1127**	**0.83**	**0.87**	**0.85**
UML for derivational morphology	**332**	**0.87**	**0.94**	**0.90**
Language : *Konkani*				
Data Set: Konkani lexicon with 25838 entries was extracted from the Konkani WordNet[3]				
p-similar with stems size >5	**1088**	**0.75**	**0.77**	**0.75**
UML for derivational morphology	**274**	**0.87**	**0.87**	**0.87**

Table 1: Results for English, Hindi and Konkani Language

[1] http://wordnet.princeton.edu/wordnet/download/
[2] http://www.cfilt.iitb.ac.in/wordnet/webhwn/
[3] http://konkaniwordnet.unigoa.ac.in

6.1 Effect of stem length on recall

We list below in Table 2, a few examples of how recall is reduced as words with short stem length are not segmented, when the minimum stem size is five.

Language	Suffix for which word not segmented	Number of words not segmented	Few examples of words not segmented
English	er	9	eater, farmer, owner...
Hindi	ी[4] (I;;Hindi suffix)	35	अरबी (arabic; arab; name of a country), आलसी (aalas; lazy;), आसानी (aasani; easiness;)
Konkani	ी (I;;Konkani suffix)	43	आनंदी (anandi; being happy;), आरोपी (aaropi; accused;)

Table 2: Effect of stem length

We observe that number of words not segmented in English is relatively very less as compared to the Indian languages Hindi and Konkani. Thus the restriction on stem-length works efficiently for English as compared to the Indian languages Hindi and Konkani.

6.2 Effect of stem length on precision

When we restrict the stem-length to five we observe that some wrong segmentation of words are pruned. Listed below in Table 3, are some examples

Language	Suffix for which word not segmented	Number of words not segmented	Few examples of words not segmented (wrongly)
English	er	32	bother, boxer, cater, sober …
Hindi	ी (I;;Hindi suffix)	8	चाँदी (chandi; silver;), चोटी (choti; peak;)
Konkani	ी (I;;Konkani suffix)	6	आजी (Aaji; grandmother;), काळी (kaalli; black;)

Table 3: Effect of stem-length on precision

We observe that for English, many word segmentations with stems-length less than five, identified by p-similar technique are correctly pruned by applying the restriction. We observe that wrong segmentations in case of Indian languages Hindi and Konkani are less when compared to English.

7 Conclusion

Unsupervised Morphology Learner framework thus can be effectively used to generate paradigms for Indian languages which have low frequency suffixes and words with short stem lengths. Suffix Association Matrix and heuristics H_1 is advantageous over p-similar technique with stem length restriction for languages like Konkani and Hindi which have many short length valid stems. The derivational suffixes obtained from UML with Lexicon as input can be used to distinguish from inflectional morphology suffixes when the framework is used with a corpus as input.

[4] A word in Indian language is followed by transliteration in Roman Script, translation in English and gloss in brackets

Reference

Bacchin, M., Ferro, N., and Melucci, M. (2005). A probabilistic model for stemmer generation. Information Processing and Management, 41(1):121–137.

Beesley K & Karttunen Lauri. 2003. Finite State Morphology. Stanford, CA: CSLI Publications.

Chan, E. 2008. Structures and Distributions in Morphology Learning. Ph.D thesis, University of Pennsylvania.

Dreyer, M. 2011. A non-parametric model for the discovery of inflectional paradigms from plain text using graphical models over strings. Ph.D thesis, The Johns Hopkins University, Baltimore, Maryland

Freitag, D. 2005. Morphology induction from term clusters. In Proceedings of the Ninth Conference on Computational Natural Language Learning (CoNLL-2005), pages 128–135, Ann Arbor, Michigan. Association for Computational Linguistics.

Gaussier Eric. 1999. *Unsupervised learning of derivational morphology from inflectional lexicons*. In ACL'99 Workshop Proceedings: Unsupervised Learning in Natural Language Processing : 24–30 ACL

Gelbukh, A. F., Alexandrov, M., and Han, S.-Y. (2004). Detecting inflection patterns in natural language by minimization of morphological model. In Sanfeliu, A., Trinidad, J. F. M., and Carrasco-Ochoa, J. A., editors, Proceedings of Progress in Pattern Recognition, Image Analysis and Applications, 9th Iberoamerican Congress on Pattern Recognition, CIARP '04, volume 3287 of Lecture Notes in Computer Science, pages 432–438. Springer-Verlag, Berlin.

Goldsmith J A. 2001. *Unsupervised learning of the morphology of a natural language*. Computational Linguistics 27(2): 153–198

Hammarstrom Harald and Lars Borin. 2011. Unsupervised learning of morphology. *Computational Linguistics*, (2):309–350.

Koskenniemi, K. 1983. *Two-level morphology: a general computational model for word-form recognition and production*. Helsinki, Department of General Linguistics, University of Helsinki.

Koskenniemi, K. 1996. *Finite-state morphology and information retrieval*. Proceedings of the ECAI-96 Workshop on Extended Finite State Models of Language ECAI, Budapest, Hungary : 42-56

Lindén, K. 2008. A probabilistic model for guessing base forms of new words by analogy. In Proceedings of CICLing-2008: 9th International Conference on Intelligent Text Processing and Computational Linguistics, volume 4919 of Lecture Notes in Computer Science, pages 106–116. Springer.

Lindén, K. and Tuovila, J. 2009 Corpus-based Paradigm Selection for Morphological Entries. In Proceedings of NODALIDA 2009, Odense, Denmark, May 2009

Loftsson, H. 2008. Tagging Icelandic text: A linguistic rule-based approach. Nordic Journal of Linguistics 31(1). 47–72.

Lovins J. B. 1968. *Development of a stemming algorithm*. Mechanical Translation and Computer Linguistic., vol.11, no.1/2: 22-31.

Maung, Zin Maung & Yoshiki Mikami. 2008. A rule-based syllable segmentation of myanmar text. In Proceedings of the IJCNLP-08 Workshop on NLP for Less Privileged Languages, 51–58. Hyderabad, India: Asian Federation of Natural Language Processing.

Paice, C.D. 1990. *Another stemmer*. SIGIR Forum, 24: 56-61

Porter, M. F. 1980. *An algorithm for suffix stripping*. Program 14 : 130-7.

Sharma U, (2006). Unsupervised Learning of Morphology of a Highly Inflectional Language, Ph.D. thesis, Tezpur University, Assam, India

English to Urdu Statistical Machine Translation: Establishing a Baseline

Bushra Jawaid, Amir Kamran and Ondřej Bojar
Charles University in Prague
Faculty of Mathematics and Physics
Institute of Formal and Applied Linguistics
Malostranské nám. 25, Praha 1, CZ-118 00, Czech Republic
`jawaid,kamran,bojar@ufal.mff.cuni.cz`

Abstract

The aim of this paper is to categorize and present the existence of resources for English-to-Urdu machine translation (MT) and to establish an empirical baseline for this task. By doing so, we hope to set up a common ground for MT research with Urdu to allow for a congruent progress in this field. We build baseline phrase-based MT (PBMT) and hierarchical MT systems and report the results on 3 official independent test sets. On all test sets, hierarchial MT significantly outperformed PBMT. The highest single-reference BLEU score is achieved by the hierarchical system and reaches 21.58% but this figure depends on the randomly selected test set. Our manual evaluation of 175 sentences suggests that in 45% of sentences, the hierarchical MT is ranked better than the PBMT output compared to 21% of sentences where PBMT wins, the rest being equal.

1 Introduction

Statistical Machine Translation (SMT) has always been a challenging task for language pairs with significant word ordering differences and rich inflectional morphology. The language pair such as English and Urdu, despite of descending from the same family of Indo-European languages, differs heavily in syntactic strucure and morphological characteristics. English is relatively fixed word order language and follows subject-verb-object (SVO) structure whereas Urdu uses restricted free word order language and most commonly follows the SOV pattern. Urdu word order is restricted for only few parts of speeches such as adjectives always precede nouns and postpositions follow nouns. Unlike English, Urdu is a pro-drop language. The morphology of Urdu is similar to other Indo-European languages, e.g. by having inflectional morphological system.

To the best of our knowledge, the research on English-to-Urdu machine translation has been very much fragmented, preventing the authors to build upon the works of others. Our underlying motivation for this paper is to establish a common ground and provide a concise summary of available data resources and set up reproducible baseline results of several available test sets. With this basis, future Urdu MT research should be able to stepwise improve the state of the art, in contrast with the scattered experiments done so far (Khan et al., 2013; Ali et al., 2013; Ali and Malik, 2010).

In Section 2, the experimental setup and data processing tools are described. Existing corpora are introduced in Section 3, automatic results are reported in Section 4 and manual evaluation is discussed in Section 5.

2 Experimental Setup

This section briefly introduces the selection of SMT models that are used to build the baseline English-Urdu SMT system and also explains the processing of parallel data before passing it to the MT system.

Proceedings of the 5th Workshop on South and Southeast Asian NLP, 25th International Conference on Computational Linguistics, pages 37–42,
Dublin, Ireland, August 23-29 2014.

2.1 Two Models of SMT

The state-of-the-art MT toolkit Moses[1] (Koehn et al., 2007), offers two mainstream models of SMT: phrase-based (PBMT) and syntax-based (SBMT) that includes the hierarchical model.

The PBMT model operates only on mapping of source phrases (short sequences of words) to target phrases. For dealing with word order differences, two rather weak models are available: lexicalized and distance-based. The lexicalized reordering models (Tillmann, 2004) are considered more advanced as they condition reordering on the actual phrases, whereas the latter model makes the reordering cost (paid when picking source phrases out of sequence) dependent only on the length of the jump. The distance-based model is suited well for local reordering but it is fairly weak in capturing any long distance reorderings.

The syntax-based model (SBMT) builds upon Synchronous Context-Free Grammar (SCFG) that synchronously generates source and target sentences. The grammar rules can either consist of linguistically motivated non-terminals such as NP, VP etc. or the generic non-terminal "X" in which case the model is called "hierarchical phrase-based" (Chiang, 2005; Chiang, 2007). In either case, the model is capable of capturing long-distance reordering much better than the lexicalized reordering of PBMT.

2.2 Data Processing and MT Training

For the training of our en-ur translation systems, the standard training pipeline of Moses is used along with the GIZA++ (Och and Ney, 2000) alignment toolkit and a 5-gram SRILM language model (Stolcke, 2002). The source texts were processed using the Treex platform (Popel and Žabokrtský, 2010)[2], which included tokenization and lemmatization.

The target side of the corpus is tokenized using a simple tokenization script[3] by Dan Zeman and it is lemmatized using the Urdu Shallow Parser[4] developed by Language Technologies Research Center of IIIT Hyderabad.

The alignments are learnt from the lemmatized version of the corpus. In all other cases, word forms (i.e. no morphological decomposition) in their true case (i.e. names capitalized but sentence starts lowercased) are used. The lexicalized reordering model uses the feature set called "msd-bidirectional-fe".

3 Dataset

Parallel and monolingual data resources are very scarce for low-resource language pairs such as English-Urdu. This section highlights the existing parallel and monolingual data resources that can be utilized for training SMT models. The number of official test sets are also exhibited.

3.1 Parallel Corpus

Our parallel corpus consists of around 79K sentences collected from five different sources. The collection comes from several domains such as News, Religion, Technology, Language and Culture etc. 95% of the data is used for training, whereas the rest is evenly split into dev and test sets.

- **Emille:** EMILLE (Enabling Minority Language Engineering) (Baker et al., 2002) is a collection of monolingual (written and spoken), parallel and annotated corpora of fourteen South Asian languages which is distributed by the European Language Resources Association (ELRA). The Urdu-English part are documents produced by the British Departments of Health, Social Services, Education and Skills, and Transport, Local Government and the Regions of British government translated into Urdu.

  In this work, the manually sentence aligned version of English-Urdu Emille corpus Jawaid and Zeman (2011) is used.

[1] `http://statmt.org/moses/`

[2] `http://ufal.mff.cuni.cz/treex/`

[3] The tokenization script can be downloaded from: http://hdl.handle.net/11858/00-097C-0000-0023-65A9-5

[4] `http://ltrc.iiit.ac.in/showfile.php?filename=downloads/shallow_parser.php`

- **IPC:** The Indic Parallel Corpus (Post et al., 2012)[5] is a collection of Wikipedia documents of six Indian sub-continent languages translated into English through crowdsourcing in the Amazon Mechanical Turk (MTurk) platform.

  The English-Urdu part generally contains four (in some cases three) English translations for each Urdu sentence. In a separate MTurk task, the Turkers voted which of the English translations is the best one. The official training, dev and devtest sets is first merged and afterwards the voting list is used to retrieve only the winning English sentence ignoring sentences with no votes altogether. The official testset is left unaltered to report our final results on this data.

- **Quran:** The publicly available parallel English and Urdu translation of Quranic data[6] is used, which is collected by Jawaid and Zeman (2011) in their work. The data consists of 6K aligned parallel sentences.

- **Penn Treebank:** Penn Treebank (Marcus et al., 1993) is an annotated corpus of around 4.5 million words originating from Wall Street Journal (WSJ), Brown corpus, Switchboard and ATIS. The entire treebank in English is released by the Linguistic Data Consortium (LDC). A subset of the WSJ section whose Urdu translations are provided by Center for Language Engineering (CLE)[7] is used. Out of 2,499 WSJ stories in the Treebank, only 317 are available in Urdu.

- **Afrl:** Afrl, the largest of the parallel resources we were able to get, is not publicly available. The corpus originally consists of 87K sentences coming from mix of several domains mainly news articles. The sentence alignments are manually checked of almost two thirds of the corpus, around 4K misaligned and 30K duplicate sentences are discarded.

The statistics shown in Table 1 are reported after removing duplicated sentences from each source. Almost all parallel corpora contained at least tens or hundreds of duplicate sentences. Afrl on the other hand contained larger chunks of Emille and also smaller subset of Penn Treebank. Around 3K sentences from Afrl that were seen in Emille are discarded but the Penn Treebank subset of Afrl is left intact because it provides different Urdu translations.

Each parallel corpus is randomly split into train, dev and test sets according to its relative size.

Corpus	Sentences	Tokens		% of Data	Train	Dev	Test
		EN	UR				
AFRL	50,313	960,683	1,022,563	63.6%	47,769	1,272	1,272
EMILLE	8,629	152,273	199,320	10.9%	8,193	218	218
IPC	7,478	118,644	132,968	9.46%	7,098	190	190
QURAN	6,364	251,387	269,947	8.05%	6,040	162	162
PENN	6,204	158,727	179,457	7.86%	5,888	158	158
TOTAL	78,988	-	-	100%	74,988	2,000	2,000

Table 1: Statistics of English-Urdu parallel corpora.

3.2 Monolingual Corpus

Jawaid et al. (2014) release[8] a plain and annotated Urdu monolingual corpus of around 95.4 million tokens distributed in around 5.4 million sentences. The monolingual corpus is a mix

[5] http://joshua-decoder.org/data/indian-parallel-corpora/
[6] http://ufal.mff.cuni.cz/legacy/umc/005-en-ur/
[7] http://www.cle.org.pk/software/ling_resources/UrduNepaliEnglishParallelCorpus.htm
[8] http://hdl.handle.net/11858/00-097C-0000-0023-65A9-5

of domains such as News, Religion, Blogs, Literature, Science, Education etc. Only plain text monolingual data is used to build our language model.

3.3 Official Testsets

In addition to the testset that is created from the parallel corpora resources, results are reported on three official testsets.

NIST 2008 Open Machine Translation (OpenMT) Evaluation[9] has distributed test data from 2 domains: Newswire and Web. The Web data is collected from user forums, discussion groups and blogs, whereas Newswire data is a mix of newswire stories and data from web. The test data contain 4 English translations for each Urdu sentence, the first English translation is picked in all cases. Because the majority of test sets are created in order to faciliatate Urdu-to-English MT, most of them contain multiple English references against each Urdu source.

Another testset is released with the IPC. Only those sentences are used whose ids are present in the voting list. The domain of the IPC test set is discussed in Section 3.1.

CLE[10] has published small test set from News domain specifically for MT evaluation. The test data contains 3 Urdu references against each source. All reference translations are used for the evaluation.

Table 2 shows the number of sentences in each test set that are used for the final evaluation. We also report the coverage of each test set (calculated on vocabulary size) i.e. how many source words in a test set were seen in the training data. The notions used in Table 2 to introduce coverage are explained in Section 4.

		NIST 2008		IPC	CLE
		NewsWire	Web Test		
Sentences		400	600	544	400
Coverage	ALL	84%	91%	90%	87%
	Except-Afrl	80%	87%	88%	84%

Table 2: Statistics of official English-Urdu test sets.

4 Results

The BLEU metric (Papineni et al., 2002) has been used to evaluate the performance of the systems. Models are trained on two different datasets: all parallel corpora (referred as "ALL") and parallel data excluding Afrl corpus (referred as "Except-Afrl"). The latter model is trained due to the fact that Afrl corpus is publicly not available. The community working on English-Urdu machine translation can thus have one common baseline that could be used to evaluate their improved systems in the future. Including Afrl allows us to see the gains in performance thanks to the additional data.

Table 3 shows the baseline results of phrase-based and hierarchical systems when trained on both datasets. The results are reported on two test sets: the test set of 2,000 sentences (called Large in Table 3) as shown in Table 1 and its subset of 728 sentences which excludes 1,272 test sentences from Afrl (called Small in Table 3).

PBMT performs better when integrated with lexicalized reordering model but Hierarchical MT outperforms both PBMT setups on both smaller and larger test sets. The absolute BLEU scores drop by up to 6 points when Afrl is removed from the training data, however they return back to ~20 when Afrl is also removed from the test set. This highlights the importance of data overall and the match in domain in particular, as supported by the differences in vocabulary coverage (see the column "Coverage" in Table 3).

Table 4 shows the results of the best performing setups (i.e. phrase-based with lexicalized reordering model and hierarchical model) trained on both training datasets and evaluated on the

[9] `http://catalog.ldc.upenn.edu/LDC2010T21`

[10] `http://www.cle.org.pk/software/ling_resources/testingcorpusmt.htm`

Parallel Corpora	Test Set	Phrase-based	Phrase-based-LexReo	Hierarchical	Coverage
ALL	Large	18.30±0.74	19.19±0.72	21.35±0.84	92%
Except-Afrl	Large	12.85±0.74	13.78±0.73	15.11±0.82	78%
Except-Afrl	Small	18.41±1.25	19.67±1.27	21.21±1.55	91%

Table 3: Results of Phrase-based, Phrase-based with Lexical Reordering and Hierarchical MT systems.

official test sets. The BLEU score for CLE test set is reported using all 3 reference translations at once as well as the average of single-reference BLEUs, taking each reference translation separately. IPC and NIST2008 results are evaluated on a single reference.

The hierarchical MT performs significantly better than the phrase-based MT on all test sets. The lowest scores were achieved on the NIST2008 test set but it is difficult to pinpoint any specific reason (other than some domain difference) because the coverage is comparable to other test sets (see Table 2). Across all the test sets, Afrl corpus brings about 2 points BLEU absolute.

		CLE		IPC	NIST2008
		3 refs	1 ref (avg.)	1 ref	1 ref
ALL	Phrase-based-LexReo	18.19±1.19	11.12±1.02	15.82±1.36	15.13±0.95
	Hierarchical	19.29±1.31	11.81±1.09	18.70±1.64	16.69±1.06
Except-Afrl	Phrase-based-LexReo	16.53±1.13	9.92±0.96	13.82±1.20	11.65±0.87
	Hierarchical	18.48±1.28	11.30±1.03	16.91±1.54	13.01±0.84

Table 4: Results of Phrase-based and Hierarchical systems on official test sets.

5 Manual Evaluation

To manually analyze the output of best performing models sample of 175 sentences is randomly selected from the large test set translated using both PBMT with lexical reordering and hierarchical models trained on "ALL" data sets. QuickJudge[11] is used to rank the outputs. The annotator is shown the source, reference and output from both machine translation systems, the identity of the MT systems is not known. There are four permitted outcomes of the ranking: both systems marked as equally good; both systems are equally bad or the output of one of the systems is better than the other one. Here is the summary of annotation by a single annotator:

- Out of 175 sentences, 41 sentences received equally bad translations from both systems.
- 17 items are marked as equally good.
- In 79 cases, the hierarchical MT is ranked better than the phrase-based MT.
- In the remaining 38 cases, the phrase-based MT is ranked better than the hierarchical MT.

The results from the manual ranking show that the hierarchical systems wins twice more often than PBMT. The two systems tie in about one third of input sentences, of which about 70 % are cases where the translations are bad.

6 Conclusion

In this work, a collection of sizeable English-Urdu corpora is summarized for statistical machine translation. These resources are used to build baseline phrase-based and hierarchical MT systems for translation into Urdu and the results are reported on 3 independent official test sets. This

[11] `http://ufal.mff.cuni.cz/project/euromatrix/quickjudge/`

can hopefully serve as a baseline for a wider community of researchers. The output of both translation models is manually analyzed and it confirms that the hierarchical model is preferred over phrase-based MT for English-to-Urdu translation.

Acknowledgments

This work has been using language resources developed and/or stored and/or distributed by the LINDAT-Clarin project of the Ministry of Education of the Czech Republic (project LM2010013). This work was also supported by the grant FP7-ICT-2011-7-288487 (MosesCore) of the European Union.

References

Aasim Ali and Muhmmad Kamran Malik. 2010. Development of parallel corpus and english to urdu statistical machine translation. *Int. J. of Engineering & Technology IJET-IJENS*, 10:31–33.

Aasim Ali, Arshad Hussain, and Muhammad Kamran Malik. 2013. Model for english-urdu statistical machine translation. *World Applied Sciences*, 24:1362–1367.

Paul Baker, Andrew Hardie, Tony McEnery, Hamish Cunningham, and Robert J. Gaizauskas. 2002. Emille, a 67-million word corpus of indic languages: Data collection, mark-up and harmonisation. In *LREC*. European Language Resources Association.

David Chiang. 2005. A hierarchical phrase-based model for statistical machine translation. In *Proc. of ACL*, pages 263–270.

David Chiang. 2007. Hierarchical phrase-based translation. *Comput. Linguist.*, 33(2):201–228, June.

Bushra Jawaid and Daniel Zeman. 2011. Word-order issues in english-to-urdu statistical machine translation. Number 95, pages 87–106, Praha, Czechia.

Bushra Jawaid, Amir Kamran, and Ondřej Bojar. 2014. A Tagged Corpus and a Tagger for Urdu (to appear). Reykjavík, Iceland. European Language Resources Association. In print.

Nadeem Khan, Waqas Anwar, Usama Ijaz Bajwa, and Nadir Durrani. 2013. English to urdu hierarchical phrase-based statistical machine translation. In *The 4th Workshop on South and Southeast Asian NLP (WSSANLP), IJCNLP*, pages 72–76, Nagoya, Japan.

Philipp Koehn, Hieu Hoang, Alexandra Birch, Chris Callison-Burch, Marcello Federico, Nicola Bertoldi, Brooke Cowan, Wade Shen, Christine Moran, Richard Zens, Chris Dyer, Ondřej Bojar, Alexandra Constantin, and Evan Herbst. 2007. Moses: Open Source Toolkit for Statistical Machine Translation. In *Proc. of ACL Companion Volume, Demo and Poster Sessions*, pages 177–180, Prague, Czech Republic.

Mitchell P. Marcus, Mary Ann Marcinkiewicz, and Beatrice Santorini. 1993. Building a large annotated corpus of english: The penn treebank. *Comput. Linguist.*, 19(2):313–330, June.

Franz Josef Och and Hermann Ney. 2000. A Comparison of Alignment Models for Statistical Machine Translation. In *Proc. of COLING*, pages 1086–1090. ACL.

Kishore Papineni, Salim Roukos, Todd Ward, and Wei-Jing Zhu. 2002. BLEU: a Method for Automatic Evaluation of Machine Translation. In *Proc. of ACL*, pages 311–318.

Martin Popel and Zdeněk Žabokrtský. 2010. TectoMT: Modular NLP Framework. In *Lecture Notes in Artificial Intelligence, Proceedings of the 7th International Conference on Advances in Natural Language Processing (IceTAL 2010)*, volume 6233 of *Lecture Notes in Computer Science*, pages 293–304. Springer.

Matt Post, Chris Callison-Burch, and Miles Osborne. 2012. Constructing parallel corpora for six indian languages via crowdsourcing. In *Proc. of WMT, ACL*, pages 401–409, Montréal, Canada.

Andreas Stolcke. 2002. Srilm - an extensible language modeling toolkit. In *In Proceedings of the 7th International Conference on Spoken Language Processing (ICSLP) 2002*, pages 901–904.

Christoph Tillmann. 2004. A unigram orientation model for statistical machine translation. In *Proc. of HLT-NAACL Short Papers*, pages 101–104.

A hybrid approach for automatic clause boundary identification in Hindi

Rahul Sharma, Soma Paul
Language Technology Research Centre, IIIT-Hyderabad, India
rahul.sharma@research.iiit.ac.in, soma@iiit.ac.in

Abstract

A complex sentence, divided into clauses, can be analyzed more easily than the complex sentence itself. We present here, the task of clauses identification in Hindi text. To the best of our knowledge, not much work has been done on clause boundary identification for Hindi, which makes this task more important. We have built a Hybrid system which gives 90.804% F1-scores and 94.697% F1-scores for identification of clauses' start and end respectively.

1 Introduction

Clause is the minimal grammatical unit which can express a proposition. It is a sequential group of words, containing a verb or a verb group(verb and its auxiliary), and its arguments which can be explicit or implicit in nature (Ram and Devi, 2008) . This makes clause an important unit in language grammars and emphasis the need to identify and classify them as part of linguistic studies.
Analysis and processing of complex sentences is a far more challenging task as compared to a simple sentence. NLP applications often perform poorly as the complexity of the sentence increases. "It is impossible, to process a complex sentence if its clauses are not properly identified and classified according to their syntactic function in the sentence" (Leffa, 1998). Further, identifying clauses, and processing them separately are known to do better in many NLP tasks. The performance of many NLP systems like Machine Translation, Parallel corpora alignment, Information Extraction, Syntactic parsing, automatic summarization and speech applications etc improves by introducing clause boundaries in a sentence (e.g., Ejerhed, 1988; Abney, 1990; Leffa, 1998; Papageorgiou, 1997; Gadde et al., 2010).
We present a hybrid method which comprises of Conditional random fields(CRFs) (Lafferty et al., 2001) based statistical learning followed by some rules to automatically determine *'clause'* boundaries (beginnings and ends) in complex or compound sentences. CRFs is a framework for building undirected probabilistic graphical models to segment and label sequence data (Lafferty et al., 2001). In past, this framework has proved to be successful for sequence labeling task (Sha and Pereira, 2003; McCallum and Li, 2003). Van Nguyen et al. (2007) used CRFs for clause splitting task with some linguistic information giving 84.09% F1-score.

Our system has minimum dependency on linguistic resources,only part of speech (POS) and chunk information of lexical items is used with a fair performance of the system. As far as we know, not much work has been done on clause boundary identification for Hindi and this makes this task more significant. This paper is structured as follows: In Section 2, we discuss the related works that has been done earlier on clause identification. Section 3 describes the creation of dataset for various system use. In Section 4, we talk about methodology of our system. Section 5 outlines the system performance. In section 6, some issues related clause identification are discussed. In Section 7, we conclude and talk about future works in this area.

Proceedings of the 5th Workshop on South and Southeast Asian NLP, 25th International Conference on Computational Linguistics, pages 43–49, Dublin, Ireland, August 23-29 2014.

2 Related works

Studies in identifying clauses date back to (Ejerhed, 1988) work, where they showed how automatic clause boundary identification in discourse can benefit a parser's performance. However her experiments could detect only basic clauses. Later (Abney, 1990) used clause filter as part of his CASS parser. (Papageorgiou, 1997) used hand crafted rules to identify clause boundaries in a text. (Leffa, 1998) is another rule based method which was implemented in an English-Portuguese MT system.
Some more recent works in this area are: (Puscasu, 2004), in which she proposed a multilingual method of combining language independent ML techniques with language specific rules to detect clause boundaries in unrestricted texts. The rules identify the finite verbs and clause boundaries not included in learning process. (Ram and Devi, 2008) proposed a hybrid based approach for detecting clause boundaries in a sentence. They have used a CRF based system which uses different linguistic cues. After identifying the clause boundaries they run an error analyzer module to find false boundary markings, which are then corrected by the rule based system, built using linguistic clues. (Ghosh et al., 2010) is another rule based system for clause boundary identification for Bengali, where they use machine learning approach for clause classification and dependency relations between verb and its argument to find clause boundaries. Dhivya et al. (2012) use dependency trees from maltparser and the dependency tag-set with 11 tags to identify clause boundaries. Similar to (Dhivya et al., 2012), Sharma et al. (2013) showed how implicit clause information present in dependency trees can be used to extract clauses in sentences. Their system have reported 94.44% accuracy for Hindi.Gadde et al. (2010) reported improvement in parser performance by introducing automatic clause information in a sentence for Hindi in 'Improving data driven dependency parsing using clausal information'. However their approach for identifying clause information has not been discussed. Thus a comparison is not possible here.

3 Dataset

In Hindi, We don't have any data available annotated with clause boundary, So to generate clause annotated corpora we have used (Sharma et al., 2013) technique where they have showed how implicit clause information present in dependency trees can be used to extract clauses in sentences. By this technique we have automatically generated 16000 sentences of Hindi treebank (Palmer et al., 2009) marked with clause boudaries. Out of which, 14500 sentences were taken as training set, 500 for development set and remaining 1000 sentences for testing set. As these sentences were generated automatically there are chances of noises in form of wrongly marked clause boundaries, so for proper evaluation of the system, we have manually corrected the wrongly marked clauses in development and testing sets.

4 Methodology

We propose a hybrid system which identifies the clause(s) in the input sentence and marks the *'clause start position'* (**CSP**) and *'clause end position'* (**CEP**) with brackets.
Hindi usually follows the SOV word order, so ends of the clauses can be found by just using verb information, in most of the cases. The language also has explicit relative pronouns, subordinating conjuncts, coordinate conjunctions etc. which serve as cues that help to identify clause boundaries of the clauses. Apart from the lexical cues we have also used POS tag and chunk information to built our system.
Our system comprise of two main modules; first modules is stochastic model which have been trained on 14500 sentences, and second module which is built using hand crafted rules.

4.1 Stochastic Models

We have used two techniques to built two different models; 1) step-by-step model and 2) merged model, using CRF machine learning approach. Both the models take word, word's POS tag and its suffix as word's features for training. Table (1) shows the common features used for training models. These feature are syntactic in nature, and relative pronoun, verb, conjunctions etc. plays important role in identifying boundaries. suffixes help to learn morphological feature of the word.

Present word's Lexicon, POS tag, last character, last two character, and last three character
Previous four words' Lexicon and POS tags
Next four words' Lexicon and POS tags
Next three words' last character, last two character, last three character

Table 1: Features

4.1.1 step-by-step model

This model comprises of two models; end model and start model. First one identifies the end of a clause and then later one takes the output of former model as input and identifies the start of the clause. In this technique we can notice that both models have to only mark whether a word is a boundary of a clause or not. For example 'end model' has to check whether a given word is a end(boundary) of a clause or not. Below example (1) explains this further.

(1) raam jisne khaanaa khaayaa ghar gayaaa
Ram who food eat+past home go+past
'Raam who ate food, went home'

In example (1), end model first marks 'gayaa' and 'khaayaa' as the end of clause. Then start model takes this additional information also as the feature, and marks 'raam' and 'jisne' as the start of clause.

4.1.2 Merged Model

This model marks the clauses' start and end in one go. Unlike the step-by-step model, it check whether a word is clause's start, clause's end or none. For above example (1), it will mark 'gayaa' and 'khaayaa' as the end of clause, and 'raam' and 'jisne' as the start of clause respectively in one go.

-- Keeping post-processing module(discussed below) same, we have evaluated our system using both stochastic models separately, and observed, system with step-by-step model gives high F1-score value than the system with merged model.

4.2 Post-processing Module

This module processes the output from stochastic model, and mark the boundaries of clauses in sentences. As we know, in a sentence CSPs should always be equal to CEPs. So on the basis of difference between CSPs and CEPs, we have formalized our rules. Below is the description of rules used in this module.

1. Rules, when CSPs are greater than CEPs are:
   (a) Check for 'ki' complement clause: The verb in a sentence which contain 'ki' compliment clause is not the end of its clause whereas its end is same as of end of 'ki' complement clause. Below example (2) will make this rule more clearer.

   (2) raam ne kahaa ki vaha ghar gayaa
   Ram+arg say+past that he home go+past
   'Raam said that he went home'

   In this example (2), Stochastic models will mark 'raam' and 'ki' as the start of clause, and 'gayaa' as the end of clause, making CSPs more than the CEPs. We can notice that 'gayaa' is the end for both the clauses in a sentence, so using this rule, we will add one more end of clause to 'gayaa' word. The resultant sentence with clauses marked will be:
   (raam ne kahaa (ki vaha ghar gayaa))

   (b) Check for finite verb: If a verb is finite and does not have any 'ki' complement clause in it then that verb should be marked as the end of clause. So if this type verb is unmarked by the stochastic model then this rule will handle this.

   (c) Check for non-finite verb: If a non-finite verb is present in a sentence and word next to it does not mark start of another clause then this rule will mark that word as the start of that clause.

–It should be noted that rules are applied in specific order, and once the number of CSPs and CEPs become same at any point of rule we stop applying more rules from this type where CSPs and CEPs are not same.

2. Rules, When CEPs are greater than CSPs are:

   (a) If there is a 'non-finite' verb in a sentence then we check for its start and mark them using regular expressions if not marked by stochastic models. for example:

   (3) raam khaanaa khakara ghar gayaa
   Ram+arg food having eaten home go+past
   'having eaten food, Ram wen home'

   In example (3), if stochastic models does not able to mark 'khaanaa' as the start of non-finite clause 'khaanaa khakara'. Then this rules will capture these type of situations and add a new CSP in a sentence.

   (b) If a word before conjunction, not a verb, is marked as end of a clause then this rule will remove that end, reducing number of CEP.

3. Rules, when CSPs and CEPs are same:

   (a) If there are more than one clauses in one single 'ki' complement clause than this rules marks one bigger boundary as clause which will contain all the embedded clauses. For example:

   (4) raam ne kahaa ki shaam ne khaanaa khaayaa aur paani piyaa
   Ram+arg say+past that Shaam+arg food eat+past and water drink+past
   'Raam said that Shaam ate food and drank water'

   The situation discussed in this rule can be observed in example (4). The system output before this rule may be,
   "(raam ne kahaa (ki shaam ne khaanaa khaayaa) aur (paani piyaa))", Which this rule will convert to
   "(raam ne kahaa (ki (shaam ne khaanaa khaayaa) aur (paani piyaa)))"

– Having these rules applied, the output sentence will contain start and end of clauses in a sentence.

5 Evaluation and Results

As mentioned earlier we have used (Sharma et al., 2013) technique to automatically generate 16000 sentences of Hindi treebank marked with clause boundaries. Out of these 16000 sentences, a set of 1500 sentences with average length of 16 words was randomly selected. This set was then manually corrected at the level of clause boundary for accurate evaluation of the system. It should be noted that this set was not used in training of the models. Further we have divided this set into two set; development set which consist of 500 sentences and testing set which consist of 1000 sentences. We have evaluated the system with both models (step-by-step and merged) along with post-processing module, and we have noticed system with step-by-step model performs better than the system with merged model. Table (2) and Table (3) show the results on development set and testing set respectively.

Model Type	**Start of clause**			**End of clause**		
	Precision	Recall	F1-measure	Precision	Recall	F1-measure
Step-by-step model	91.493	89.816	90.646	95.129	93.482	94.298
Merged Model	92.171	89.918	91.030	90.927	92.871	91.888

Table 2: Results on development set.

Model Type	Start of clause			End of clause		
	Precision	Recall	F1-measure	Precision	Recall	F1-measure
Step-by-step model	92.051	89.590	90.804	95.969	93.458	94.697
Merged Model	91.779	88.907	90.320	90.919	92.263	91.586

Table 3: Results on testing set.

6 Error Analysis and Discussion

While evaluating our both systems (system with step-by-step model and system with merged model), we come across some constructions which were not handled by them. which are:

1. Ellipses of verb: when a verb is omitted in a sentence then it is not possible for our system to mark boundaries correctly. For example:

   (5) raam ne kitaab <V> aur maine kavitaa padhii
   Ram+erg book <read+past> and I+erg poem read+past
   'Ram read a book and I read a poem'

   In example (5), there is an ellipses of the verb 'padhi' in the clause 'raam ne kitaab'. Thus, though the sentence has two clauses–'raam ne kitaab' and 'maine kavitaa padhii', our system incorrectly identifies the whole sentence as one clause due to the ellipses of the verb (denoted by <V>).

2. Scrambling in the usual word order, which is SOV in Hindi, is likely to induce incorrect identification of the clauses in our system. For Example:

   (6) ghar gayaa raam, vaha bolaa.
   home go+past Ram, he say+past
   'He said Ram went home'

   In example (6), Our system is unable to identify the clause boundaries correctly for any of the two clauses, 'ghar gayaa raam' and 'ghar gayaa raam,vaha bolaa', due to scrambling in the word order. Its output for the sentence is '(ghar) (gayaa raam, vaha bolaa)', though the output should be '((ghar (gayaa raam,) vaha bolaa)'.

3. Missing subordinate conjunction 'ki' in a sentence also leads to incorrect identification of clause boundaries by our system. For example:

   (7) raam ne kahaa tum ghar jaao
   Ram+erg say+past you home go
   'Ram said you go home'

   The missing subordinate conjunction 'ki' in example (7) leads to incorrect marking of the clause boundaries as: '(raam ne kahaa) (tum ghar jaao)'. The correct clause boundaries for the sentence are '(raam ne kahaa (tum ghar jaao))'.

4. **Start of non-finite clause**: As we don't find any syntactic cues for start of non-finite clause, our systems does not perform much efficiently in finding start of non-finite clauses. For example:

   (8) ab hum alag maslon para khulkara baatchit kar rahe hain
   now we different matters/topics on openly discussion do+conti+present
   'Now we are discussing openly on different matters'

Both system marks ‘khulkara’ and ‘kar rahe hain’ verbs as the end of clauses accurately but start of non-finite clause which is ‘alag’ is not identified correctly. Output by the systems is, ‘(ab hum alag maslon para khulkara) (baatchit kar rahe hain)’ , where as the correct output is, ‘(ab hum (alag maslon para khulkara) baatchit kar rahe hain)’

-- Overall we observed that the system with step-by-step model which statistically first identifies end and then start, followed by rules performs better than the system with merged model.

7 Conclusion and Future Work

We have discussed our work on clause boundary identification in Hindi and the issues pertaining to them, in the course of this paper. Clausal information in a sentence is known to improve the performance of many NLP systems, thus the need for this task. We observed that the system with step-by-step model which statistically, first identifies end and then start of clauses, followed by rules, performs better than the system with merged model. The step-by-step model system, showing a satisfactory performance in terms of F1 scores of 91.53% for clause boundary identification, and the merged model system showing 80.63% for the same. Since this task is a promising resource for NLP systems such as Machine Translation, Text-to-Speech and so on, and can contribute to their better performance, applying this system for betterment of NLP tools seems quite a favorable prospect as a future work. (Gadde et al., 2010) report that even minimal clause boundary identification information leverages the performance of their system. We would like to test the performance of our system in terms of leveraging the performance of other NLP systems

References

Steven Abney. 1990. Rapid incremental parsing with repair. pages 1–9.

R Dhivya, V Dhanalakshmi, M Anand Kumar, and KP Soman. 2012. Clause boundary identification for tamil language using dependency parsing. pages 195–197. Springer.

Eva I Ejerhed. 1988. Finding clauses in unrestricted text by finitary and stochastic methods. pages 219–227. Association for Computational Linguistics.

Phani Gadde, Karan Jindal, Samar Husain, Dipti Misra Sharma, and Rajeev Sangal. 2010. Improving data driven dependency parsing using clausal information. pages 657–660. Association for Computational Linguistics.

Aniruddha Ghosh, Amitava Das, and Sivaji Bandyopadhyay. 2010. Clause identification and classification in bengali. In *23rd International Conference on Computational Linguistics*, page 17.

John Lafferty, Andrew McCallum, and Fernando CN Pereira. 2001. Conditional random fields: Probabilistic models for segmenting and labeling sequence data.

Vilson J Leffa. 1998. Clause processing in complex sentences. volume 1, pages 937–943.

Andrew McCallum and Wei Li. 2003. Early results for named entity recognition with conditional random fields, feature induction and web-enhanced lexicons. In *Proceedings of the seventh conference on Natural language learning at HLT-NAACL 2003-Volume 4*, pages 188–191. Association for Computational Linguistics.

Martha Palmer, Rajesh Bhatt, Bhuvana Narasimhan, Owen Rambow, Dipti Misra Sharma, and Fei Xia. 2009. Hindi syntax: Annotating dependency, lexical predicate-argument structure, and phrase structure. pages 14–17.

Harris V Papageorgiou. 1997. Clause recognition in the framework of alignment. pages 417–426.

Georgiana Puscasu. 2004. A multilingual method for clause splitting.

R Vijay Sundar Ram and Sobha Lalitha Devi. 2008. Clause boundary identification using conditional random fields. In *Computational Linguistics and Intelligent Text Processing*, pages 140–150. Springer.

Fei Sha and Fernando Pereira. 2003. Shallow parsing with conditional random fields. In *Proceedings of the 2003 Conference of the North American Chapter of the Association for Computational Linguistics on Human Language Technology-Volume 1*, pages 134–141. Association for Computational Linguistics.

Rahul Sharma, Soma Paul, Riyaz Ahmad Bhat, and Sambhav Jain. 2013. Automatic clause boundary annotation in the hindi treebank.

Vinh Van Nguyen, Minh Le Nguyen, and Akira Shimazu. 2007. Using conditional random fields for clause splitting. *Proceedings of The Pacific Association for Computational Linguistics, University of Melbourne Australia.*

RBMT as an alternative to SMT for under-resourced languages

Guillaume de Malézieux
INaLCO, Paris
guillaume2l2m@gmail.com

Amélie Bosc
INaLCO, Paris
amelie.bosc@gmail.com

Vincent Berment
INaLCO, Paris
LIG/GÉTALP, Grenoble
Vincent.Berment@imag.fr

Abstract

Despite SMT (Statistical Machine Translation) recently revolutionised MT for major language pairs, when addressing under-resourced and, to some extent, mildly-resourced languages, it still faces some difficulties such as the need of important quantities of parallel texts, the limited guaranty of the quality, etc. We thus speculate that RBMT (Rule Based Machine Translation) can fill the gap for these languages.

1 Introduction

In this paper, we present an ongoing work that aims at assessing the relevance of specific methods to reach "quick and quality" machine translation for under-resourced languages. These methods include working in parallel on several languages, reusing software and linguistic resources, relying on a pivot architecture, opening our linguistic sources and letting any group of users the possibility to "do it themselves". We also chose to adopt the old fashioned RBMT approach.

More concretely, we are applying Vauquois' methodology [Vauquois and Chappuy, 1985] to the development of analysers for Khmer, Lao, Thai and Hindi, which we plan to "connect" to existing and open source syntheses of French and English through three means: deep transfer, deep hybrid transfer and UNL pivot representation. In order to elaborate easy-to-understand guidelines for new comers, we chose to create a primer methodological step involving the small novel of Saint-Exupéry "The Little Prince", which has been translated into 270 languages and dialects. Doing so, the principles for developing dictionaries and grammars that follow Vauquois' methodology become much simpler to understand.

2 Tools and methodology

2.1 The Heloise RBMT framework

The RBMT framework we are using is called Heloise. It has been presented at COLING 2012 [Berment and Boitet, 2012]. Heloise is an online environment available to anyone wishing to design his or her own operational expert MT system, especially for under-resourced pairs of languages. It is upward-compatible with Ariane-G5's languages, so the open-source modules developed under this environment can be reused in any new system. For example, in order to add a new language X, an existing generation of French language can be taken as such for a new X-French system, limiting the effort to an analyser of language X and to a transfer from X to French. Figure 1 represents the usual phases involved in a development under Ariane-G5.

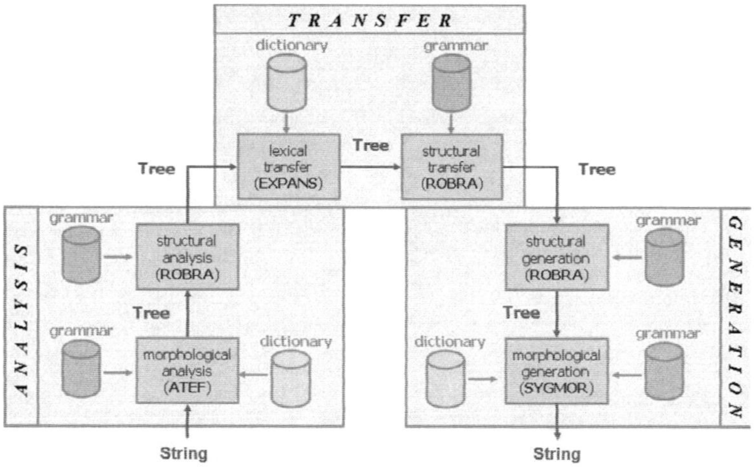

FIGURE 1 – Ariane-G5 phases.

Proceedings of the 5th Workshop on South and Southeast Asian NLP, 25th International Conference on Computational Linguistics, pages 50–54, Dublin, Ireland, August 23-29 2014.

2.2 GÉTA's methodology

The approach of the GÉTA group of Grenoble (France), who created Ariane-G5, is a second generation MT, in which the text to be translated is first transformed into an abstract representation, as independent of any language as possible, so this abstract representation can then be translated in any other language. The abstract representation is a multi-level structure (m-structure) ideally containing the logic (predicate-argument) and semantic data that are the most language-independent computed in this approach. As this deep level is not always reached, two other (lower) levels are borne by the m-structure: the syntagmatic level and the syntactic dependency level, so the translation system will output the best it can do.

As one can see in Figure 1, the development is made of modules corresponding to the different steps of the translation. If we concentrate on the analysis (the systems we are working on are X-French and X-English systems so firstly on analysers for the X languages), the work consists in developing monolingual dictionaries containing all the information necessary for the analysis, as well as structural analysers. As such linguistic descriptions are rather complex, one first needs to specify what will be programmed, especially for the structural part. GÉTA's answer to this issue consists in making a list of the different structural phenomena found in the language, each one being represented as a correspondence between a string and its abstract representation ("charts"), and establishing links between the charts so the charts can include references to other charts. One can think it roughly as derivation rules in formal grammars in which terminal elements are classes of words and non-terminal elements are charts. For example, a noun phrase (the string) such as [adjective+noun] can be represented as NP(AP,noun) where AP refers to a chart of general adjective phrases, possibly containing adverbs as in "a very cute cat". The formalism for those charts has initially been called "static grammar" and later SCSG (Static Correspondence Specification Grammar).

3 Parallel work on Khmer, Hindi, Lao and Thai languages

This work aims at elaborating an efficient and simple methodology for developing MT systems for groups of under-resourced languages. We are using for that purpose a small corpus consisting in Saint-Exupéry's *Little Prince* in Khmer, Hindi, Lao and Thai which are our source languages, and our target languages are French and English. Two of the authors, Guillaume de Malézieux and Vincent Berment, are working on Khmer and Lao, as two other persons, Jennifer Wong and Satenik Mkhitaryan, are working on Thai and Hindi.

3.1 Reuse of existing linguistic modules

The systems developed under Ariane-G5 are made of linguistic module dedicated to each step of the translation process (analysis, transfer, generation). In GÉTA's approach, analyses are independent from generations so an analyser for a specific language can be used with a generation of any other language. As French an English modules are available under BSD licence (among many others), we are using them for our work so the analysers and the transfers have to be developed.

3.2 Segmentation and POS tagging

In the case of Khmer, Lao and Thai, one needs to segment into words first, as the writing systems do not include spaces between words. This is done by Motor, a segmenter performing a maximum matching algorithm. It is currently available for Burmese, Khmer, Lao, Thai and Tibetan. Within the limits of our small corpus, the obtained segmentation is 100% correct (the figure reached for general corpora is significantly lower). In order to create the first step called "morphological analysis" in Figure 1, we need a list of words with a number of features that will be used for the analysis. To achieve that, we fill an Excel file with the required data. The following figure is an extract of the Excel file that describe a noun phrase with a possessive attribution. Note that Hindi is not completed and was not included is this paper.

Lao	UL	CAT	Thaï	UL	CAT	Khmer	UL	CAT
ຮູບແຕ້ມ	image	N	รูป	image	N	គំនូរ	image	N
ຂອງ	of	S	ของ	of	S	របស់	of	S
ຂ້ອຍ	I	R	ฉัน	I	R	ខ្ញុំ	I	R

FIGURE 2 – Khmer, Lao and Thai data used in the "morphological analysis"

We used parts of speech often found in GÉTA systems: V verb, N noun, A adjunct, R pronoun, S subordination (preposition, subordinating conjunction and linking word), C coordinating conjunction. In Figure 2, LU stands for Lexical Unit, which is a generalisation of lemma that groups together words deriving from the same base such as build, building, builder, etc. That notion is very useful, for example during transfers where it eases paraphrasing.

The example in Figure 2 is an ideal case where the three languages involved are aligned word for word. When it is not the case, we have different lines for the parts in the different languages that are not aligned and we mark them as "similar" thanks to a colour given to those parts. That is used later when specifying the structural analysers as blocks of words that are not aligned may share common structures (see the next section).

After the Excel file is completed, we can then generate automatically the "morphological analysis" source code written in ATEF language, thanks to a tool we developed for that aim. Note that segmenting and POS tagging have their own dictionaries so a special care is needed to ensure their consistency.

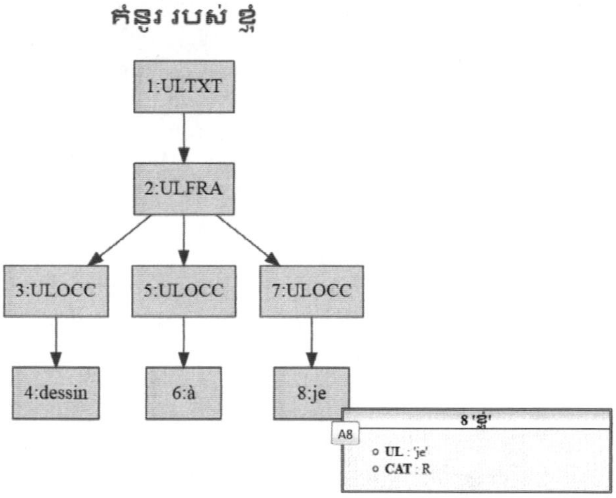

FIGURE 3 – Result of the morphological analysis for គំនូររបស់ខ្ញុំ (Khmer)

3.3 Structural analysis

In order to perform the structural analysis of a text, one needs a formal description of the language. This description, that we call a specification, will be written according to the formalism given by Bernard Vauquois and Sylviane Chappuy [Vauquois et Chappuy, 1985] and mentioned in section 2.2: the static grammars. After we get such specification, we can start programming the analyser in the Ariane-G5 language called ROBRA, which performs tree transformations.

Now let us have a closer look at what a static grammar is like. It is a series of charts, each chart describing a family of strings by associating it to a tree. The charts may refer to each other. For example in order to recognise a complex noun phrase such as "gaz reaction", the two nouns have to be first recognised as separate valid noun phrases (for example, "gaz" is a word that makes sense on its own) so that then they can be gathered into the same tree in order to take a new meaning. So that means the chart describing complex noun phrases refers to the chart describing simple noun phrases. As a consequence, all the charts have to be organised in the grammar so that the ones describing elementary phrases, that are the ones that do not need referring to another chart, come first. Then come the charts describing simple phrases, because they can only refer to lower charts in this hierarchy. At last come the charts for complex groups, they can refer to any chart in the grammar.

Now to write the charts, we need a list of variables to gather all the information we need. They can be of different types, but for the purpose of our study, we will only need basic information. Because we use the limited vocabulary of the *Little Prince*, we won't have to work much on disambiguation. So for now we are only using POS information, with some refinements to recognise mass nouns from countable nouns, and some subcategories of verbs. As an example, we will present the chart describing the possession noun phrases, that are built identically in the three languages: noun + particle "of " + personal pronoun. Here in order to write a chart that could apply to Lao, Thai and Khmer languages at a time, we will use the variable OF to refer to របស់ in Khmer, ของ in Thai, and ຂອງ in Lao. A static chart is divided into three zones. The first one is a string-tree correspondence, describing the structure to be recognised. Each node and leaf receives a number. In FIGURE 4, the root node of our noun phrase is the number 1. Numbers 2, 3 and 4 are the leaves, and each cross below represents a word of the string. The square brackets around number 3 mean that it is optional. The last two lines at the bottom of the tree give information about the words. For example leave 2 is a noun, and more precisely a common noun, leave 3 is a subordinating and its LU is the particle OF, and at last, leave 4 is a personal pronoun. One particularity in this tree is the fact that the node 3 is not linked to the root. This is because although the particle needs to be taken into account during the analysis, we chose not to have it appear into the tree. All the information it carries will be transferred into other nodes. Zone 2 of the static chart provides complementary information on the condition necessary for the structure to be correct. This could be semantic information on one of the nodes, or the presence of one node excluding another, etc. But we do not need any information of this type in the chart we are studying. At last, it is in zone 3 that we present the actions to be taken on the tree. In our case, we store in a variable the possession relation. We also assign the noun of leave 2 to be the governor, that is to say the head, of the phrase.

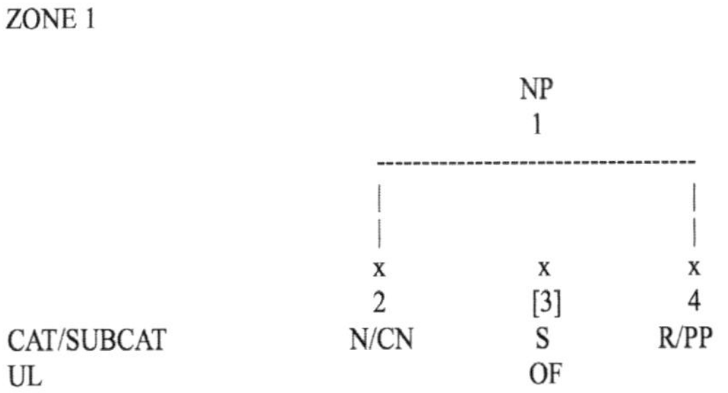

FIGURE 4 – String-tree correspondence

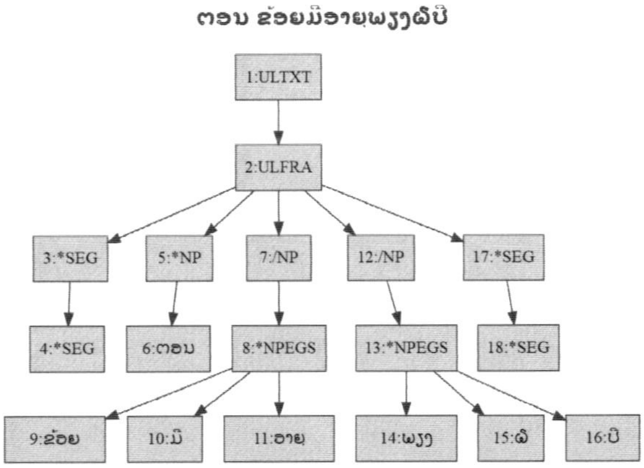

FIGURE 5 – Example of structural analysis for a Lao phrase

3.4 Lexical transfer

In transfers, we transform the Lexical Units and their variables from the source to the target lexical spaces. As we found lexical similarities between Thai, Lao and Khmer languages — ULs are between 50% and 70% common —, a large part of the transfers is also common to those languages.

4 Conclusion

In this paper, we presented an ongoing work. A lot remains to be done but we already observe that working in parallel on several languages brings a lot of advantage. For example, when a question raises on the methodology, on how we can build a specific static chart, etc., people working on any language can answer. For this purpose, the Ariane/Heloise community has set-up a Web site and enriches it continuously: lingwarium.org. Also, as for the structural phases, we noted that many structures were common between Khmer Lao and Thai (Hindi development is late because of the few common features shared with the other languages), thus reducing the effort for making the static grammars. We also noted that the time to develop the transfers were dramatically reduced as a large part of them were common to the three languages. That remains to be further evaluated but we are already convinced it is a way that will help reaching Christian Boitet's prediction that 600 languages will have access to machine translation [Boitet, 2013].

Acknowledgements

We would like to thank Jennifer Wong and Satenik Mkhitaryan for their contribution, as well as Michel Antelme who helped a lot for the work on the Khmer language.

References

Bachut D., Le projet EUROLANG : une nouvelle perspective pour les outils d'aide à la traduction, TALN 1994 Proceedings ,PRC-CHM Days, Marseille University, April 7-8th 1994.

Bachut D., Verastegui N., Software tools for the environment of a computer aided translation system, COLING-1984, Stanford University, pages 330 to 333, July 2-6th 1984.

Berment V., Méthodes pour informatiser des langues et des groupes de langues « peu dotées », PhD Thesis, Grenoble, May 18th 2004.

http://portal.unesco.org/ci/fr/files/16735/10914394223these_Berment.pdf/these_Berment.pdf

Berment V., Boitet C.: Heloise — A reengineering of Ariane-G5 SLLPs for application to π-languages, COLING 2012, Bombay, December 2012

Boitet C., Le point sur Ariane-78 début 1982 (DSE-1), vol. 1, partie 1, le logiciel, ADI Contract report n° 81/423, April 1982.

Boitet C., Guillaume P., Quézel-Ambrunaz M., A case study in software evolution: from Ariane-78.4 to Ariane-85, Proceedings of the Conference on Theoretical and Methodological Issues in Machine Translation of Natural Languages, Colgate University, Hamilton, New York, August 14-16th 1985.

Boitet C., Current machine translation systems developed with GETA's methodology and software tools, Translating and the Computer 8, November 13-14th 1986.

Boitet C., La TAO à Grenoble en 1990, 1980-90 : TAO du réviseur et TAO du traducteur, LATL and CNET, Lannion, 1990.

Boitet C., A research perspective on how to democratize machine translation and translation aids aiming at high quality final output, MT Summit VII, Kent Ridge Digital Labs, Singapour, pages 125 to 133, September13-17th 1999.

Boitet C., A roadmap for MT: four « keys » to handle more languages, for all kinds of tasks, while making it possible to improve quality (on demand), International Conference on Universal Knowledge and Language (ICUKL 2002), Goa, November 25-29th 2002.

Boitet C., Les architectures linguistiques et computationnelles en traduction automatique sont indépendantes, TALN 2008, Avignon, June 9-13th 2008.

Boitet C., Les logiciels traduiront 600 langues dans dix ans, Les dossiers de la Recherche, n°4, June-July 2013.

Chappuy S. Formalisation de la description des niveaux d'interprétation des langues naturelles, Thesis, 1983

Delavennat E., Comparaison des systèmes de décoration des linguiciels traitant les langues FRA, ENG, ALD, RUS, final report, Traouiero project, 2010

Del Vigna C., Berment V., Boitet C., La notion d'occurrence de formes de forêt (orientée et ordonnée) dans le langage ROBRA pour la traduction automatique, Approches algébrique, logique et algorithmique, ATALA, ENST Paris, December 1st 2007.

Collective work, Maquette Pédagogique du BEX FEX, GETA Document, 1983

Guillaume P., Ariane-G5 : Les langages spécialisés TRACOMPL et EXPANS, GÉTA document, June 1989.

Guilbaud J.-P., Ariane-G5 : Environnement de développement et d'exécution de systèmes (linguiciels) de traduction automatique, GDR I3 ATALA, Paris, November 1999.

Tang E.K., Natural languages Analysis in machine translation (MT) based on the STCG, PhD thesis, Sains Malaysia University, Penang, March 1994

Vauquois B., Aspects of mechanical translation in 1979, Conference for Japan IBM Scientific program, July 1979.

Vauquois B., Computer aided translation and the Arabic language, First Arab school on science and technology, Rabat, October 1983.

Vauquois B., Chappuy S., Static grammars, A formalism for the description of linguistic models, Proceedings of the Conference on Theoretical and Methodological Issues in Machine Translation of Natural Languages, Colgate University, Hamilton, New York, August 14-16, 1985.

Zaharin Yusoff, Strategies and heuristics in the analysis of a natural language in machine translation, PhD thesis, Sains Malaysia University, Penang, March 1986.

Developing an interlingual translation lexicon using WordNets and Grammatical Framework

Shafqat Mumtaz Virk
University of Gothenburg,
University of Eng. & Tech. Lahore
virk.shafqat@gmail.com

K.V.S. Prasad
Chalmers University of Technology
prasad@chalmers.se

Aarne Ranta
University of Gothenburg
aarne@chalmers.se

Krasimir Angelov
University of Gothenburg
krasimir@chalmers.se

Abstract

The Grammatical Framework (GF) offers perfect translation between controlled subsets of natural languages. E.g., an abstract syntax for a set of sentences in school mathematics is the interlingua between the corresponding sentences in English and Hindi, say. GF "resource grammars" specify how to say something in English or Hindi; these are re-used with "application grammars" that specify what can be said (mathematics, tourist phrases, etc.). More recent robust parsing and parse-tree disambiguation allow GF to parse arbitrary English text. We report here an experiment to linearise the resulting tree directly to other languages (e.g. Hindi, German, etc.), i.e., we use a language-independent resource grammar as the interlingua. We focus particularly on the last part of the translation system, the interlingual lexicon and word sense disambiguation (WSD). We improved the quality of the wide coverage interlingual translation lexicon by using the Princeton and Universal WordNet data. We then integrated an existing WSD tool and replaced the usual GF style lexicons, which give one target word per source word, by the WordNet based lexicons. These new lexicons and WSD improve the quality of translation in most cases, as we show by examples. Both WordNets and WSD in general are well known, but this is the first use of these tools with GF.

1 Introduction

1.1 Translation via an interlingua

Interlingual translation scales easily up to a large number of languages. Google translate, for example, deals with all pairs of 60 languages mostly by using English as a pivot language. In this way, it can do with just 2 * 59 = 118 sets of bilingual training data, instead of 60 * 59 = 3540 sets. It would be hard to collect and maintain so many pairs, and in many cases, there is very little data to be found.

The roots of an inter-lingua are perhaps in the medieval idea of a universal grammar (Lyons, 1968), in which a universal representation of meaning can be expressed. Translating via this interlingua then also means that meaning is conserved in going from the source to the target language. In recent decades, this idea appears in (Curry, 1961) where the interlingua is called tectogrammar, in the Rosetta project (Rosetta, 1994), building on the semantic models of (Montague, 1974), and in the UNL (Universal Networking Language) project.

Incidentally, interlingua is also the heart of modern compiler technology. For instance, the GNU Compiler Collection (Stallman, 2001) uses a shared tree representation to factor out the majority of compilation phases between a large number of source and target languages. Compiler writers save work, and semantics is preserved by design. A compiler, then, is built as a pipeline with **parsing** from a source language to an **abstract syntax tree**, which is analyzed and optimized in the language-independent phases, and finally **linearized** to a target language.

Proceedings of the 5th Workshop on South and Southeast Asian NLP, 25th International Conference on Computational Linguistics, pages 55–64, Dublin, Ireland, August 23-29 2014.

It is easy to see an analogy between this pipeline and the way a human language translator could work. But how to make it real? How to scale up to the full size of natural languages?

1.2 WordNets

In current machine translation research, interlingual methods are marginal, despite the wide use of pivot languages in systems like Google translate. Closest to the mainstream perhaps is the development of linked WordNets. The original Princeton Wordnet for English (Miller, 1995) defines a set of word senses, which many other wordnets map to other languages. Implementations of this idea are Finnish (Lindén and Carlson., 2010) and Hindi (Hindi-WordNet, 2012).

In the linked Wordnet approach, the Princeton WordNet senses work as an interlingua, albeit only on the level of the lexicon. (Lindén and Carlson., 2010) give strong arguments why in fact this is a good way to go, despite the often emphasized fact that different languages divide the world in different ways, so that the senses of their word don't map one to one. The evidence from the English-Finnish case shows that 80% of the mappings are one-to-one and un-problematic. As this part of the lexicon can be easily reused, linguists and system builders can concentrate their effort on the remaining 20%.

The Universal WordNet (de Melo and Weikum, 2009) works on the same lines. Building on the Princeton WordNet, it populates the mappings to over 200 different languages by collecting data from different sources (such as the Wikipedia) and using supervised machine learning techniques to propagate the knowledge and infer more of it. What makes it a particularly interesting resource is that it is freely available under the most liberal licenses, as is the original Princeton WordNet,

1.3 GF

Grammatical Framework (GF)(Ranta, 2004) is a grammar formalism tool based on Martin Löf's type theory (Martin-Löf, 1982). It can be seen as a tool to build interlingua based translation systems. GF works like a compiler: the source language is parsed to an abstract syntax tree, which is then linearized to the target language. The parsing and linearization component are defined by using Parallel Multiple Context-Free Grammars (PMCFG, (Seki et al., 1991), (Ljunglöf, 2004)), which give GF an expressive power between mildly and fully context-sensitive grammars. Thus GF can easily handle with language-specific variations in morphology, word order, and discontinuous constituents, while maintaining a shared abstract syntax.

Historically, the main use of GF has been in controlled language implementations, e.g., (Ranta and Angelov, 2010; Angelov and Enache, 2010; Ranta et al., 2012) and natural language generation, e.g., (Dymetman et al., 2000), both applied in multilingual settings with up to 15 parallel languages. In recent years, the coverage of GF grammars and the processing performance has enabled open-domain tasks such as treebank parsing (Angelov, 2011) and hybrid translation of patents (Enache et al., 2012). The general purpose Resource Grammar Library (RGL)(Ranta, 2011) has grown to 30 languages. It includes the major European languages, South Asian languages like Hindi/Urdu (Prasad and Shafqat, 2012), Nepali and Punjabi (Shafqat et al., 2011), the Southeast Asian language Thai, and Japanese and Chinese.

However, GF has yet not been exploited for arbitrary text parsing and translation. To do this, we have to meet several challenges: robust parsing, parse-tree disambiguation, word sense disambiguation, and development of a wide-coverage interlingual translation lexicon. This paper focuses on the latter two. We report first a method of using the WordNets (Princeton and Universal) to build an interlingual full-form, multiple sense translation lexicon. Then, we show how these lexicons together with a word sense disambiguation tool can be plugged in a translation pipeline. Finally, we describe an experimental setup and give many examples to highlight the effects of this work.

1.4 South Asian languages

While the work described here can apply to any language, it is particularly interesting for South Asian languages. In these languages, statistical tools do not have much bilingual training data to work on, so Google translate and similar tools are not as useful as they are with better resourced languages. At the same time, there is an urgent and widely recognised need for translations from English to the various languages of South Asia. Fortunately, word nets are being built for many of them, so that the techniques described here can be applied.

2 From Universal WordNet to a GF Lexicon

The original Princeton WordNet (Miller, 1995) defines a set of word senses, and the Universal WordNet (de Melo and Weikum, 2009) maps them to different languages. In this multilingual scenario, the Princeton WordNet senses can be seen as an abstract representation, while the Universal WordNet mappings can be seen as concrete representation of those senses in different languages. GF grammars use very much the same technique of one common abstract and multiple parallel concrete representations to achieve multilingualism. Due to this compatibility, it is easy to build a multilingual GF lexicon using data from those two resources (i.e. Princeton and Universal WordNets). This section briefly describes the experiment we did to build one abstract and multiple concrete GF lexicons for a number of languages including German, French, Finnish, Swedish, Hindi, and Bulgarian. The method is very general, so can be used to build a similar lexicon for any other language for which data is available in the Universal WordNet.

2.1 GF Abstract Lexicon

The Princeton WordNet data is distributed in the form of different database files. For each of the four lexical categories (i.e. noun, verb, adjective, and adverb), two files named 'index.pos' and 'data.pos' are provided, where 'pos' is noun, verb, adj and adv. Each of the 'index.pos' files contains all words, including synonyms of the words, found in the corresponding part of speech category. Each of the 'data.pos' files contains information about unique senses belonging to the corresponding part of speech category. For our purposes, there were two possible choices to build an abstract representation of the lexicon:

1. To include all words of the four lexical categories, and also their synonyms (i.e. to build the lexicon from 'index.pos' files)

2. To include only unique senses of the four categories with one word per sense, but not the synonyms (i.e. to build the lexicon from the data.pos' files)

To better understand this difference, consider the words 'brother' and 'buddy'. The word 'brother' has five senses with sense offsets '08111676', '08112052', '08112961', '08112265' and '08111905' in the Princeton WordNet 1.7.1[1], while the word 'buddy' has only one sense with the sense offset '08112961'. Choosing option (1) means that we have to include the following entries in our abstract lexicon.

```
brother_08111676_N
brother_08112052_N
brother_08112961_N
brother_08112265_N
brother_08111905_N
buddy_08112961_N
```

We can see that the sense with the offset '08112961' is duplicated in the lexicon: once with the lemma 'brother' and then with the lemma 'buddy'. However, if we choose option (2), we end up with the following entries.

[1]We choose WordNet 1.7.1, because the word sense disambiguator that we are using in our translation pipeline is based on WordNet 1.7.1

```
brother_08111676_N
brother_08112052_N
brother_08112265_N
brother_08111905_N
buddy_08112961_N
```

Since the file 'data.noun' lists the unique senses rather than the words, their will be no duplication of the senses. However, the choice has an obvious effect on the lexicon coverage, and depending on whether we want to use it as a parsing or as a linearization lexicon, the choice becomes critical. Currently, we choose option (2) for the following two reasons:

1. The Universal WordNet provides mappings for synsets (i.e. unique senses) but not for the individual synonyms of the synsets. If we choose option (1), as mentioned previously, we have to list all synonyms in our abstract representation. But, as translations are available only for synsets, we have to put the same translation against each of the synonyms of the synset in our concrete representations. This will not gain us anything (as long as we use these lexicon as linearization lexicons), but will increase the size of the lexicon and hence may have reduce the processing speed of the translation system.

2. At the current stage of our experiments we are using these lexicons as linearization lexicons, so one translation of each unique sense is enough.

Our abstract GF lexicon covers 91516 synsets out of around 111,273 synsets in the WordNet 1.7.1. We exclude some of the synsets with multi-word lemmas. We consider them more of a syntactic category rather than a lexical category, and hence deal with them at the syntax level. Here, we give a small segment of our abstract GF lexicon.

```
abstract LinkedDictAbs = Cat ** {
  fun consecutive_01624944_A  : A ;
  fun consequently_00061939_Adv : Adv ;
  fun conservation_06171333_N : N ;
  fun conspire_00562077_V : V ;
  fun sing_01362553_V2  : V2 ;
  ........
 }
```

The first line in the above given code states that the module 'LinkedDictAbs' is an abstract representation (note the keyword 'abstract'). This module extends (achieved by '**' operator) another module labeled 'Cat[2]' which, in this case, has definitions for the morphological categories 'A', 'Adv', 'N' and 'V'. These categories correspond to the 'adjective', 'adverb', 'noun', and 'verb' categories in the WordNet respectively. However, note that in GF resource grammars we have a fine-grained morphological division for verbs. We sub-categorize them according to their valencies i.e 'V' is for intransitive, and 'V2' for transitive verbs. We refer to (Bringert et al., 2011) for more details on these divisions.

Each entry in this module is of the following general type:

```
fun lemma_senseOffset_t : t ;
```

Keyword 'fun' declares each entry as a function of the type 't'. The function name is composed of lemma, sense offset and a type 't', where lemma and sense offset are same as in the Princeton WordNet, while 't' is one of the morphological types in GF resource grammars.

This abstract representation will serve as a pivot for all concrete representations, which are described next.

[2]This module has definitions of different morphological and syntactic categories in the GF resource grammar library

2.2 GF Concrete Lexicons

We build the concrete representations for different languages using the translations obtained from the Universal WordNet data and GF morphological paradigms (Détrez and Ranta, 2012; Bringert et al., 2011). The Universal WordNet translations are tagged with a sense offset from WordNet 3.0[3] and also with a confidence score. As, an example consider the following segment form the Universal WordNet data, showing German translations for the noun synset with offset '13810818' and lemma 'rest' (in the sense of 'remainder').

```
n13810818 Rest           1.052756
n13810818 Abbrand        0.95462
n13810818 Ruckstand    0.924376
```

Each entry is of the following general type.

```
posSenseOffset translation confidence-score
```

If we have more than one candidate translation for the same sense (as in the above case), we select the best one (i.e. with the maximum confidence score) and put it in the concrete grammar. Next, we give a small segment from the German concrete lexicon.

```
concrete LinkedDictGer of LinkedDictAbs = CatGer ** open
 ParadigmsGer, IrregGer,Prelude in {
  lin consecutive_01624944_A =  mkA "aufeinanderfolgend" ;
  lin consequently_00061939_Adv =  mkAdv "infolgedessen" ;
  lin conservation_06171333_N =  mkN "Konservierung" ;
  lin conspire_00562077_V = mkV "anzetteln" ;
  lin sing_01362553_V2 = mkV2 (mkV "singen" ) ;
  ......
 }
```

The first line declares 'LinkedDictGer' to be the concrete representation of the previously defined abstract representation (note the keyword 'concrete' at the start of the line). Each entry in this representation is of the following general type:

```
lin lemma_senseOffset_t = paradigmName "translation" ;
```

Keyword 'lin' declares each entry to be a linearization of the corresponding function in the abstract representation. 'paradigmName' is one of the morphological paradigms defined in the 'ParadigmsGer' module. So in the above code, 'mkA', 'mkAdv', 'mkN', 'mkV' and 'mkV2' are the German morphological paradigms[4] for different lexical categories of 'adjective', 'adverb', 'noun', 'intransitive verb', and 'transitive verb' respectively. "translation" is the best possible translation obtained from the Universal WordNet. This translation is passed to a paradigm as a base word, which then builds a full-form inflection table. These tables are then used in the linearization phase of the translation system (see section 3)

Concrete lexicons for all other languages were developed using the same procedure. Table 1 gives some statistics about the coverage of these lexicons.

Language	Number of Entries	Language	Number of Entries
Abstract	91516	German	49439
French	38261	Finnish	27673
Swedish	23862	Hindi	16654
Bulgarian	12425		

Table 1: Lexicon Coverage Statistics

[3]However, in our concrete lexicons we match them to WordNet 1.7.1 for the reasons mentioned previously

[4]See (Bringert et al., 2011) for more details on these paradigms

3 System architecture

Figure 1 shows an architecture of the translation pipeline. The architecture is inter-lingual and uses the Resource Grammar Library (RGL) of Grammatical Framework (Ranta, 2011) as the syntax and semantics component, Penn Treebank data for parse-tree disambiguation and IMS(It Makes Sense)(Zhong and Ng, 2010) as a word sense disambiguation tool. Even though the syntax, semantics and parse-tree disambiguation are not the main topics of this paper, we give the full architecture to show where the work reported in this paper fits. Internal GF resources (e.g. resource grammars and dictionaries) are shown in rectangles while the external components (e.g. PennTreebank and IMS(Zhong and Ng, 2010): a wide coverage word sense disambiguation system for arbitrary text.) are shown in double-stroked rectangles.

With reference to Figure 1: The input is parsed using English resource grammar (EngRG) and a comprehensive English dictionary (DictEng). If the input is syntactically ambiguous the parser will return more than one parse-tree. These trees are disambiguated using a statistical model build from the PennTreebank data. The best tree is further processed using the input from the IMS to tag the lexical nodes with best sense identifiers. This tree is finally linearized to the target language using the target language resource grammar (TLRG) together with the target language lexicon (LinkedDict) discussed in section 2.

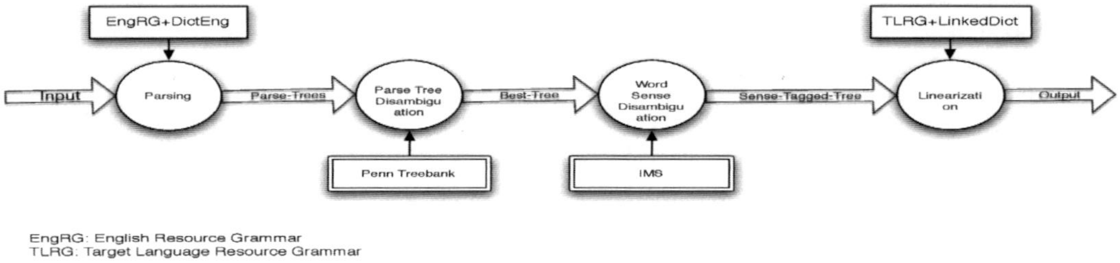

Figure 1: The translation pipeline.

4 Experimental Setup and Evaluation

Our experimental setup is as follows: We take some English text as source, and translate it to a target language (German and Hindi in these experiments) by passing it through the translation pipeline described in section 3. To show the usefulness of the lexicons described in section 2 and for comparison, we translate the same source twice: with and without word sense disambiguation.

For the first attempt, we used exactly the same translation pipeline as shown in Figure 1, except that to overcome the deficiencies of our existing parse-tree disambiguator, for some of the examples, we used trees directly from the PennTreebank, which are supposed to be correct. However, this should not damage the claims made in this paper which is about developing wide coverage interlingual translation lexicons and then using them for WSD in an interlingual translation pipeline.

For the second attempt, we plugged out the word sense disambiguation form the translation pipeline and used our old GF style lexicons (one target word per source word irrespective of its sense) in the linearization phase.

Finally, we compared both candidate translations to see if we have gained anything. We did both manual and automatic evaluations to confirm our findings.

For a set of 25 sentences for English-German pair we got marginal BLEU score improvements (from 0.3904 to 0.399 with 'old' and 'new' dictionaries). Manual inspection, however, was much more encouraging, and explained the reasons for very low improvements in the BLEU scores in some cases. The reason was that even if the word sense disambiguation, and hence, our new lexicon gives a better lexical choice, it will still be considered 'wrong" by the evaluation tool if the gold-standard has a different choice. It was also observed that there were cases where the 'old' lexicon produced a much better translation than the 'new' one. The reasons for this are obvious. The word sense disambiguator has its own limitations and is known to make mistakes. Also, as explained in Section 5, the lexicon cannot be guaranteed to always give the right translation.

Next, we give a number of example sentence with comments[5] to show that how the new lexicons improved the quality of translations, and also give some examples where it worked the other way around.

4.1 German

1. **Source** He increases the board to seven

   Without WSD `er erhöht das Brett nach einigen sieben`

   With WSD `er vergrößert die Behörde nach einigen sieben`

   Comments `das Brett` is a wooden board (wrong); `erhöht` means "to raise". while `vergrößert` means "increases the size". Note the wrong preposition choice ("to" should be `zu` rather than `nach`). Also, an indefinite determiner (`einige`, some) has been wrongly added to the cardinal number is used as a noun phrase.

2. **Source** the index uses a base of 100 in 1,982

   Without WSD `das Verzeichnis verwendet eine Base nach einige 100 in einigen 1982`

   With WSD `der [index_11688271_N] nutzt einen Operationsbasis von einigen 100 in einigen 1982`

   Comments Note the untranslated word in the WSD version. `Base` means a chemical base, the wrong meaning here. `Operationsbasis` is not the best choice, but acceptable.

3. **Source** fear is the father of panic

   With WSD Angst ist der Papa von Angst

   Comment The traditional hilarious example, saying "fear is fear's daddy".

4.2 Hindi

To represent Hindi, we use an IPA style alphabet, with the usual values and conventions. Retroflexed sounds are written with a dot under the letter: `ṭ`, `ḍ`, and `ṛ` (a flap) are common, while `ṇ` and `ṣ` occur in Sanskritised Hindi (though many dialects pronounce them `n` and `š`). The palatalised spirant is shown `š` and aspirated stops are shown thus: `kʰ`. A macron over a vowel denotes a long vowel, and ˜, nasalisation. In Hindi, `e` and `o` are always long, so the macron is dropped. Finally, we use `ñ` to mean the nasal homorganic with the following consonant.

Here are examples from our evaluation showing that the WSD system works well; the versions without WSD merely pick the first synonym in the lexicon.

1. **Source** Mr Baris is a lawyer in New York .

   Without WSD `Mr Baris New York mẽ kānūn kā pañḍit hæ`

   With WSD `Mr Baris New York mẽ vakīl hæ`

   Word order `Mr Baris New York in lawyer is`

   Comments `kānūn kā pañḍit` is "expert/teacher in law", while `vakīl` means "lawyer".

2. **Source** we don't depend on pharmaceutical companies for our support

   Without WSD `ham auṣadʰīya sahyōgī par hamāre bʰaraṇ pōṣaṇ ke liye nahī nirte hæ̃.`

[5] For the comments on German, we are indebted to Erzsebet Galgoczy and Wolfgang Ahrendt, our colleagues and German informants.

With WSD `ham auṣadʰīya kañpanī par hamāre nirvāh vyay ke liye nahī̃ ūte hæ̃.`

Word order `We pharmaceutical companies on our subsistence expenditure for not ??? do`

Comments `sahyōgī` means "company" in the sense of "colleagues", `nirvāh vyay` means "subsistence expenditure" , while `bʰaraṇ pōṣaṇ` means "weight bearing". The penultimate word in both versions is nonsense, and the lexicons need to be debugged.

3. **Source** you may recall that a triangle is also a polygon

Without WSD `tum "recall may" ho ki ṭrāyengl "also" bahubʰuj hæ`

With WSD `tum smaraṇ kar sakte ho ki trikoṇ bʰī bahubʰuj hæ`

Word order `You recall do can that triangle also polygon is`

Comments The version without WSD has several missing words. The WSD version of "recall" is not idiomatic, but understandable.

It should be noted that the coverage of the Hindi lexicon is lowest of all the lexicons given in Table 1. The result is that many sentences have missing words in the translations. Also, there is considerable interference with Urdu words (some stemming from the shared base grammar (Prasad and Shafqat, 2012)). Further, some mappings coming from the Universal WordNet data are in roman, as opposed to Devanagari (the usual script for Hindi, and what the grammar is based on), so these need to be transcribed. Finally, idiomatic phrases are a problem ("before the law" is likely to be rendered "(temporally) before the law" rather than "in the eyes of the law").

5 The next steps

Since the Universal WordNet mappings are produced from parallel data by machine learning techniques, the translations are not always accurate and do not always make the best possible choice. This leaves a window for improvement in the quality of the reported lexicons. One way of improvement is the manual inspection/correction, not an easy task for a wide-coverage lexicon with around 100 thousand entries, but not impossible either. This would be a one-time task with a strong impact on the quality of the lexicon. Another way is to use manually built WordNets, such as the Finnish and Hindi WordNets. In our work, the availability of some of these resources was an issue, so we leave it for the future. Further, as mentioned in Section 4, the Hindi lexicon has some script-related issues which should be fixed in future.

When it comes to interlingua-based arbitrary machine translation, an important concern is the size of lexicons. We are aware of the fact that the size of our lexicons is not comparable to some of the other similar systems such as ATLAS-II (Fujitsu), where the size of lexicons is in millions. We have plan to extend the size of lexicons using some of the other publicly available resources (such as Hindi WordNet) and/or using parallel corpus. The development of bilingual lexicons form parallel corpus have been previously explored (Delpech et al., 2012; Qian et al., 2012), and the same ideas can be applied in our case.

6 Conclusion

We have shown how to use existing lexical resources such as WordNets to develop an interlingual translation lexicon in GF, and how to use it for the WSD task in an arbitrary text translation pipeline. The improvements in the translation quality (lexical), shown by examples in Section 4, are encouraging and motivate further work in this direction. However, it should be noted that there is still a lot of work to be done (especially in the open domain text parsing and parse-tree disambiguation phases of the translation pipeline) to bring the translation system to a competitive level. For the reasons noted in the introduction, we expect our techniques to be particularly useful for South Asian languages.

References

Angelov, K. (2011). *The Mechanics of the Grammatical Framework.* PhD thesis, Chalmers University Of Technology. ISBN 978-91-7385-605-8.

Angelov, K. and Enache, R. (2010). Typeful Ontologies with Direct Multilingual Verbalization. In Fuchs, N. and Rosner, M., editors, *CNL 2010, Controlled Natural Language.*

Bringert, B., Hallgren, T., and Ranta., A. (2011). GF resource grammar library synopsis. www.grammaticalframework.org/lib/doc/synopsis.html.

Curry, H. B. (1961). Some logical aspects of grammatical structure. In Jakobson, R., editor, *Structure of Language and its Mathematical Aspects: Proceedings of the Twelfth Symposium in Applied Mathematics*, pages 56–68. American Mathematical Society.

de Melo, G. and Weikum, G. (2009). Towards a Universal Wordnet by learning from combined evidence. In *Proceedings of the 18th ACM Conference on Information and Knowledge Management (CIKM 2009)*, pages 513–522, New York, NY, USA. ACM.

Delpech, E., Daille, B., Morin, E., and Lemaire, C. (2012). Extraction of domain-specific bilingual lexicon from comparable corpora: Compositional translation and ranking. In *Proceedings of COLING 2012*, pages 745–762, Mumbai, India. The COLING 2012 Organizing Committee.

Détrez, G. and Ranta, A. (2012). Smart paradigms and the predictability and complexity of inflectional morphology. In *EACL*, pages 645–653.

Dymetman, M., Lux, V., and Ranta, A. (2000). XML and multilingual document authoring: Convergent trends. In *Proc. Computational Linguistics COLING, Saarbrücken, Germany*, pages 243–249. International Committee on Computational Linguistics.

Enache, R., España-Bonet, C., Ranta, A., and Márquez, L. (2012). A hybrid system for patent translation. In *Proceedings of the 16th Annual Conference of the European Association for Machine Translation (EAMT12), Trento, Italy.*

Hindi-WordNet (2012). *Hindi Wordnet. 2012. Universal Word—Hindi Lexicon.* http://www.cfilt.iitb.ac.in.

Lindén, K. and Carlson., L. (2010). Finnwordnet—wordnet på finska via översättning. *LexicoNordica—Nordic Journal of Lexicography*, 17:119–140.

Ljunglöf, P. (2004). *The Expressivity and Complexity of Grammatical Framework.* PhD thesis, Dept. of Computing Science, Chalmers University of Technology and Gothenburg University. `http://www.cs.chalmers.se/~peb/pubs/p04-PhD-thesis.pdf`.

Lyons, J. (1968). Introduction to theoretical linguistics. *Cambridge: Cambridge University Press.*

Martin-Löf, P. (1982). Constructive mathematics and computer programming. In Cohen, Los, Pfeiffer, and Podewski, editors, *Logic, Methodology and Philosophy of Science VI*, pages 153–175. North-Holland, Amsterdam.

Miller, G. A. (1995). Wordnet: A lexical database for English. *Communications of the ACM*, 38:39–41.

Montague, R. (1974). *Formal Philosophy.* Yale University Press, New Haven. Collected papers edited by Richmond Thomason.

Prasad, K. V. S. and Shafqat, M. V. (2012). Computational evidence that Hindi and Urdu share a grammar but not the lexicon. In *The 3rd Workshop on South and Southeast Asian NLP, COLING.*

Qian, L., Wang, H., Zhou, G., and Zhu, Q. (2012). Bilingual lexicon construction from comparable corpora via dependency mapping. In *Proceedings of COLING 2012*, pages 2275–2290, Mumbai, India. The COLING 2012 Organizing Committee.

Ranta, A. (2004). Grammatical Framework: A Type-Theoretical Grammar Formalism. *The Journal of Functional Programming*, 14(2):145–189. `http://www.cse.chalmers.se/~aarne/articles/gf-jfp.pdf`.

Ranta, A. (2011). *Grammatical Framework: Programming with Multilingual Grammars.* CSLI Publications, Stanford. ISBN-10: 1-57586-626-9 (Paper), 1-57586-627-7 (Cloth).

Ranta, A. and Angelov, K. (2010). Implementing Controlled Languages in GF. In *Proceedings of CNL-2009, Athens*, volume 5972 of *LNCS*, pages 82–101.

Ranta, A., Détrez, G., and Enache, R. (2012). Controlled language for everyday use: the MOLTO phrasebook. In *CNL 2012: Controlled Natural Language*, volume 7175 of *LNCS/LNAI*.

Rosetta, M. T. (1994). *Compositional Translation*. Kluwer, Dordrecht.

Seki, H., Matsumura, T., Fujii, M., and Kasami, T. (1991). On multiple context-free grammars. *Theoretical Computer Science*, 88:191–229.

Shafqat, M., Humayoun, M., and Aarne, R. (2011). An open source Punjabi resource grammar. In *Proceedings of the International Conference Recent Advances in Natural Language Processing 2011*, pages 70–76, Hissar, Bulgaria. RANLP 2011 Organising Committee. http://aclweb.org/anthology/R11-1010.

Stallman, R. (2001). *Using and Porting the GNU Compiler Collection*. Free Software Foundation.

Zhong, Z. and Ng, H. T. (2010). It makes sense: A wide-coverage word sense disambiguation system for free text. In *Proceedings of the ACL 2010 System Demonstrations*, pages 78–83, Uppsala, Sweden. Association for Computational Linguistics. http://www.aclweb.org/anthology/P10-4014.

A Dictionary Data Processing Environment and Its Application in Algorithmic Processing of Pali Dictionary Data for Future NLP Tasks

Dipl. Inf. Jürgen Knauth
Trier Center for Digital Humanities
Universitätsring 15
54296 Trier
Germany
knauth@uni-trier.de

David Alfter
Trier Center for Digital Humanities
Bollwerkstrasse 10
54290 Trier
Germany
s2daalft@uni-trier.de

Abstract

This paper presents a highly flexible infrastructure for processing digitized dictionaries and that can be used to build NLP tools in the future. This infrastructure is especially suitable for low resource languages where some digitized information is available but not (yet) suitable for algorithmic use. It allows researchers to do at least some processing in an algorithmic way using the full power of the C# programming language, reducing the effort of manual editing of the data. To test this in practice, the paper describes the processing steps taken by making use of this infrastructure in order to identify word classes and cross references in the dictionary of Pali in the context of the SeNeReKo project. We also conduct an experiment to make use of this data and show the importance of the dictionary. This paper presents the experiences and results of the selected approach.

1 Introduction

Pali (also written Pāli, Paḷi or Pāḷi) is a dead language from the group of Middle Indo-Aryan languages (Burrow, 1955: 2). Despite its status as dead language, Pali is still widely studied because many of the early Buddhist scriptures were written in Pali (Bloch, 1970: 8). It is also said that Buddha himself spoke Pali or a closely related dialect (Pali Text Society; Thera, 1953: 9).

SeNeReKo is a joint research project of the Trier Center for Digital Humanities (TCDH) and the Center of Religious Studies in Bochum (CERES), Germany. This project aims to process the Pali Canon – which at the same time is the only texts left of Pali – in order to research religious contacts between the early Buddhists and other religious groups and cultures.

To achieve this we aim to develop NLP tools and process this data as we believe that the concepts of interest will be found in direct verbal expressions within this corpus. From the information we aim to extract we intend to create networks that allow analysis of these concept.

Until now such an attempt has never been made. Even processing Pali using computer algorithms has not been in the focus of the scientific community yet. As we researchers in SeNeReKo try to change this we now focus on a basic building block for NLP tools: Building a machine readable dictionary that allows building sophisticated NLP tools in the long run. To attempt this a digitized copy of the dictionary of William and Davids (1997) has been provided to our team by the University of Chicago.

2 Related Work

As Pali is a low resource language not much work has yet been done in this field, especially not with the dictionary data. The only researchers we know of that have tried to use this data is a team of the

Proceedings of the 5th Workshop on South and Southeast Asian NLP, 25th International Conference on Computational Linguistics, pages 65–73,
Dublin, Ireland, August 23-29 2014.

University of Copenhagen. Their goal was to create a new digitized version of this dictionary. Unfortunately they did not succeed and stopped after having edited three letters of the Pali alphabet. To our knowledge we are the first to work with this data again.

With good success a language somehow similar to Pali has been addressed in the past: Sanskrit (Hellwig 2009). Nevertheless attempts to adapt these tools to Pali have not been possible due to the lack of a suitable dictionary.

Regarding NLP tools addressing Pali some experiments have already been performed by the members of the SeNeReKo project team and especially by David Alfter. Nevertheless no work could yet reach a state of publication due to the lack of a suitable digital dictionary that would serve as a basis for NLP tasks.

3 Technical infrastructure

As it is the nature of digital humanities projects like SeNeReKo a variety of researchers is involved into the process of processing and editing data and developing methods for the research intended. In SeNeReKo this involves Pali experts, Sociologists, Computer Linguists and Scientists (and Egyptologists for performing work with other text corpora not addressed by this paper.) An infrastructure that aims at enabling collaboration is therefore mandatory. This section describes key aspects of the infrastructure developed.

3.1 Dictionary Server

Each dictionary entry is to be understood as a single document which is self-contained and structured. A dictionary is considered to be a collection of documents.

Being self-contained all information relevant to each individual entry is stored in the same document. Each of these entries must be structured to provide information in a clearly defined way for NLP tools in the future.

To store the dictionary data a MongoDB data base is used. This NoSQL data base not only supports such kind of data model it also provides the necessary flexibility to define and change the internal structure of such dictionary document in the future as needed.

For ease of use a NodeJS-based dictionary server has been implemented that provides user authentication and high level data base operations addressing searching, inserting, updating and deleting specific to the requirements of a dictionary.

The pairing of NodeJS and MongoDB is reasonable because of performance reasons: MongoDB receives and returns data not in XML, but in JSON notation; and as NodeJS provides its functionality through a highly efficient JavaScript engine JSON data can directly be processed without any need of conversion.

For collaboration purposes a REST-API has been implemented with compatibility and interoperability in mind. As we aim for algorithmic processing of data and want to enable researchers to easily implement custom NLP tools that make use of the dictionary data independently from each other. To support this as best as possible a Java and C# library has been implemented as well as an R module for convenience.

As it is the nature of dictionary data to consist of a larger amount of individual entries, classical request-response communication models, as they would be imposed by HTTP, are unsuitable for processing (in the sense of algorithm based editing). Following that approach would result in notable performance degradation. Fortunately single processing steps as we intend them for pattern matching and enriching of dictionary entries have largely no relation between individual entries. Therefore the dictionary server provides an interface for bulk communication: A large amount of individual protocol function calls can be packed into a single package. As the server processes them in parallel and returns the response to all requests again in a single response we are capable of overcoming the problem of summation of network latencies and end up with good performance in updating data.

3.2 Data Processing Tool

In SeNeReKo we need to process the original - near plaintext - dictionary entries. This data is inserted into the dictionary server beforehand and then various analysing and processing steps need to be taken. To perform these, we implemented a processing environment that makes developing of individual processing units very easy, gives high performance and great transparency about data modifications intended by these units.

Our data processing tool is a programming environment for creating small processing units in C#. Data management issues do not need to be addressed: This is done by the programming environment automatically. The individual units are compiled to native .Net code for speed of processing. On execution data from the dictionary server is retrieved and passed through these units and – if necessary – sent back to the server after modifications have been applied. Together with the bulk processing supported by the dictionary server the compilation of the code units speeds up any processing. By directly making use of C# this approach we achieve great flexibility: It allows making use of all kinds of existing libraries if desired and enables researchers to implement all kinds of data specific pattern matching and processing for research tasks.

As it is the nature of dictionary data to consist of a large amount of individual entries, applying pattern matching and transformation tasks require a great deal of transparency. Researchers performing these tasks need to be able to identify which rule is applied to which entry in what form and see what modification an entry will receive. To achieve this transparency our data processing tool collects information about all modifications applied to each individual data record and presents them in a large list that can be filtered by some criteria. Thus our tool aids in debugging by allowing insight into every details of the tasks a researcher is going to perform.

4 Processing of Pali Dictionary Data

Prior to any processing we converted the original digitized dictionary entries we received from the University of Chicago into JSON data structures and inserted them into our dictionary server. In the next sections we present our processing steps applied to the individual dictionary data records within the infrastructure described above.

4.1 Transliteration of Lemmas

As it turned out the digitized version of the Pali Dictionary we received was not entirely in accordance with the current transliteration conventions. Therefore to be able to use the Pali dictionary for research the lemmas had to be adjusted.

To achieve a valid transformation we first had to verify that no accidental errors had been introduced by the original digitization process done by the Pali Text Society. We therefore implemented an alphabet model that follows the old transliteration schema used to represent glyphs of the Sinhalese alphabet. For these single letters one or two Latin ligatures (with diacritics) are used today. Modelling each word with the original alphabet is mandatory to be able to identify possible errors. We checked all lemmata against our model and were able to identify 14 of 16280 lemmata violating our model. The errors could be identified to be printing errors or misinterpretation during digitalization and were then corrected manually before continuing processing.

The next step was to perform substitutions of the letters 'ŋ'. To ensure correct processing this was not done on the Unicode based character representation of the data directly but on the original letters modelled by our alphabet model. Substitution is performed on that basis taking the phonetic context into account as necessary:

```
ŋ followed by j, c, h or e => ñ
ŋ followed by k or kh => ṅ
ŋ followed by d, dh or n => n
ŋ followed by m, p, bh or b => m
ŋ followed by s => ṃ
ŋ followed by ṭ, ṭh => ṇ
ŋ followed by l => l
ŋ followed by v, y or r => ṃ
ŋ followed by a, e, i, o, u, ā, ī, ū => ṃ
ŋ not followed by any character => ṃ
```

5 Pattern Recognition and Enriching Dictionary Entries

5.1 Pattern Matcher

In processing Pali we had to take our own pattern matching approach in order to avoid problems encountered with regular expressions in C#. We found that some Pali specific diacritics did not get processed as the official regular expression syntax specification suggested. To overcome these limitations we implemented an own pattern matcher.

Nevertheless we were not interested in dealing with space characters as they do not provide any valuable information to our pattern recognition tasks. And for easy communication with Indologists a pattern syntax was required that would be easy to understand. So these requirements specific to our field of application were taken into account in building the pattern matcher.

The pattern matching system we designed does not process character streams but token streams. The system can distinguish between the following concepts:

- A whitespace – which is automatically left out during tokenizing the dictionary articles
- A word – which is an alphanumeric character including all diacritics
- A delimiter – which is any kind of character not being to a word or whitespace

As we aimed for an iterative process in order to identify relevant pattern it helped greatly to be able to express patterns to be matched in the form of expressions that are easy readable by non-computer experts. Our syntax supports the following forms:

- Match a specific word token
- Match any word token
- Match a specific delimiter token
- Match any delimiter token

Examples of this syntax are given in the next sections which address specific pattern recognition tasks individually.

5.2 Cross References

As Pāli grammar is not standardized to the same extent as, e.g., Sanskrit, various alternative word forms occur. The Pali dictionary at hand addresses this problem to some extent by containing several versions of some lemmas. These entries then contain purely textual information of a reference to the dictionary entry having more information about the selected lemma. In the Pali dictionary this is expressed in forms like this:

```
... in general see <b>buddha<b> ...
```

Such a form is matched by a pattern like this:

```
'in'  'general'  'see'  <  'b'  >  W*!  <  /  'b'  >
```

The pattern specified is easy to understand: This is a sequence of individual patterns matching specific tokens. Words in inverted commas express an exact match of a single word. “`W*!`” indicates that a word of any kind is expected here (and it should be available for further use after a match has been found). Other characters match specific delimiter tokens.

Two real world examples of dictionary entries:

```
anumatta
    see <b>aṇu°</b> .

ano
    is a frequent form of comp<superscript>n.
```

```
</superscript><b>an--ava</b> , see <b>ava</b> .
```

As there exist various different forms of patterns like this in the dictionary specifying multiple possible variants was required. Within an iterative process we were able to identify 46 different kinds of patterns which we could make use of for automatic identification.

To further help manual processing of the dictionary we implemented a verifier that tries to identify the lemmas each cross reference refers to within the dictionary. This is done by direct dictionary lookup. References that do not seem to point to a valid lemma are listed together with candidates based on Levenshtein distance for manual processing later by Indologists.

5.3 Extracting word class information

As we aim for lemmatizing and part of speech tagging of the Pali Canon, in the long run having information about the word class of each lemma is mandatory. Therefore we used pattern matching to aid the generation of data for this purpose.

Our algorithmic approach of classification is basically performed in three steps described next.

Word class information mainly manifests itself in expressions enclosed in rounded brackets. E.g.:

```
apāra
      (nt.) [a + pāra] 1. the near bank of a river ...

sīhaḷa
      Ceylon; (adj.) Singhalese ...

susira
      (adj.--nt.) [Sk. śuṣira] perforated, full
      of holes, hollow ...

pītika
      (--°) (adj.) [fr. pīti] belonging to joy; ...
```

Unfortunately round bracket expressions are used in different semantic contexts within dictionary entries. In a first step we therefore extracted all content enclosed in round brackets and identified expressions that represent word class information. Though an old printed edition of the dictionary contained a clear definition of these word class expressions used we encountered some variety of writing, of combination and of misspelling: Building a list of relevant expressions was the only way to address all phenomena in sufficient quality.

Secondly we know from Pali grammars that verb lemmata typically end with "-ti" in the dictionary. But not all lemmata ending with "-ti" are verbs. Therefore we implemented the following algorithm that was able to clearly identify lemmata correctly as verbs:

```
for all lemmas do
    if lemma does not end with "-ti" -> reject it
    if bracket expression in data matches a pattern clearly
          classifiable as non-verb -> reject it
    if entry does not contain the (English) word "to" -> reject it
    otherwise -> recognize this lemma as being a verb
```

After having identified verbs successfully we then were able to address dictionary entries of other word forms purely according to expressions in round brackets. The following list gives an overview of how many kinds of patterns have been identified and were involved in this process:

Word Class	Number of Patterns
adjective	26 incl. one misspelling
indeclinable	1
adverbs	4 incl. one misspelling

pronouns	1
numerals and ordinals	2
nouns	8

6 Word class recognition

In order to evaluate the importance of the dictionary, we designed the following task: for each word in a manually tagged subset of the Pali Canon, we tried to recognize the word class using a generation-based and a heuristic approach. We then compared the results of both approaches.

For the generation-based approach, we generated all possible word forms, including morphological information, for every word in the dictionary using the morphological generator. The generator uses paradigms to generate regularly inflected word forms. Furthermore, the generator uses the dictionary to look up morphological information about a word and, if present, uses this information to restrict the generation to grammatically adequate forms. However, since the dictionary entries do not always present this information, or because it's not always possible to easily extract this information, we over-generated in cases where no information can be retrieved from the dictionary. We also generated rare forms according to information presented in available grammars on Pali. In total, we were able to generate 11447206 word forms for all words. This averages to about 702 word forms per dictionary entry. In compact notation, this resulted in about 1.5 GByte of data.

As we generated possible morphological forms from lemmas, we then reversed the data structure to arrive at a morphological form lookup table. We saved these results locally for later efficient lookup.

As a test corpus for our word class recognition task we used a manually annotated set of 500 sentences (about 4600 words). These sentences have been extracted earlier in the SeNeReKo project, choosing three consecutive sentences at random from the whole Pali corpus. This preparatory step has been started about a year ago to assist future computational linguistic tasks (a further 500 sentences are work in progress). Thus, the data is representative of the whole corpus and is not biased.

We then stepped through our corpus and checked for each word whether one or more of the generated forms corresponded to the word at hand. If this was the case, we retrieved the relevant entries including all attached morphological information. From these entries, we then retrieved the word class information for the word.

For the heuristic approach, we built a morphological analyzer. The analyzer can only rely on its internal heuristic for guessing the word class of a word. The heuristic is ending based and uses paradigms to determine to which word class a word could belong. The analyzer tries to identify and separate possible endings occurring in different paradigms. Based on these analyses, the word class is guessed.

Before we could start the experiment, we had to map the word classes used by the generator/analyzer and the word classes used in the annotated corpus onto a common set of classes. The reference corpus uses a fine-grained tag set that's standardized for use in more than one corpus in the SeNeReKo project. The dictionary uses a simple tag set, which has been created independently of the SeNeReKo tag set many decades ago. The tag sets follow different principles and goals. It is therefore not always straightforward to map one tag set onto the other.

We tried to assign each word of the reference corpus a word class and checked the results against the manual annotations. The results of this algorithmic output are evaluated in the result section below.

7 Discussion

7.1 Performance of the processing environment

As a server we use an older 32 bit Linux machine with an Intel Core Duo at 2.4 GHz and 4 GByte of memory which runs the dictionary server with its data base.

Due to bulk processing of requests we were able to bring down the average time for a single write operation to about 0.7ms per dictionary entry from a client's point of view under ideal circumstances. In a real world application such as our data processing tool this enables us to process all 16280 dictionary entries within about 10 seconds if no changes are applied and to about 20 seconds if all entries must be read and written back to server. We found this delay very acceptable during our design and implementation of individual processing units for the dictionary data.

The following performance measurement chart for data write requests gives an insight into how performance is affected by network latency:

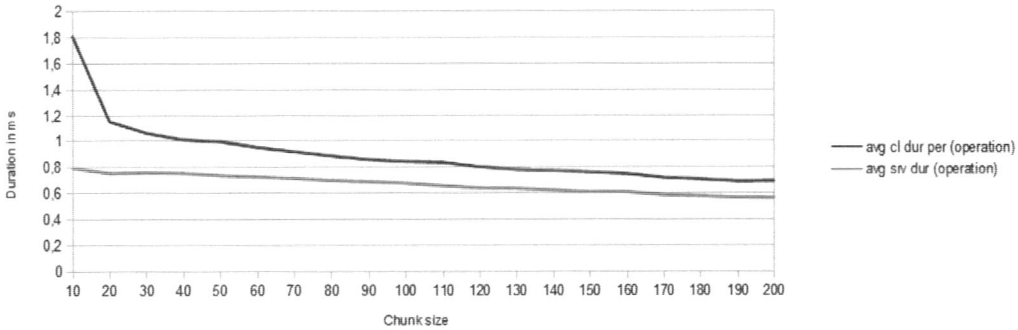

(If the above chart is displayed in black and white: The top line represents the client duration measured per operation, the bottom line measures the server duration per individual insert operation.)

This measurement is taken by inserting all Pali dictionary data 10 times with different chunk sizes and averaging the duration as measured by the test software. For convenience the server performs performance measurements on his own and sends his results 9together with the response to the client, so that such a kind of analysis can be performed easily. The difference between both measurements indicate the overhead introduced (mainly) by network latencies.

Please note that the chart starts at a chunk size of 10. This is for a reason: It turned out that lower values will introduce significantly more delay.

7.2 Results of pattern matching

Our attempts to process the 16280 dictionary entries resulted in being able to recognize word forms in 10016 of all entries. This is about 61.5% of all dictionary data.

Regarding cross references we were able to extract 457 cross references to existing lemmas within the dictionary, 52 references to lemmas not in the dictionary and 75 references containing only incomplete information and cannot be resolved automatically.

At first hand these values do not seem to be very high. But as we can only rely on clearly identifiable patterns within the dictionary entries these values are even better than we hoped at the beginning of our work. It has been clear right from the start that a greater amount of dictionary entries would need to be the centre of manual work in the future by Pali experts: Many entries simply do not contain any information that can be recognized by the algorithmic approaches taken.

As Pali is a largely dead language we have to consider that our data processing described in this paper is a one-time task. The only relevant dictionary at hand is the one we used, containing exactly those words we have. We successfully identified word classes for lemmas leaving 6264 for manual processing for our Indological colleagues. If even more time would be spent in finding even more patterns within the dictionary entries, we might improve our performance by a few percent, but there is no real reason to do this: We have come to a point where finding more patterns will take considerably more time than identifying word classes and assigning them manually to the dictionary entries.

7.3 Results of Word Class recognition

We tried to recognize word classes based on the generation-based approach and on the heuristic approach as described above. We faced the problem that word forms can be analysed in more than one way, even by using paradigms, which represent regular inflections. This degree of ambiguity cannot be resolved currently due to the particularities of Pali, such as a high degree of homonymy. Furthermore, different paradigms yield the same surface form, even though they belong to totally different word classes.

Therefore, we evaluated the resulting data in two different ways. First, we used "is-any" matching. If a test corpus word has been assigned more than one word class by our algorithms, we consider the word classes to match if the two sets share at least one common element. This way we address the problem of ambiguities. Second, we used "exact" matching. In this case, we consider the result to be a positive match if and only if the proposed word class corresponds exactly to the assigned word class. By using this approach, we try to determine the degree of unambiguousness with which we can propose a word class. If a word is assigned a word class and the program suggests two word classes, of which one corresponds to the assigned word class, we count this as a failure.

Please note that, since it's not always possible to distinguish clearly between nouns and adjectives in Pali, we aggregated these word classes into one class. To this class we also counted words tagged as ordinal adjectives, since they are inflected like regular adjectives.

The following tables illustrate our results:

"is any" matching		
	Generation based	Heuristic
Noun-adjective-ordinalAdjective	63.30%	99.96%
Numeral	61.04%	76.62%
Pronoun	82.75%	88.57%
Verb	51.24%	63.37%

As you can gather from the table, the performance of the word form generation based approach did not match the performance of our heuristic approach in the first experiment. Further investigation showed that this is mainly due to the fact that not all necessary word forms encountered in the reference corpus could be generated. There are several reasons for this: First, the exact ways to generate word forms are not yet completely covered by literature and in some areas are still under research: e.g. at least regarding verb forms, there is still ongoing research. Second, our generation process was not able to handle irregular forms well because this information is not yet represented in the dictionary. This data will probably be entered by Pali experts next year. Third, most of the forms we could not recognize are sandhi and other compound forms. This is a task the generation process cannot handle well in general. A heuristic approach does not encounter these problems.

To better judge our algorithms, we therefore evaluated the results only for word forms that could be addressed by these algorithms. The following tables give an overview about these results:

"is any" matching (processable words)		
	Generation based	Heuristic
Noun-adjective-ordinalAdjective	97.31%	99.96%
Numeral	81.03%	76.62%
Pronoun	86.61%	88.57%
Verb	76.25%	63.37%

As you can see, on word forms that could be processed, both approaches work similarly well.

With the current state of the dictionary, these results are as good as can be. Please note that while the heuristic approach must be considered to be final the generation based approach will improve over time as the dictionary will be improved by the Pali experts in the next years.

Our "exact" evaluation operator revealed that word forms in the reference corpus that uniquely belong to a single word class can be recognized much better by the generation based approach than by the heuristic approach. Interestingly, though we are still lacking information about irregular verb forms in the dictionary, we achieved up to 60.37% precision on verbs in exact word class recognition, while the heuristic approach surprisingly did not succeed very well.

The approaches we took can surely be improved. However, these approaches rely heavily on a dictionary, which is more detailed and even more complete. Pali experts will provide this data in the future but this is an ongoing process which will take a few years.

7.4 Conclusion and Future Work

In this paper we have addressed the task of extracting cross references and word class information from dictionary entries in a Pali dictionary. For this task as well as for future computer linguistic tasks, we have built an infrastructure suitable for data management and processing. We have experienced that even if the individual articles are not written in a consistent and clear way, some information still can be extracted. We therefore propose that similar approaches might be taken with dictionaries of other dead languages as well in the future based on the technical infrastructure we created.

We tried to complement our approach with taking the English translations, contained in most of the dictionary entries, into consideration. Unfortunately this did not work well due to the nature of our data: Most of the dictionary entries do contain a discussion of a lemma in English, but as the individual dictionary entries don't follow a clearly defined structure and even discuss various related words within these entries it turned out this approach is too incomplete and too error prone to be usable in practice.

We found the processing environment to be of great help in order to shorten the time consuming manual processing of data. Three aspects we like to point out in this context: The concept of having an integrated development environment that takes data management work off the shoulders of researchers and allows writing small units of code for processing turned out to aid in this process. Furthermore the transparency given by the system about processing details for every single word helps greatly to avoid mistakes and therefore saves time of researchers.

Our experiment concerning word class recognition showed that the dictionary is essential. While the dictionary data is still relatively incomplete, we were able to get good results. Future work needs to be done in this area, especially the correction of lemmas and part of speech tags in the future. However, this is a future task that goes beyond the scope of this paper.

A custom dictionary editor has been built that connects to the dictionary infrastructure at hand. With this tool our Indological collegues intend to perform the unavoidable manual improvement in the next years. If this process is completed at some point in the future we intend to address lemmatizing and part of speech tagging again, something that can not yet been done to a fully satisfying extent right now. Nonetheless, as our word class experiment showed, we were able to achieve good results despite the problems encountered. It is to be expected that with the improvement of the dictionary, the results will also improve in the future.

Reference

Alfter, David. 2014. *Morphological analyzer and generator for Pali.*

Critical Pāli Dictionary. Web.

Collins, Steven. 2006. *A Pali grammar for students.* Chiang Mai: Silkworm Books. Print.

Geiger, Wilhelm. 1943. *A Pali Grammar.* Pali Text Society. Print.

Helwig, Oliver. 2009. *SanskritTagger, a stochastic lexical and POS tagger for Sanskrit.*

Stede, William and Davids , Rhys. 1997. *Pali-English Dictionary.* 2nd ed, Motilal Banarsidass. Print.

Pali Text Society. Web.

Thera, Nārada. 1953. *An elementary Pāḷi course.* 2nd ed. Colombo: Associated Newspapers of Ceylon. BuddhaNet eBooks. Web. N.d.

Constituent structure representation of Pashto Endoclitics

Azizud Din
Faculty of Computer Science and Information Technology
UNIMAS, Malaysia
University of Peshawar, Pakistan
aziz621@gmail.com

Bali Ranaivo-Malancon
Faculty of Computer Science and Information Technology
UNIMAS, Malaysia
mbranaivo@fit.unimas.my

M. G. Abbas Malik
Faculty of Computing and IT – North Jeddah Branch
King Abdulaziz University
Jeddah, Saudi Arabia
mgmalik@kau.edu.sa

Abstract

Pashto is one of the widely spoken languages in Pakistan, Afghanistan and by the diaspora around the world, especially in Middle East. This paper presents an initial study of Pashto endoclitics, the constituent structure representation of Pashto endoclitics and the context free grammar rules. Subsequently, this study will help in the development of clitics generation system for Pashto language. The special focus is on the development of CFG rules for the generation of endoclitics which would finally be incorporated into a Text Generation System for Pashto language.

1 Introduction

This paper examines the phenomenon of Pashto second position (endo)clitics as described by Tegey (1977). Pashto is an Eastern Iranian language spoken in parts of Afghanistan, Pakistan and by the diaspora around the world, especially in Middle East. It is the mother tongue of more than 40 million people. It is the official language of Afghanistan. In Pakistan, it is mainly spoken in the province of Khyber Pakhtunkhwa, but it also significant number of mother tongue speakers in Sindh (Karachi, Hyderabad) (Din *et. al.*, 2012).

Clitics have been defined in many ways, both phonologically and syntactically, often as semi-independent forms which attach to phrases rather than words. The technical details of different definitions are not relevant for this paper; here clitics can be described simply as a part of speech somewhere between affixes and particles, attached to hosts like affixes, yet behave at the same time as independent words, like particles.

The two most common types of clitic, found in other languages besides Pashto, are enclitic and proclitic. Enclitic is attached at the end of the host (parallel to suffixes or postpositions) whereas, proclitic is attached at the beginning (parallel to prefixes or prepositions). Pashto has several proclitics, including و (waw,perf), نه (na, not), را(raa, 1p),) در (der, 2p), and ور (wer, 3p) (Kopris, 2009). They are also classified as oblique pronominal clitics.

The third type of clitics is the endoclitic, which attaches itself to the middle of a word like an infix. Endoclitics are not simply inserted in a word at a grammatical boundary (in which case they would simply be affixes) but rather they can split morphemes into separate chunks (called *partials* here). Part of a morpheme may end up in one *partial* while the rest of the morpheme may end up in another, potentially separated by multiple words in between. In linguistic theory, they are generally considered to be impossible, a violation of lexical integrity (Kopris and Davis, 2005). This theoretical impossibility may explain why the only languages claimed to have endoclitics are Pashto, Udi (Harris, 2002) and Degema (Kari, 2003). The existence of Endoclitics is still a major controversial issue in today's linguistic theory. Putting aside the status of Endoclitics in linguistics, this paper focuses on the develop-

Proceedings of the 5th Workshop on South and Southeast Asian NLP, 25th International Conference on Computational Linguistics, pages 74–79,
Dublin, Ireland, August 23-29 2014.

ment of Context Free Grammar (CFG) rules for endoclitic generation in natural language generation systems.

2 Context-free Grammar and C-Structure

Different models in computational linguistics have been used to process natural languages at lexical, syntactic and semantic levels. CFG is one such model that is commonly employed to represent language syntax (grammar) rules for natural languages (Jurafsky and Martin,2002). In this paper, a CFG for parsing and generating Pashto endoclitics is presented. In the contemporary linguistic approach, a sentence is an acceptable if native speakers accept the sentence as sounding good. Thus, if a majority of native people accept a sentence to be valid, then the sentence is considered good and valid. In the view of formal language theorists, the sentence is grammatical with respect to a grammar under consideration, if the grammar permits it, by generating the parse tree of the sentence. A good grammar should not only accept valid sentences but also reject invalid sentences. A grammar is also required to have fewer rules and the derived parse trees should be compact. Languages like Pashto, Urdu and Sindhi have complex syntactic structures. Formal language models like CFGs are not able to handle all the syntactic complexities for these languages. Despite these limitations, CFG can be used as an effective tool for dealing with the most sentence types in these languages (Rehman and Shah, 2003). Like Lexical Functional Grammar (LFG) (Joan, 2001), my approach for the creation of context free grammar is based on the idea of phrase structure and constituent structures. In the LFG, the phrase structures are in the form of a tree diagram, called c-structure (Joan, 2001).

3 PASHTO VERBS FORMS AND CFG PRODUCTION RULES

Pashto is an argument-dropping language (Miriam, 2007); therefore sentences may consist of only a verb and a clitic. The endoclitics mainly appear in short sentences in the context of a stress alternation that accompanies a difference in the aspect as shown in the example (1) parse tree in Figure 1 with constituent structure (c-structure) representation. Two syntactically aligned terminal nodes may share one lexical item, a representation similar to Figure 1.

وهو	مې	تک	(1)
Waho	mee	ta'k	
Shook	I	shook-1(Perf)	

I shook it.

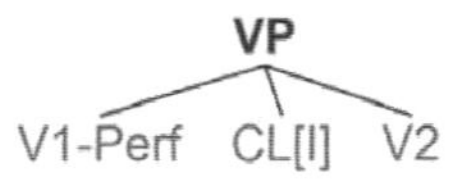

Figure 1. Clitics as postlexical elements

In Pashto language, the perfective aspect of the verb is accompanied by a verb-internal stress shift, placing the main stress on the first foot of the verb, while the verb in the imperfective aspect carries the main stress on the last foot of the verb. Verbs are split by clitics and each sub part of the verb is called root. With regard to the stress shift, Pashto verbs fall roughly into three classes based on their *word-internal structure*. Since these structures are essential to the correct placement of the clitic, it is necessary to analyse them more closely in order to find the appropriate (prosodic or syntactic) unit on which the clitic depends. Based on the morphological structure of different verbs, verb classes have to be defined. These verb classes and their internal characteristics and behaviour concerning the placement of clitic are described next.

3.1 Monomorphemic Verbs

Monomorphemic verbs are classified as **Class-I** verbs. Imperfective monomorphemic verbs bear stress on the last foot; the clitic is placed after the verb as shown in (2a). On the other hand, the perfective Class-I verbs take on a perfective prefix (و,wa) - which receives the main stress. In this case, the clitic occurs between the prefix and the stem, as shown in (2b).

Imperfective (2a)

مې   تښنوله

me   *texnawala*

I   tickle

I was tickling (her).

Perfective (2b)

تښنوله   مې   و

Texnawala   *me*   *wa*

Tickle   CLT   PERF

I tackled her

The infinitive of تښنوله "təxnaw´ əla" is تښنول "təxnaw´ əl". To make it masculine, morpheme و "wa" is added to the infinitive and ه "ha" is added to make it feminine in Pashto. The CFG production Rules for monomorphemic verbs are specified below:

```
S    → VP*
VP   → Perf NP*
NP   → CL V*
V    → V_sg_mas
V    → V_sg_fem
V    → V_pl
```

Each production consists of a rewrite rule. Each symbol on the left hand side of arrow (→) called non-terminals can be replaced with symbols on the right hand side of the arrow. The Kleene star (*) denotes zero or more repetitions. The Symbol S stands for sentence, NP for noun-phrase, CL for endo-clitic, VP for verb phrase and Perf for perfective marker. The verb V in Pashto is usually a derived form of the stem, called "مصدر" [maSder] in Pashto, using morphological rules. It contains information about tense, gender and number. The words or lexical items like w'ə, mee and təxnawəla are terminals. Each non-terminal must be replaced with a terminal to generate a sentence. Using bottom-up parsing technique, the phrase structure tree of sentence (2b) is shown in Figure 2.

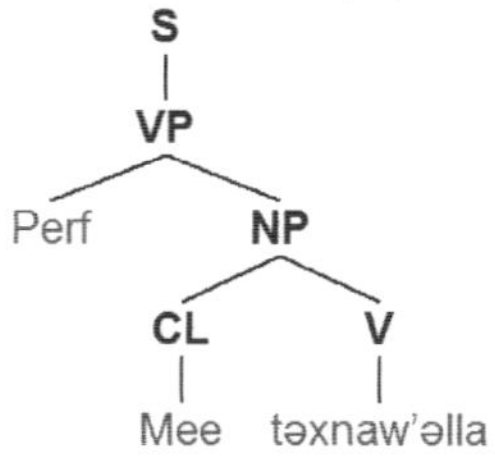

Figure 2. Phrase structure tree of sentence (2b)

The prosodic surface representation of (2b) is shown in Figure *33*.

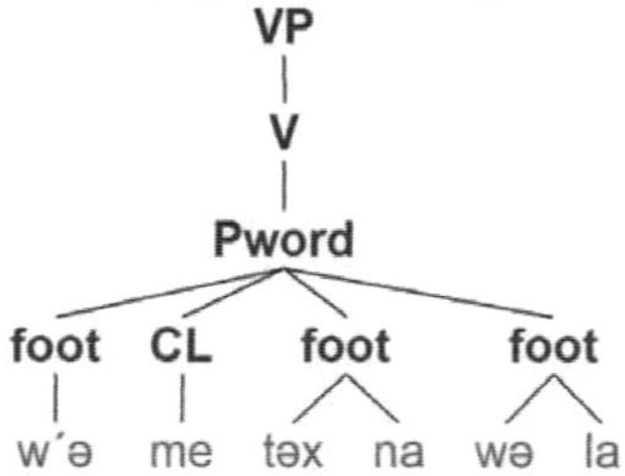

Figure 3. Prosodic surface representation of (2b)

3.2 Bimorphemic Verbs

Class-II and III are bimorphemic verbs. They form the perfective verb by means of a stress shift from the last to the first foot of the verb without adding a perfective prefix. Class-II verbs consist of a derivational prefix and a root. In the bimorphemic imperfective verb, the stress is on the second foot of the verb and the clitic is placed after it as exemplified in (3a). The perfective verb is formed via a stress shift from the last to the first foot of the verb. The clitic is then placed after the first foot, i.e. after the derivational prefix as shown in (3b).

Imperfective (3a)
مې تيل وهو
mee telwah΄ə
CLT-I Pushing-him
I was pushing.

Perfective (3b)
وهو مې تيل
Waho mee t'el(Perf)
Push-past I Push
I pushed it.

Class-III verbs are complex predicates consisting of an adjective, adverb or noun and a light verb. They form the largest group of verbs in Pashto. Noun-verb combinations such as obə lagawəl 'to water' (see Figure for parse tree), suč wahəl 'to guess, think', paysé lagawəl 'to deposit money', and qadám wahəl 'to walk' are frequently used in Pashto.

These noun-verb combinations are structured as compound verbs or verbal phrases and often correspond to simple verbs in English. Their behaviour with respect to clitics is the same as with the Class-II verbs, because there is also a verb internal stress shift that goes along with a change in the aspect. The clitic is positioned after the first foot in the perfective, as shown in (4), and after the whole verb in the imperfective.

Perfective (4)
کو مې پوښ
Ko mee pox'
Did I cook
I cooked (it)

Tree models are helpful in the derivation of phrase structure rules. Such a tree model is also called a phrase marker. Here forth, we will give the additional CFG rules using phrase markers.

کو مې اوبه
Ko mee obə
Did I water
I watered (it).

With Class-III verbs, one can easily identify the individual elements of a word because they are complex predicates. Thus, an analysis in favour of treating all three elements as post-lexically independent items seems likely. On the other hand with Class-II verbs, the separation of the elements is not clear, but one could argue that the derivational prefix might itself be a 'lexical word', e.g. a clitic (Stephen. 2005). Assuming that clitics are post-lexical elements that occupy separate syntactic nodes, the Class-II verb in (3b) would thus lead to a c-structure representation similar to **Error! Reference source not found.**.

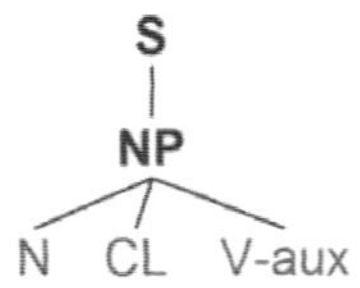

Figure 4. Phrase Stucture Tree for Noun phrase

```
S → NP*
NP → N CL V-aux
```

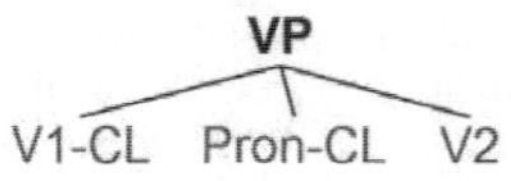

Figure 5. Clitics as Post-Lexical elements

Similarly, Adjective-verb combinations are structured as compound verbs or verbal phrases and often correspond to simple verbs in English. The phrase structure tree for this is given in figure 6.

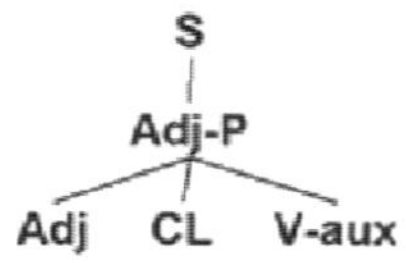

Figure 6. Phrase Stucture Tree

S → Adj-P*
Adj-P → Adj CL V-aux

However, there is a group of verbs within Class-II, which do not contain any identifiable derivational prefix, i.e., the element after which the clitic is placed as in the (5a) 'bay', does not constitute a morpheme with a separate meaning. It is therefore rather difficult to argue in favour of a clitic status of 'bay' as in Figure 1, if the morpheme is not clearly identifiable and furthermore holds a unique position within the language, i.e. it cannot be found in any other word.

Imperfective (5a)
بيلود مي
Mee bəylod´e
I Lose
I was losing (it).

Perfective (5b)
بي مي لود
Lode mee b´əy
Lose2- I -lose(1)
I lost (it).

3.3 The Special Class of A-initial Verbs

Apart from the three classes introduced above, there is a small group of verbs that can have alternating stress in the imperfective, but form the perfective with the perfective prefix of Class-I verb (wa-), thus adopting properties of all three classes. Within this group, there are verbs that begin with consonants, which do not show any special behaviour in the imperfective: even if the stress is on the front vowel, the clitic is placed after the verb.

However, there is a small number of verbs in this group with an initial vowel a- which show a very distinct behaviour with respect to the alternating stress shift in the imperfective. If the stress falls on the second foot, the clitic is placed after the verb as in (6a). If it falls on the initial vowel a-, the clitic is placed directly after the vowel as in (6b), thus acting similar to class of bimorphemic verbs.

Imperfective — stress on the second foot (6a)
ا غستل مي
Mee aˇgust´əl
I wear
I was wearing it.

Imperfective — stress on the first foot (6b)
ا مي غستل
ˇgust´əl mee a
Wear-2 I wear-1
I was wearing it.

Partials are much less in use in writing and in speaking. It indicates that speakers can find a way around using them. This raises the possibility of converting sentences with partials into equivalent sentences, which do not contain partials. One way is to avoid using endoclitics altogether, and the other is to rephrase such that the verb is not split into partials. We present a solution to the above problem in 6, which is commonly used by speakers of Pashto. Table *1* shows the rearrangement based on the addition of strong pronoun هغه, at the start of the sentence. This allows the endoclitic to appear in second position without necessitating verb-splitting. Parsing of such sentence with strong pronoun at the start can be done easily.

Original	With partials	ا مي غستل I was wearing them.
Modified	Without partials	هغه مي اغستل I was wearing them.

Table 1. Solution for a'Intial words

Production for such modified sentence is given as follows.

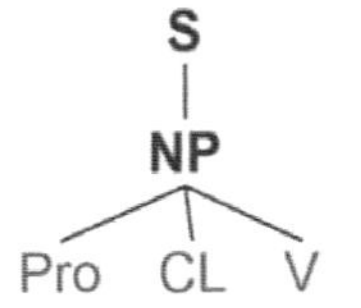

Figure 7. Phrase structure tree for modified sentence in table.1

```
S  → NP*
NP → Pro CL V
```

4 Conclusion

This paper presented endoclitics in Pashto language, solution to A-initial Verbs, Constituent structure representation and CFG rules for Pashto endoclitics. However, this paper is only a first proposal for the development of CFG grammar for the grammatical phenomena of the Pashto language. Further research is necessary, especially implementation of these rules for the generation of Pashto endoclitics.

Reference

Anderson, Stephen. 2005. Aspects of the Theory of Clitics. Oxford University Press.

Bresnan, Joan (2001). Lexical Functional Syntax. Blackwell. ISBN 0-631-20973-5

Butt, Miriam. 2007. The Role of Pronominal Suffixes in Punjabi. In Annie Zaenen, Jane Simpson, Tracy HollowayKing, Jane Grimshaw, JoanMaling and ChrisManning (eds.), Architecture, Rules, and Preferences, pages 341–368, CSLI Publications.

Craig Kopris, AppTek, Inc. Endoclitics in Pashto: Can They Really Do That?

Craig A. Kopris and Anthony R. Davis. 2005. Endocliticsin Pashto: Implications for Lexical Integrity.Presented at the Fifth Mediterranean Morphology Meeting, Sept. 15-18, 2005, Fréjus, France.

Daniel Jurafsky & James H. Martin. Speech and Language Processing An Introduction to Natural Language Processing, Computational Linguistics and Speech Recognit ion. Pearson Education Series 2002.

Din, A. Malancon, B and Yeo, A. 2012. Pashto Endoclitic Generation. In proceedings of IEEE conference, Pages 248-252, ICCIS Publication (Volume:1).

Rahman,M and Shah,A. Grammar Checking Model for Local Languages. In proceedings to the SCONEST (Student Conference on Engineering Sciences and Technology) 2003. SCON-S15, Hamdard & Bahria University Karachi Pakistan, October 2003.

Tagey, Habibullah. 1977. "The Grammar of Clitics: Evidence from Pashto and Other Languages" PhD Dissertation University of Illinois.

Real Time Early-stage Influenza Detection with Emotion Factors from Sina Microblog

Xiao SUN
School of Computer and Information
Hefei University of Technology
Hefei, Anhui, China
Anhui Province Key Laboratory of Affective Computing and Advanced Intelligent Machine
suntian@gmail.com

Jiaqi YE
School of Computer and Information
Hefei University of Technology
Hefei, Anhui, China
Anhui Province Key Laboratory of Affective Computing and Advanced Intelligent Machine
lane_3000@163.com

Fuji REN
School of Computer and Information
Hefei University of Technology
Hefei, Anhui, China
Faculty of Engineering, University of Tokushima
Tokushima, Japan
ren2fuji@gmail.com

Abstract

Influenza is an acute respiratory illness that occurs every year. Detection of Influenza in its earliest stage would reduce the spread of the illness. Sina microblog is a popular microblogging service, provides perfect sources for flu detection due to its real-time nature and large number of users. In this paper we investigate the real-time flu detection problem and describe a Flu model with emotion factors and sematic information (em-flu model). Experimental results show the robustness and effectiveness of our method and we are hopeful that it would help health organizations in identifying flu outbreak and take timely actions to control.

1 Introduction

Influenza is a highly contagious acute respiratory disease caused by influenza virus. As the highly genetic variation, influenza can cause global epidemic, which not only brought huge dis-asters to people's life and health, but also have significant disruptions to economy. There are about 10-15% of people who get influenza every year and results in up to 50 million illnesses and 500,000 deaths in the world each year. Influenza is a worldwide public health problem and there are no effective measures to control its epidemic at present. The prevalence of influenza in China is one of the most notable problems.

The epidemic of SARS, H1N1 and H5N9 influenza make us realized that people really need to expand surveillance efforts to establish a more sensitive and effective precaution indicator system for infectious disease forecasting. In order to detect influenza epidemic timely and im-prove the ability of early precaution, the research of early forecasting technique is urgently needed.

Nowadays influenza surveillance systems have been established via the European Influenza Surveillance Scheme (EISS) in Europe and the Centre for Disease Control (CDC) in the US to collect data from clinical diagnoses. The research of forecasting methods started relatively late in China and these systems have about two-week delay. The need for efficient sources of data for forecasting have increased due to the Public health authorities' need to forecast at the earliest time to ensure effective treatment. Another surveillance system is Google's flu trends service which is web-based click flu reporting system. Google's flu trend uses the linear model to link the influenza-like illness visits.

Proceedings of the 5th Workshop on South and Southeast Asian NLP, 25th International Conference on Computational Linguistics, pages 80–84, Dublin, Ireland, August 23-29 2014.

Sina Weibo is a Chinese popular microblog service that can potentially provide a good source for early stage flu detection due to its large data scale and real-time features. When flu breaks out, infected users might post related microblog with corresponding emotions in a timely way which can be regarded as indicators or sensors of Influenza. Based on the real-time data of mi-croblog, there has been many applications such as earthquake detection (Sakaki T et al., 2010), public health tracking (Collier N, 2012; Paul M J et al., 2011) and also flu detection (Achrekar H et al., 2011; Culotta A,2010).

The measures of collecting clinical diagnoses and web-based clicks on key word with linear model are quite good but not fair enough. Our research tries to use the big real-time data as re-sources and design a machine learning mode with the emotional factors and sematic information to help find the break point of influenza.

The rest of this paper is organized as follows: In section 2, we describe our Flu model with emotion factors (em-flu model). We describe the preparation of our dataset in Section 3. Exper-imental results are illustrated in Section 4. We conclude this paper in Section 5.

2 Em-flu Model

Existing works on flu prediction suffer the following limitations: Spatial information is seldom considered and sematic or emotion factors are out of consideration. To address this problem, in this paper, we try to introduce an unsupervised approach called Em-flu Markov Network for early stage flu detection. Spatial information are modelled in a four-phase Markov switching model, i.e. non-epidemic phase (NE), rising epidemic phase (RE), stationary epidemic phase (SE) and declining epidemic phase (DE). Our approach assumes microblog users as "sensors" and collective posts containing flu keywords as early indicators. Our algorithm can capture flu outbreaks more promptly and accurately compared with baselines. Based on our proposed algorithm, we create a real-time flu surveillance system. For early stage flu detection, we use a probabilistic graphical Bayesian approach based on Markov Network. The key of the flu detection task is to detect the transition time from non-epidemic phase to epidemic phase.

Basically, our model is based on a segmentation of the series of differences into an epidemic and a non-epidemic phase using a four-stage Markov switching model. Suppose we collect flu related microblog data from N location. For each location i∈[1,N], we segment the data into a time series. $Z_{i,t}$ denotes the phase location i takes on at time t. $Z_{i,t}$=0,1,2,3 correspond to the phase NE, RE SE and DE. $Y_{i,t}$ is the observant variable, which denotes the number of flu related microblog at time t, join in location i. $\Delta Y_{i,t} =(Y_{i,t} - Y_{i,t-1})/ Y_{i,t-1}$. The underlying idea of Markov switching models is to associate each $Y_{i,t}$ with a random variable $Z_{i,t}$ that determines the conditional distribution of $Y_{i,t}$ given $Z_{i,t}$. In our case, each $Z_{i,t}$. is an unobserved random variable that indicates which phase the system is in. Moreover, the unobserved sequence of $Z_{i,t}$. follows a four-stage Markov chain with transition probabilities. For location i, N(i) denotes the subset containing its neighbors. We simplify the model by only considering bordering states in N(i).

We model the spatial information in a unified Markov Network, where the phase for location i at each time is not only dependent upon its previous phase, but its neighbors. In this work, for simplification, we only treat bordering States as neighbors. Since the influence from non-bordering States can be transmitted through bordering ones, such simplification makes sense and experimental results also demonstrate this point. A Generalized Linear Model is used to integrate the spatial information in a unified framework. For location i at time t, the probability that Zi,t takes on value Z is illustrated as follows:

$$\mathrm{P} = \Pr(Z_{i,t} \mid Z_{j,t+1}, Z_{i,t-1}) = \frac{\exp(\psi Z_{i,t-1}, Z_{i,t} + \psi Z_{i,t}, Z_{i,t+1} + \sum \Theta Z_{j,t}, Z_{i,t})}{\sum_z \exp(\sum \Theta Z_{j,t}, Z_{i,t} + \psi Z_{i,t-1}, Z_{i,t} + \psi Z_{i,t}, Z_{i,t+1})}, j \in N(i) \qquad (1)$$

Where ψ and Θ respectively correspond to parameters that control temporal and spatial influence. We give a non-informative Gaussian prior for each element in ψ and Θ:

$$\Theta_{i,j} \sim N(0, \delta^2_{i,j}) \qquad \psi_{i,j} \sim N(0, \Phi^2_{i,j}) \qquad (2)$$

Next, we describe the characteristics for the dynamics of different phases. Generally speaking, the course of influenza may last a week or two, for a single microblog user, we believe his or her microblog contents will record a series of feelings when user is sick or catching flu. When a person got the flu, he will go through NE, RE, SE, DE phases; the main emotion in these four phases would naturally change by the phase change to another phase. All these individuals' data could be combined into datasheet segmented by time. From the statistics theories, the dynamics for NE, RE, DE and SE can be characterized as Gaussian process:

$$\Pr(\Delta Y_{i,t} \mid z) \sim N(E_{day(t)}, \delta^2_{day(t)}) \quad (3)$$

Where $E_{day(t)}$ corresponds to the average microblog records' number every day, and $\delta^2_{day(t)}$ corresponds to the variance of the records.

3 Data Preparation

We extend our earlier work on Sina microblog data acquisition and developed a crawler to fetch data at regular time intervals. We fetched microblog records containing indicator words shown in Table 1 and collect about 4 million flu-related microblog starting from January 2013 to January 2014. Location details can be obtained from the profile page. We select tweets whose location are in China and discard those ones with meaningless locations.

Indicator words	止咳药(pectoral),输液(transfusion),伤风(cold),流涕(running nose),流感(flu),咳嗽(cough),抗生素(antibiotic),喉咙疼(Sore throat),感冒(influenza),发烧(fever),发高烧(high fever),鼻涕(snot)

Table 1: Indicator seed words set for data collection

Not all microblog containing indicator keywords indicate that the user is infected. Meanwhile the indicator words list may not be perfect, so the indicator words list needs to expand from the data we have and the dataset needs to be processed before be used for our task.

The words in Table 1 will be used as seed words to find the initial dataset and then computing vector in the dataset to find other keyword which can be the representations of seed words. In this way, words list could be expanded and adapt the changes of cyber word. The necessity of filtering in real-time task has been demonstrated in many existing works (Aramaki E et al., 2011; Sakaki T et al., 2010).To filter out these bias tweets, we first prepared manually labeled training data, which was comprised of 3000 microblog records containing key words. We manually annotate them as positive examples and negative ones.

We built a classifier based on support vector machine. We use SVMlight with a polynomial kernel, and employ the following simple text-based features.

Feature A: Collocation features, representing words of the query word within a window size of three.

Feature B: unigrams, denoting the presence or absence of the terms from the dataset.

Performances for different combinations of features are illustrated at Table 2. We observe that A+B is much better than A or B. So in our following experiments, microblog are selected according to a classifier based on feather A+B.

Features	Accuracy	Precision	Recall
A	84.21%	82.31%	89.40%
B	85.10%	84.92%	87.00%
A+B	87.40%	88.75%	**89.64%**

Table 2: Result of different combinations of features for filtering

We briefly demonstrate the relatedness between microblog data and CNIC (Chinese National Influenza Center) surveillance weekly report data, which would support the claim that microblog data can be used for the flu detection task. We observe that performing svm filtering and microblog selection would definitely make microblog data more correlated with real world CNIC data.

For these flu-related microblog records, we generate another microblog web crawler to deal with every record. For every record's user, we use this tool to backup user's microblog content and cut records by a window of time with one week before and after the flu-related microblog record which we had captured. Then the emotional SVM is established to help get the trend of these series of microblog records.

4 Experiments and Data Analysis

The main goal of our task is to help raise an alarm at those moments when there is a high probability that the flu breaks out. In real time situations, for each time, available data only comes from the previous days, and there is no known information about what will happen in the following days or week. By adding the data day by day, we calculate the posterior probability for transiting to epidemic states based on previous observed data. The sum over parameter $Z_{i,t-1}$ and $Z_{j,t}$ makes it infeasible to calculate. We use Gibbs Sampling by first sampling $Z_{i,t-1}$ and $Z_{j,t}$ first and then attain the value of $Z_{i,t}$ given Zi,t-1,Zi,t-1,...:

$$Z_{i,t} = \arg\max P(Z_{i,t} = z \mid Z_{j,t}, Z_{i,t-1}, \ldots, Y_{j,t}, Y_{i,t-1}, \ldots) \qquad (3)$$

Figure 1 shows the global distribution of DE, SE and RE in the year of 2013. The left hand side figure corresponds to number of flu-related microblog records overtime. Purple symbols denote the phase of RE, red symbols denote the phase of SE and white symbols denote the phase of DE.

Figure 2 shows the result of searching key words like influenza on Baidu Index platform. Compared to Figure 1 seems our influenza curve matches well. The interesting thing we observe from figure 1 is that if the percentage of RE > 0.5, there is strong possibility to convince the flu alarm is coming.

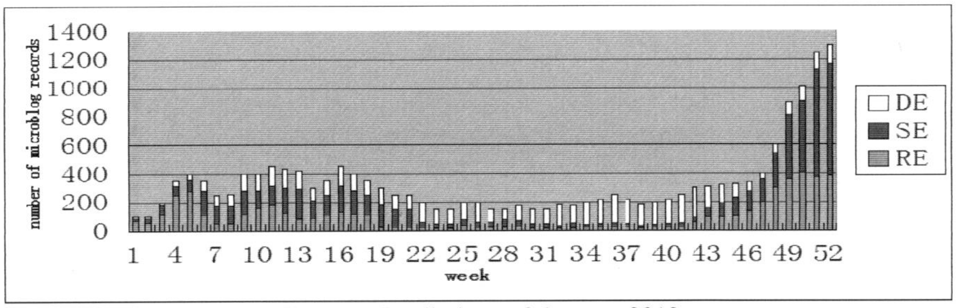

Figure 1: Predictions of the year 2013

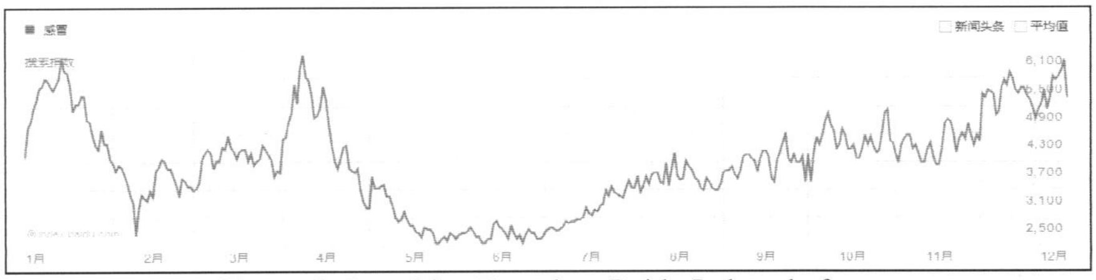

Figure 2: Searching Resutl on Baidu Index platform

For comparison, we employ the following baseline in this paper:

Average: Uses the averager frequency of micrblog records containing keywords based on previous years as the threshold.

Two-Phase: A simple version of our approach but using a simple two-phase in Markove network.

We only report partial experimental results for one province. As we can see from figure 3, our model can best fit the actual microblog data and semms stable. The other two measures also represent the actual truth but not stable enough.

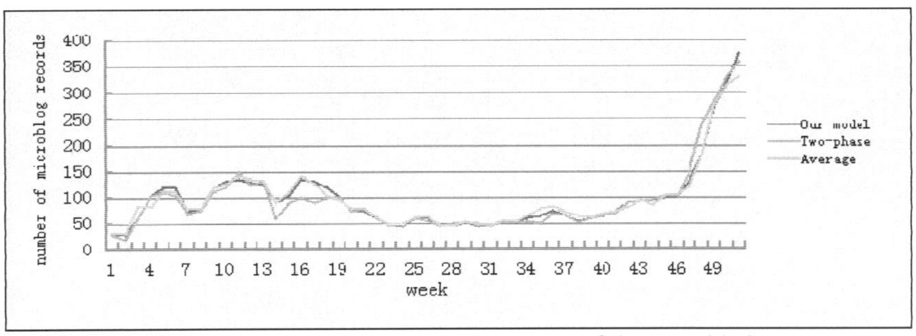

Figre 3: Prediction of Anhui province of the year 2013

5 Conclusions

In this paper, we introduced an unsupervised Bayesian model based on Markov Network based on four phases and microblog emotional factors are appended in the model to help detect early stage flu detection on Sina Microblog. We test our model on real time datasets for multiple applications and experiments results demonstrate the effectiveness of our model. We are hopeful that our approach would help to facilitate timely action by those who want to decrease the number of unnecessary illnesses and deaths. At present, the method also has a few shortcomings; we will continually develop it for further research and exploration.

ACKNOWLEDGMENT

The work is supported by National Natural Sci-ence Funds for Distinguished Young Scholar(No.61203315) and 863 National Advanced Tech-nology Research Program of China (NO. 2012AA011103), and also supported by the Funding Project for AnHui Province Key Laboratory of Affective Computing and Advanced Intelligent Machine, HeFei University of Technology.

Reference

Sakaki T, Okazaki M, Matsuo Y. 2010. Earthquake shakes Twitter users: real-time event detection by so-cial sensors[C]//Proceedings of the 19th international conference on World wide web. ACM, 851-860.

Collier N. 2012. Uncovering text mining: A survey of current work on web-based epidemic intelli-gence[J]. Global public health, 7(7): 731-749.

Paul M J, Dredze M. You are what you Tweet: Analyzing Twitter for public health[C]//ICWSM. 2011.

Achrekar H, Gandhe A, Lazarus R, et al. 2011. Predicting flu trends using twitter data[C]//Computer Communications Workshops (INFOCOM WKSHPS), 2011 IEEE Conference on. IEEE, 702-707.

Culotta A. 2010. Towards detecting influenza epidemics by analyzing Twitter messag-es[C]//Proceedings of the first workshop on social media analytics. ACM, 115-122.

Aramaki E, Maskawa S, Morita M. 2011. Twitter catches the flu: detecting influenza epidemics using Twitter[C]//Proceedings of the Conference on Empirical Methods in Natural Language Processing. Asso-ciation for Computational Linguistics, 1568-1576.

Lamb A, Paul M J, Dredze M. 2013. Separating fact from fear: Tracking flu infections on twitter[C]//Proceedings of NAACL-HLT.789-795.

Sakaki T, Okazaki M, Matsuo Y. 2010. Earthquake shakes Twitter users: real-time event detection by so-cial sensors[C]//Proceedings of the 19th international conference on World wide web. ACM, 851-860.

Achrekar H. 2012. ONLINE SOCIAL NETWORK FLU TRACKER A NOVEL SENSORY APPROACH TO PREDICT FLU TRENDS[D]. University of Massachusetts,

Aschwanden C. 2004.Spatial Simulation Model for Infectious Viral Diseases with Focus on SARS and the Common Flu[C]//HICSS.

Building English-Vietnamese Named Entity Corpus with Aligned Bilingual News Articles

Quoc Hung Ngo
University of Information Technology
Vietnam National Universiry - HCM City
Ho Chi Minh City, Vietnam
`hungnq@uit.edu.vn`

Dinh Dien
University of Sciences
Vietnam National Universiry - HCM City
Ho Chi Minh City, Vietnam
`ddien@fit.hcmus.edu.vn`

Werner Winiwarter
University of Vienna
Research Group Data Analytics and Computing
Währinger Straße 29, 1090 Wien, Austria
`werner.winiwarter@univie.ac.at`

Abstract

Named entity recognition aims to classify words in a document into pre-defined target entity classes. It is now considered to be fundamental for many natural language processing tasks such as information retrieval, machine translation, information extraction and question answering. This paper presents a workflow to build an English-Vietnamese named entity corpus from an aligned bilingual corpus. The workflow is based on a state of the art named entity recognition tool to identify English named entities and map them into Vietnamese text. The paper also presents a detailed discussion about several mapping errors and differences between English and Vietnamese sentences that affect this task.

1 Introduction

Named entity recognition (NER) is a basic task in natural language processing and one of the most important subtasks in Information Extraction. It is really essential to identify objects and extract relations between them. Moreover, recognizing proper names from news articles or newswires is also useful in detecting events and monitoring them. The NER task aims to identify and classify certain proper nouns into some pre-defined target entity classes such as person (PER), organization (ORG), location (LOC), temporal expressions (TIME), monetary values (MON), and percentage (PCT).

Several previous works in NER have been done on languages such as English (J. Sun et al., 2002; C.W. Shih et al., 2004), Japanese (R. Sasano and S. Kurohashi, 2008), Chinese (J. Sun et al., 2002; C.W. Shih et al., 2004), and Vietnamese (N.C. Tu et al., 2005; T.X. T. Pham et al., 2007; Q.T. Tran et al., 2007); and NER systems have been developed using supervised learning methods such as Decision Tree, Maximum Entropy model (D. Nadeau and S. Sekine, 2007), and Support Vector Machine (Q.T. Tran et al., 2007), which achieved high performance. Moreover, there are several studies for bilingual named entity recognition (C.J. Lee et al., 2006; D. Feng et al., 2004; F. Huang and S. Vogel, 2002). However, for the English-Vietnamese pair, this task still presents a significant challenge in a number of important respects (R. Sasano and S. Kurohashi, 2008). Firstly, words in Vietnamese are not always separated by spaces, so word segmentation is necessary and segmentation errors will affect the level of NER performance. Secondly, some proper names of foreign persons and locations are loanwords or represented by phonetic symbols, so we can expect wide variations in some Vietnamese terms. Thirdly, there are considerably fewer available existing resources such as lexicons, parsers, word nets, etc. for Vietnamese that have been used in previous studies.

Proceedings of the 5th Workshop on South and Southeast Asian NLP, 25th International Conference on Computational Linguistics, pages 85–93, Dublin, Ireland, August 23-29 2014.

In this study, we suggest a process to build a bilingual named entity corpus from aligned news express articles. In fact, this process is applied to build an English-Vietnamese Named Entity Corpus by using available English named entity recognition to tag entities in the English text, and then map them into Vietnamese text based on word alignments. The mapping results are also corrected manually by using a visualization tool.

The remainder of this paper describes the details of our work. Firstly we address the data source for building the corpus in Section 2. Next, we present a procedure to build an English-Vietnamese Named Entity Corpus by using a bilingual corpus and mapping English entities into Vietnamese entity tags in Section 3. Experimental results and conclusion appear in Sections 4 and 5, respectively.

2 Tagset and Data Source

2.1 Tagset for Named Entities

There are many tagsets for the NER task, such as the hierarchical named entity tagset with 150 types (S. Sekine et al., 2002), the biological named entity tagset (Y. Tateisi et al., 2000; J-D Kim et al., 2003), or common named entity tagsets with 3 types and 7 tags (N. Chinchor and P. Robinson, 1998). According to the definition of the MUC-7 conference (N. Chinchor and P. Robinson, 1998), we will identify six types of named entities:

- **PERSON (PER)**: Person entities are limited to humans identified by name, nickname or alias.
- **ORGANIZATION (ORG)**: Organization entities are limited to corporations, institutions, government agencies and other groups of people defined by an established organizational structure.
- **LOCATION (LOC)**: Location entities include names of politically or geographically defined places (cities, provinces, countries, international regions, bodies of water, mountains, etc.). Locations also include man-made structures like airports, highways, streets, factories and monuments.
- **TIME (TIM)**: Date/Time entities are complete or partial expressions of time of day, or date expressions.
- **PERCENTAGE (PCT)**: Percentage entities are percentage expressions, including percentage range expressions.
- **MONEY (MON)**: Money entities include monetary expressions.

We have developed a guide for bilingual named entity tagging and published it as EnVnNEguide at http://code.google.com/p/evbcorpus/downloads/list.

2.2 Data Source

The data source for building the English-Vietnamese named entity corpus is a part of the EVBCorpus[1], which consists of both original English text and its Vietnamese translations. It contains 1,000 news articles defined as the EVBNews part of the EVBCorpus (as shown in Table 1) (Q.H. Ngo et al., 2013). This corpus is also aligned semi-automatically at the word level.

In particular, each article was translated one to one at the whole article level, so we align sentence to sentence. Then, sentences are aligned semi-automatically at the word level, including automatic alignment by class-based method (D. Dien et al., 2002) and use of the BiCAT tool (Q.H. Ngo and W. Winiwarter, 2012) to correct the alignments manually. The details of the corpus are listed in Table 1.

Parallel documents are also chosen and classified into categories, such as economy, entertainment (art and music), health, science, social, politics, and technology (percentage of each category is shown in Table 2 and Figure 1). The wide range of categories ensures that named entities in the corpus are diversified enough for other following tasks.

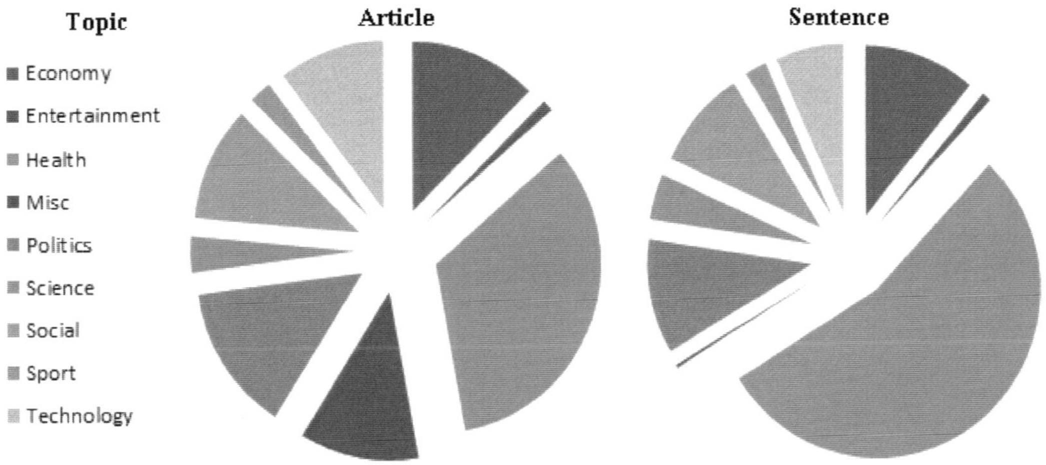

Figure 1: The distribution of articles and sentences in each topic in EVBNews

Table 1: Characteristics of EVBNews part

	English	Vietnamese
Files	1,000	1,000
Paragraphs	25,015	25,015
Sentences	45,531	45,531
Words	740,534	832,441
Words in Alignments	654,060	768,031

3 Building Named Entity Corpus

3.1 Model of Building EVNECorpus from EVBCorpus

Figure 2 shows the main modules of bilingual named entity corpus building, including three main modules: pre-processing, named entity recognition, bilingual entity mapping, and bilingual entity correction. According to this workflow, the bilingual corpus will be tagged with named entities on the English text, then, named entities are mapped from English to Vietnamese text. Finally, annotators will correct both English and Vietnamese named entities by using the BiCAT tool (Q.H. Ngo and W. Winiwarter, 2012).

At the first stage, a Named Entity Recognition system is used to tag English entities in the English sentence. Several Named Entity Recognition systems for English text are available online. For traditional NER, the most popular publicly available systems are: OpenNLP NameFinder [2] , Illinois NER[3] system by Lev Ratinov (L. Ratinov and D. Roth, 2009), Stanford NER[4] system by Jenny Rose Finkel (J.R. Finkel et al., 3005), and Lingpipe NER[5] system by Baldwin, B. and B. Carpenter (B. Carpenter, 2006). The Stanford NER reports 86.86 F1 on the CoNLL03 NER shared task data. We chose the Stanford NER to provide for the ability of our corpus for tagging with multi-type, such as 3 classes, 4 classes, and 7 classes.

The following example is the result of the Stanford NER for the English sentence "Prime Minister Gordon Brown resigned as Britain 's top politician on Tuesday evening, making way for Conservative

[1]http://code.google.com/p/evbcorpus/
[2]http://sourceforge.net/apps/mediawiki/opennlp/
[3]http://cogcomp.cs.illinois.edu/page/software_view/4
[4]http://nlp.stanford.edu/ner/index.shtml
[5]http://alias-i.com/lingpipe/index.html

Table 2: Number of files and sentences for each topic

Topic	File	Sentence
Economy	125	4,326
Entertainment	11	365
Health	336	21,107
Politics	141	4,253
Science	34	1,692
Social	110	3,699
Sport	22	838
Technology	104	2,609
Misc	117	117
Total	**1,000**	**45,531**

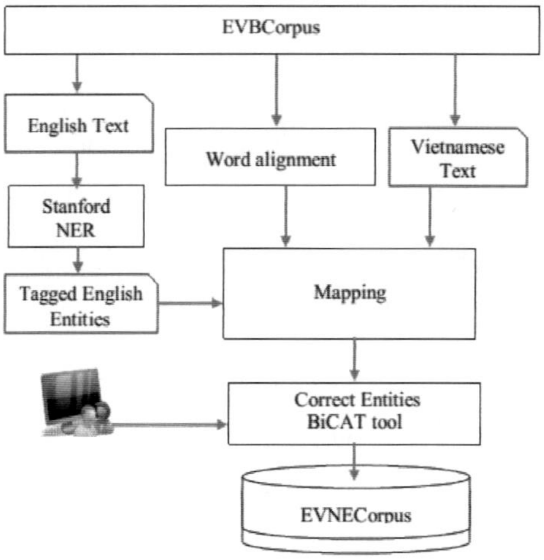

Figure 2: Architecture of building EVNECorpus from EVBCorpus

leader David Cameron." :

Prime Minister [Gordon Brown]$_{PER}$ resigned as [Britain]$_{LOC}$'s top politician on [Tuesday]$_{TIM}$ evening, making way for [Conservative]$_{ORG}$ leader [David Cameron]$_{PER}$.

and its mapped named entities in the Vietnamese sentence:

Thủ tướng [Gordon Brown]$_{PER}$ đã từ giã chức vụ cao nhất trên chính trường [Anh]$_{LOC}$ vào tối [thứ ba]$_{TIM}$, nhường chỗ cho [David Cameron]$_{PER}$ nhà lãnh đạo [Đảng Bảo thủ]$_{ORG}$.

3.2 Mapping English to Vietnamese Named Entities

At the next stage, every alignment will be mapped from English into Vietnamese tokens. Every named entity tag on linked English words is mapped to Vietnamese tokens on the target sentence. Left and right boundaries are also detected to re-build named entity chunks on the Vietnamese sentence (as shown in Figure 3):

- Remove all alignments which are not related to English named entity tokens
- Map English named entity tokens to Vietnamese text by using alignments

- Identify the boundaries of named entities and rebuild named entity script text.

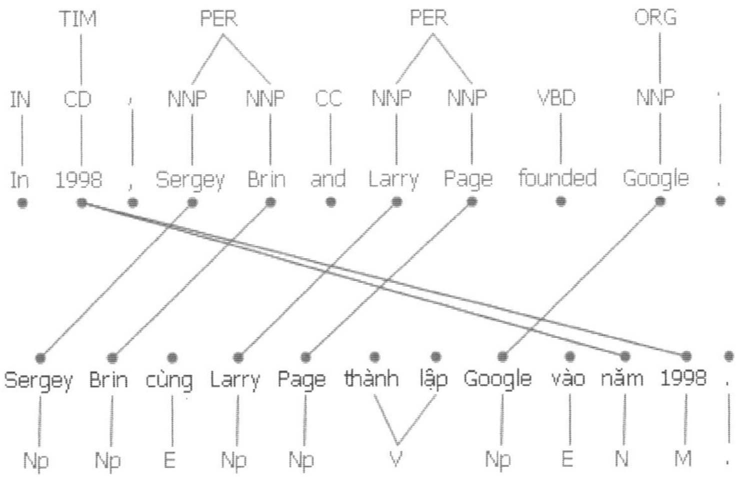

Figure 3: Mapping named entities

However, there is a difference between the number of tagged English named entities and mapped Vietnamese named entities (as shown in Table 3). Several English entities in the English sentences are not translated into the Vietnamese text, therefore, these entities are not mapped.

Table 3: Number of entities at the first stage

Tag	Name	Tagged English Entity	Mapped Vietnamese Entity	Unmapped Entity
LOC	Location	10,418	10,354	64
ORG	Organization	8,197	8,120	77
PER	Person	7,217	7,153	64
TIM	Time	4,474	4,437	37
MON	Money	1,003	992	11
PCT	Percent	1,201	1,193	8
	Total	**32,510**	**32,249**	**261**

There are several common errors of the mapping stage. The most frequent error is caused by the separation of entities from English text in Vietnamese. It means that there are several cases of one tagged English named entity being separated into two distinct Vietnamese named entities in the Vietnamese text. On the other hand, for example, the phrase "President [Bill Clinton]$_{\mathrm{PER}}$ between [1994]$_{\mathrm{TIM}}$ and [1997]$_{\mathrm{TIM}}$" has one PER entity and two TIM entities whereas the Vietnamese translated text "Tổng thống [Bill Clinton]$_{\mathrm{PER}}$ trong giai đoạn [1994-1997]$_{\mathrm{TIM}}$" has one PER entity and only one TIM entity.

Three common reasons which lead to mapping errors (these cases are discussed in the next section by analysing unmatched cases) are:

- The differences between English and Vietnamese characteristics.
- The splitting of an English named entity to two Vietnamese entities.
- The entities are replaced by pronouns and possessive pronouns in the target sentences or the other way around.

3.3 Correcting Named Entities

As shown in Figure 4, we use the BiCAT tool (Q.H. Ngo and W. Winiwarter, 2012) for correcting named entities in both English and Vietnamese sentences. The BiCAT tool is a visualization tool based on drag, drop, and edit label operations (actions) to correct the sentence pairs. It is designed for annotators to review whole phrase structures of English and Vietnamese sentences. They can compare the English named entity result with the Vietnamese named entity result and correct them in both sentences. The comparison is also used to detect incorrect named entities in both English and Vietnamese text.

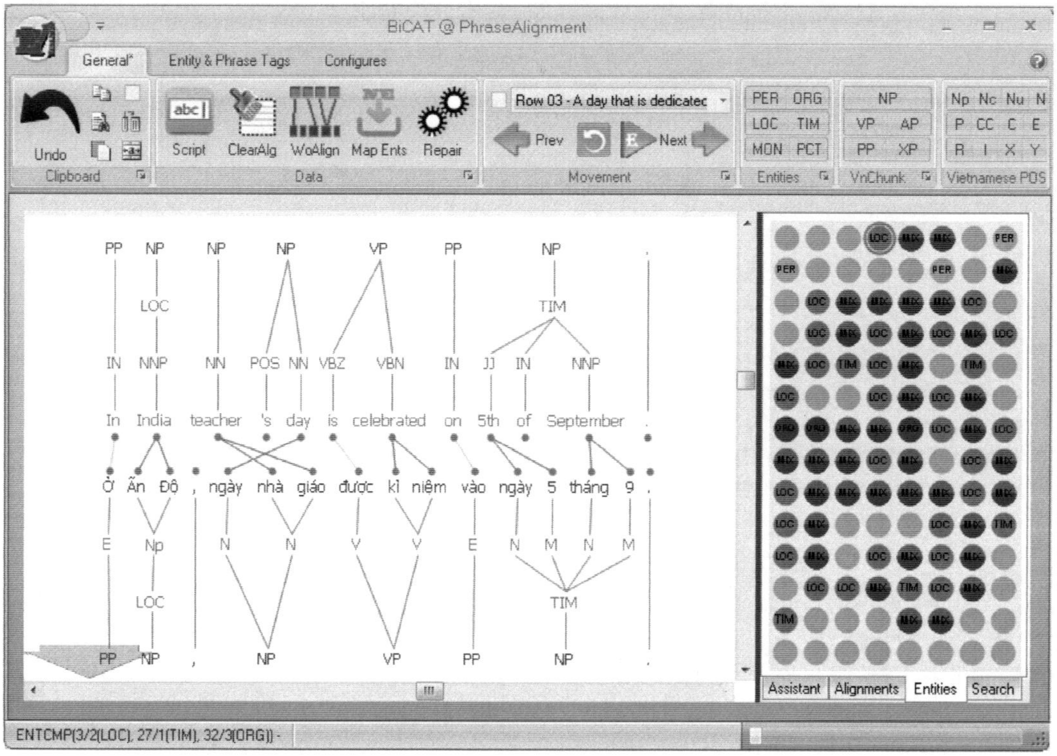

Figure 4: Screenshot of BiCAT with the named entity map

Moreover, several additional information, such as POS tagger, chunker, is also shown for building further linguistic tags. Several features are implemented on the entity matrix at the right panel of the BiCAT tool:

- Show the sentence where named entities occur.
- Highlight the pairs which have imbalance in number of entities between source sentence and target sentence.
- Quick jump to the sentence pair on which the user clicks.

4 Experiment and Results

Named entities include six tags: Location (LOC), Person (PER), Organization (ORG), Time including date tags (TIM), Money (MON), and Percentage (PCT). English text is tagged with English NER tags by Stanford NER and then mapped to Vietnamese text. Next, Vietnamese entity tags are corrected manually.

In total, the English-Vietnamese Named Entity Corpus (EVNECorpus) has 32,454 English named entities and 33,338 Vietnamese named entities in the EVBNews corpus (see Table 4 for details and its comparison in Figure 5).

Table 4: Number of entities in the EVNECorpus

Tag	Name	English Entity	Vietnamese Entity	Unmatched Entity
LOC	Location	10,406	11,343	998
ORG	Organization	8,177	8,218	189
PER	Person	7,201	7,205	199
TIM	Time	4,408	4,417	136
MON	Money	1,003	993	32
PCT	Percent	1,194	1,170	27
	Total	**32,454**	**33,338**	**1,581**

There are several common unmatched named entities in English-Vietnamese named entity corpus: the English-Vietnamese Named Entity Corpus (EVNECorpus) has 32,454 English named entities and 33,338 Vietnamese named entities in the EVBNews corpus (see Table 5). Moreover, to classify the unmatched named entities, we also tag part-of-speech for English sentences by the POS Tagger[6] of the Stanford Natural Language Processing Group (K. Toutanova and C. D. Manning, 2000).

As shown in Table 5, a large number of English adjectives (tagged JJ tag) are not tagged as named entities while their translations are tagged as locations. Most of them are coming from country names, such as French, English, and Vietnamese, and they refer to people or languages. In the English text "Cuban missile crisis", the word Cuban is not tagged as a location because Cuban is an adjective ("Cuban/JJ missile/NN crisis/NN"), while, in its Vietnamese translation, "Khủng khoảng tên lửa [Cu Ba]$_{LOC}$", "Cu Ba" is tagged as a location. Moreover, there are several English named entities that are split into two entities in the Vietnamese sentences. For example, "[Thailand]$_{LOC}$'s [Ministry of Public Health]$_{ORG}$" has two entities while its translation is [Bộ Y tế Thái Lan]$_{ORG}$. Finally, there are several named entities that are replaced by pronouns and possessive pronouns (30 cases for PRP and 11 cases for PRP$) in the translated sentences and the inverse direction (38 cases).

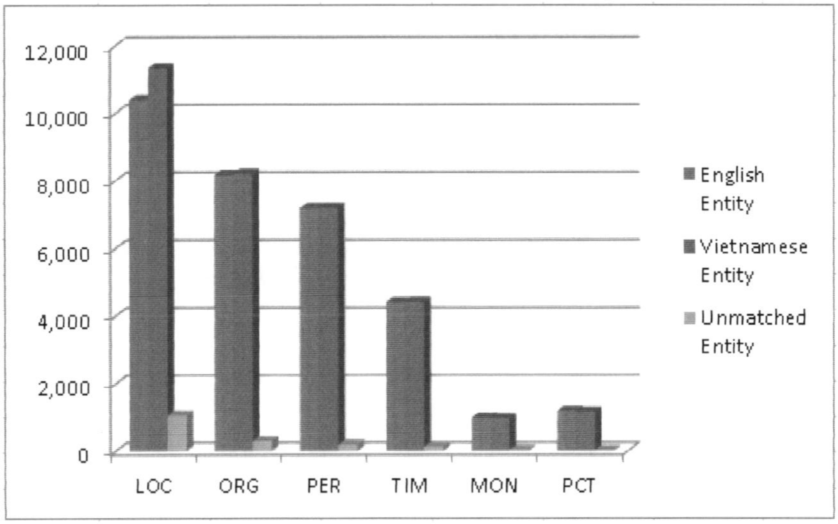

Figure 5: English entities and Vietnamese entities in the EVNECorpus

[6]http://nlp.stanford.edu/software/tagger.shtml

Table 5: Common Unmatched Named Entities

	Description/Examples	POS	Count
1	English named entities without alignments to Vietnamese words		190
2	Vietnamese named entities without alignments to English source words		106
3	English named entities with alignments to Vietnamese words rather than Vietnamese entities	NNP	38
4	Vietnamese named entities with alignments to English words rather than English entities		
	- Eurobond,	NN	10
	- Democrats, Eurobonds, Socialists	NNS	45
	- Kenyan, French,	NNP	229
	- Russians, Danish, Philippines	NNPS	107
	- They, he, she, it	PRP	36
	- Him, His, her, them	PRP$	11
	- French, English, and Fuji-based	JJ	797
	- other cases	Others	12
	Total		**1,581**

5 Conclusion

In this paper, we have shown a workflow of building an English-Vietnamese named entity corpus. This workflow is based on an aligned bilingual corpus. In addition, we built a Vietnamese word segmentation corpus for training and evaluating the system. As result, the corpus is built semi-automatically with over 45,000 sentences, and totally 32,454 English named entities and 33,338 Vietnamese named entities. Moreover, we also pointed out several differences in named entity tagging between English and Vietnamese text. These differences can be used to map named entity tags, linguistic information, and in machine translation systems.

However, adding to the six common named entity types additional names (such as product, disease, and event names) is also necessary, and we need further research for identifying them in bilingual corpora because they affect the named entity recognition process as well as the corpus.

References

Bob Carpenter 2006. *Character Language Models for Chinese Word Segmentation and Named Entity Recognition*, In Proceedings of the Fifth SIGHAN Workshop on Chinese Language Processing, pp. 169-172.

Chun-Jen Lee, Jason S. Chang, and Jyh-Shing R. Jang. 2006. *Alignment of Bilingual Named Entities in Parallel Corpora Using Statistical Models and Multiple Knowledge sources*, ACM Transactions on Asian Language Information Processing (TALIP) 5, no. 2 (2006): 121-145.

Cheng-Wei Shih, Tzong-Han Tsai, Shih-Hung Wu, Chiu-Chen Hsieh, and Wen-Lian Hsu. 2004. *The Construction of a Chinese Named Entity Tagged Corpus: CNEC1.0.*, In Proceedings of Conference on Computational Linguistics and Speech Processing (ROCLING). Association for Computational Linguistics and Chinese Language Processing (ACLCLP).

Dinh Dien, Hoang Kiem, Thuy Ngan, Xuan Quang, Nguyen V. Toan, Hung Ngo, and Phu Hoi. 2002. *Word Alignment in English – Vietnamese Bilingual Corpus*, In Proceedings of the 2nd East Asian Language Processing and Internet Information Technology (EALPIIT'02), pp. 3-11.

Donghui Feng, Yajuan Lü, and Ming Zhou. 2004. *A New Approach for English-Chinese Named Entity Alignment*, In Proceedings of Conference of the European Chapter of the Association for Computational Linguistics (EMNLP), vol. 2004, pp. 372-379. Association for Computational Linguistics.

David Nadeau, and Satoshi Sekine. 2007. *A Survey of Named Entity Recognition and Classification*, Lingvisticae Investigationes 30, no. 1 (2007): 3-26.

Fei Huang, and Stephan Vogel. 2002. *Improved Named Entity Translation and Bilingual Named Entity Extraction*, In Proceedings of the Fourth IEEE International Conference on Multimodal Interfaces, pp. 253-258. IEEE.

J-D Kim, Tomoko Ohta, Yuka Tateisi, and Jun'ichi Tsujii. 2003. *GENIA Corpus - a Semantically Annotated Corpus for Bio-Textmining*, Bioinformatics 19 (suppl. 1), pp. 80-82. Oxford University Press.

Jenny R. Finkel, Trond Grenager, and Christopher Manning. 2005. *Incorporating Non-local Information into Information Extraction Systems by Gibbs Sampling*, In Proceedings of the 43nd Annual Meeting of the Association for Computational Linguistics (ACL 2005), pp. 363-370. Association for Computational Linguistics.

Jian Sun, Jianfeng Gao, Lei Zhang, Ming Zhou, and Changning Huang. 2002. *Chinese Named Entity Identification Using Class-based Language Model*, In Proceedings of the 19th International Conference on Computational Linguistics - Volume 1, pp. 1-7. Association for Computational Linguistics.

Kristina Toutanova, and Christopher D. Manning, 2000. *Enriching the Knowledge Sources Used in a Maximum Entropy Part-of-Speech Tagger*, In Proceedings of the Joint SIGDAT Conference on Empirical Methods in Natural Language Processing and Very Large Corpora (EMNLP/VLC-2000), pp. 63-70. Association for Computational Linguistics.

Lev Ratinov, and Dan Roth. 2009. *Design Challenges and Misconceptions in Named Entity Recognition*, In Proceedings of the Thirteenth Conference on Computational Natural Language Learning (CoNLL '09), pp. 147-155. Association for Computational Linguistics.

Nguyen C. Tu, Tran T. Oanh, Phan X. Hieu, and Ho Q. Thuy. 2005. *Named Entity Recognition in Vietnamese Free-Text and Web Documents Using Conditional Random Fields*, The 8th Conference on Some Selection Problems of Information Technology and Telecommunication. Hai Phong, Vietnam.

Nancy Chinchor, and Patricia Robinson. 1997. *MUC-7 named entity task definition*, In Proceedings of the 7th Conference on Message Understanding.

Quoc Hung Ngo, and Werner Winiwarter. 2012. *A Visualizing Annotation Tool for Semi-Automatically Building a Bilingual Corpus*, In Proceedings of the 5th Workshop on Building and Using Comparable Corpora, LREC2012 Workshop, pp. 67-74. Association for Computational Linguistics.

Quoc Hung Ngo, Werner Winiwarter, and Bartholomäus Wloka. 2013. *EVBCorpus - A Multi-Layer English-Vietnamese Bilingual Corpus for Studying Tasks in Comparative Linguistics*, In Proceedings of the 11th Workshop on Asian Language Resources (11th ALR within the IJCNLP2013), pp. 1-9. Asian Federation of Natural Language Processing Associations.

Quoc Tri Tran, TX. Thao Pham, Quoc Hung Ngo, Dien Dinh, and Nigel Collier. 2007. *Named Entity Recognition in Vietnamese Documents*, Progress in Informatics, No.4, March 2007, pp. 5-13.

Ryohei Sasano, and Sadao Kurohashi. 2008. *Japanese Named Entity Recognition Using Structural Natural Language Processing*, In Proceedings of the International Joint Conference on Natural Language Processing (IJCNLP), pp. 607-612. Asian Federation of Natural Language Processing Associations.

Satoshi Sekine, Kiyoshi Sudo, and Chikashi Nobata. 2002. *Extended Named Entity Hierarchy*, In Proceedings of the Language Resources and Evaluation Conference, pp. 1818-1824. Association for Computational Linguistics.

TX. Thao Pham, Quoc Tri Tran, Dinh Dien, and Nigel Collier. 2007. *Named Entity Recognition in Vietnamese Using Classifier Voting*, ACM Transactions on Asian Language Information Processing (TALIP) 6, no. 4 (2007): 3.

Yuka Tateisi, Tomoko Ohta, Nigel Collier, Chikashi Nobata, and Jun-ichi Tsujii. 2000. *Building an Annotated Corpus in the Molecular-Biology Domain*. In Proceedings of the COLING-2000 Workshop on Semantic Annotation and Intelligent Content, pp. 28-36. Association for Computational Linguistics.

Character-Cluster-Based Segmentation using Monolingual and Bilingual Information for Statistical Machine Translation

Vipas Sutantayawalee **Peerachet Porkeaw** **Thepchai Supnithi**
Prachya Boonkwan **Sitthaa Phaholphinyo**

National Electronics and Computer Technology Center, Thailand

{vipas.sutantayawalee, peerachet.porkeaw,prachya.boonkwan, sitthaa.phaholphinyo,thepchai}@nectec.or.th

Abstract

We present a novel segmentation approach for Phrase-Based Statistical Machine Translation (PB-SMT) to languages where word boundaries are not obviously marked by using both monolingual and bilingual information and demonstrate that (1) unsegmented corpus is able to provide the nearly identical result compares to manually segmented corpus in PB-SMT task when a good heuristic character clustering algorithm is applied on it, (2) the performance of PB-SMT task has significantly increased when bilingual information are used on top of monolingual segmented result. Our technique, instead of focusing on word separation, mainly concentrate on character clustering. First, we cluster each character from the unsegmented monolingual corpus by employing character co-occurrence statistics and orthographic insight. Secondly, we enhance the segmented result by incorporating the bilingual information which are character cluster alignment, co-occurrence frequency and alignment confidence into that result. We evaluate the effectiveness of our method on PB-SMT task using English-Thai language pair and report the best improvement of 8.1% increase in BLEU score. There are two main advantages of our approach. First, our method requires less effort on developing the corpus and can be applied to unsegmented corpus or poor-quality manually segmented corpus. Second, this technique does not only limited to specific language pair but also capable of automatically adjust the character cluster boundaries to be suitable for other language pairs.

1 Introduction

Nowadays, it is admitted that word segmentation is a crucial part of Statistical Machine Translation (SMT) especially in the languages where there are no explicit word boundaries such as Chinese, Japanese or Thai. The writing system of these languages allow each word can be written continuously with no space appearing between words. Consequently, word ambiguities will arise if word boundary has been misplace which finally lead to an incorrect translation. Thus, the effective word segmentator is required to disambiguate each word separator before processing another task in SMT. Several word segmentators which focusing on word, character [1] or both [2] and [3] have been implemented to accomplish this goal.

In order to retrieve a useful information to segment or cluster the word, most of word segmentators are trained on a manually segmented *monolingual* corpus by using various approaches such as dictionary-based, Hidden Markov Model (HMM), support vector machine (SVM) or conditional random field (CRF). Although, a number of segementators are able to yield very promising results, certain of them might be unsuitable for SMT task due to the influence of segmentation scheme [4]. Therefore, instead of solely rely on monolingual corpus, various researches make use of either manually segmented [4] or unsegment[1]ed *bilingual* corpus [5] as a guideline information to perform a word segmentation task and improve the performance of SMT system.

Proceedings of the 5th Workshop on South and Southeast Asian NLP, 25th International Conference on Computational Linguistics, pages 94–101, Dublin, Ireland, August 23-29 2014.

In this paper, we propose a novel segmentation approach for Phrase-Based Statistical Machine Translation (PB-SMT) to languages where word boundaries are not obviously marked by using both monolingual and bilingual information on English-Thai language pair and demonstrate that (1) unsegmented corpus is able to provide the nearly identical result to manually segmented corpus in PB-SMT task when the good heuristics character clustering algorithm is applied on it, (2) the performance of PB-SMT task has significantly increased when bilingual information are used on top of monolingual segmented result. Our technique, instead of focusing on word separation, mainly concentrate on character clustering. First, we cluster each character from the unsegmented monolingual corpus by employing heuristic algorithm and language insight. Secondly, we enhance the segmented result by incorporating the bilingual information which are character cluster (CC) alignment, CC co-occurrence frequency and alignment confidence into that result. These two tasks can be performed repeatedly.

The remainder of this paper is organized as follows. Section 2 provides some information related to our work. Section 3 describes the methodology of our approach. Section 4 present the experiments setting. Section 5 present the experimental results and empirical analysis. Section 6 and 7 gives a conclusion and future work respectively.

2 Related Work

2.1 Thai Character Clustering

In Thai writing system, there are no explicit word boundaries as in English, and a single Thai character does not have specific meanings like Chinese, Japanese and Korean. Thai characters could be consonants, vowels and tone marks and a word can be formed by combining these characters. From our observation, we found that the average length of Thai words on BEST2010 corpus (National Electronics and Computer Technology Center, Thailand 2010) is 3.855. This makes the search space of Thai word segmentation very large.

To alleviate this issue, the notion of Thai character cluster (TCC), is introduced [1] to reduce the search space with predetermined unambiguious constraints for cluster formation. A cluster may not be meaningful and has to combine with other consecutive clusters to form a word. Characters in the cluster cannot be separated according to the Thai orthographic rules. For example, a vowel and tone mark cannot stand alone and a tone marker is always required to be placed next to a previous character only. [6] applied TCC to word segmentation technique which yields an interesting result.

2.2 Bilingually Word Segmentation

Bilingual information has also been shown beneficial for word segmentation. Several methods have used the information from bilingual corpora to perform word segmentation. As in [5], it focuses on unsegmented bilingual corpus and builds a self-learned dictionary using alignment statistics between English and Chinese language pair. On the other hands, [4] is based on the manually segmented bilingual corpus and then try to "repack" the word from existing alignment by using alignment confidence. Both works evaluated the performance in BLEU metric and reported the promising result of PB-SMT task.

3 Methodology

This paper aim to compare translation quality based on SMT task between the systems trained on bilingual corpus that contains both segmented source and target, and on the same bilingual corpus with segmented source but unsegmented target. First, we make use of *monolingual information* by employing several character cluster algorithms on unsegmented data. Second, we use *bilingual-guided alignment information* retrieved from alignment extraction process for improving character cluster segmentation. Then, we evaluate our performance based on translation accuracy by using BLEU metric. We want to prove that (1) the result of PB-SMT task using unsegmented corpus (unsupervised) is nearly identical result to manually segmented (supervised) data and (2) when bilingual information are also applied, the performance of PB-SMT is also improved.

3.1 Notation

Given a target $\{Thai\}$ sentence t_1^J consisting of J clusters $\{t_1, \dots, t_J\}$, where $|t_j| \geq 1$. If $|t_j| = 1$, we call $t_j$as a single character S. Otherwise, we call is as a character cluster T . In addition, given a English sentence e_1^I consisting of I words $\{e, \dots, e_I\}$, $A_{E \to T}$ denotes a set of English-to-Thai language word alignments between e_1^I and t_1^J. In addition, since we concentrate on one-to-many alignments, $A_{E \to T}$, can be rewritten as a set of pairs a_i and $a_i = < e_i, t_j >$ noting a link between one single English *word* and several Thai *characters* that are formed to one cluster T

3.2 Monolingual Information

Due to the issue mentioned in section 2.1, we apply character clustering (CC) technique on target text in order to reduce the search space. After performing CC, it will yield several character clusters Twhich can be grouped together to obtain a larger unit which approaches the notion of word. However, for Thai and Lao, we do not only receive T but also S which usually has no meaning by itself. Moreover, Thai, Burmese and Lao writing rule does not allow S to stand alone in most case. Thus, we are required to develop various adapted versions of CC by using *orthographic insight* and *heuristic algorithm* to automatically pack the characters that reside in a pre-defined grammatical word list handcrafted by linguists. Then, all of single consonants in Thai Burmese, and Lao are forced to group with either left or right cluster due to the Thai writing system. The decision has been made by consulting on character co-occurrence statistics (unigram and bigram frequency).

Eventually, we obtain different character cluster alignments from the system trained on various CC approaches which effect to translation quality as shown in section 5.1

3.3 Bilingually-Guided Alignment Information

We begin with the sequence of small clusters resulting from previous character clustering process. These small clusters can be grouped together in order to form "word" using bilingually-guided alignment information. Generally, small *consecutive* clusters in target side which are aligned to the same word in source data should be grouped together. Therefore, this section describes our one-to-many alignment extraction process.

For one-to-many alignment, we applied processes similar to those in phrase extraction algorithm [7] which is described as follows.

With English sentence e_1^I and a Thai character cluster T_i, we apply IBM model 1-5 to extract word-to-cluster translation probability of source-to-target $P(t|e)$ and target-to-source $P(e|t)$. Next, the alignment points which have the highest probability are greedily selected from both $P(t|e)$ and $P(e|t)$. Figure 1.a and 1.b show examples of alignment points of source-to-target and target-to-source respectively. After that we selected the intersection of alignment pairs from both side. Then, additional alignment points are added according to the growing heuristic algorithm (grow additional alignment points, [8])

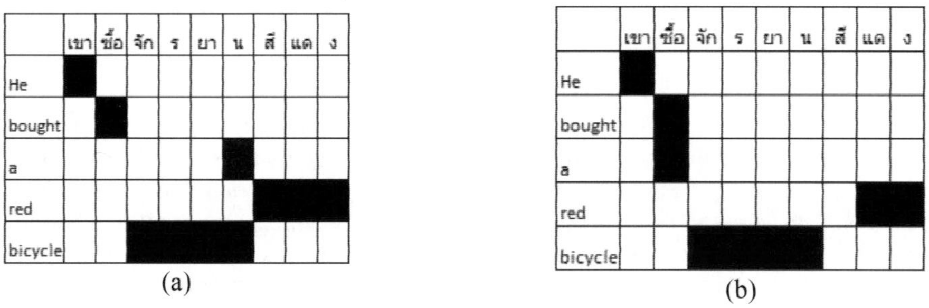

(a) (b)

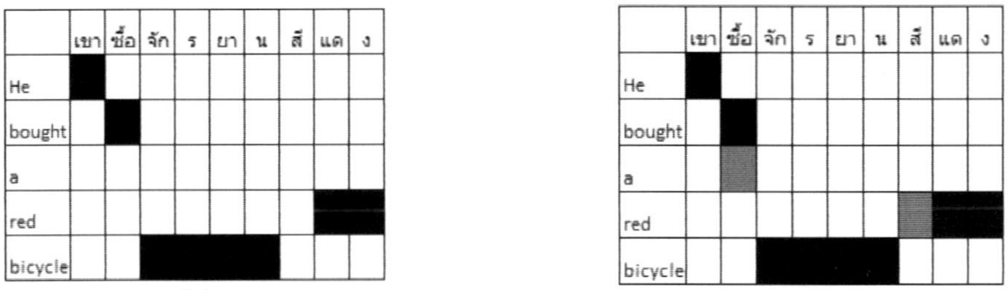

(c) (d)

Figure 1. The process of one-to-many alignment extraction (a) Source-to-Target word alignment (b) Target-to-Source word alignment (c) Intersection between (a) and (b). (d) Result of (c) after applying the growing heuristic algorithm.

Finally, we select *consecutive* clusters which are aligned to the same English word as candidates. From the Figure 1.d, we obtain these candidates (red, สีแดง) and (bicycle, จัก ร ยา น).

3.4 Character Cluster Repacking

Although the alignment information obtained from the previous step is very helpful for the PB-SMT task, there is still plenty of room to enhance the PB-SMT performance. One way of doing that is by using word repacking [4]. However, in this paper, we perform a character cluster repacking (CCR) instead of word. The main purpose of repacking technique is to group all small consecutive clusters (or word) in target side that frequently align with one word in source data. Repacking approaches uses two simple calculations which are a co-occurrence frequency $(COOC\ (e_i, T_i))$ and alignment confidence $(AC(\ a_i))$. $(COOC\ (e_i, T_i))$ is the number of times e_i and T_i co-occurr in the bilingual corpus [4] [9] and $AC(\ a_i)$ is a measure of how often the aligner aligns e_i and T_i when they co-occur. AC is defined as

$$AC(a_i) = \frac{C(a_i)}{COOC\ (e_i, T_i)}$$

where $C(a_i)$ denotes the number of alignments suggested by the previous-step word aligner.

Unfortunately, due to the limited memory in our experiment machine, we cannot find $COOC\ (e_i, T_i))$ for all possible $< e_i, T_i >$ pairs. We, therefore, slightly modified the above equation by finding $C(a_i)$ first. Secondly, we begin searching $COOC\ (e_i, T_i))$ from all possible alignments in a_i instead of finding all occurrences in corpus. By applying this modification, we eliminate $< e_i, T_i >$ pairs that co-occur together but *never* align to each other by previous-step aligner ($AC(a_i)$ equals to zero) so as to reduce the search space and complexity in our algorithm. Thirdly, we choose a_i with the highest $AC(a_i)$ and repack all character clusters in target side that similar to T_i to be a new single cluster unit. This process can be done repeatedly. However, we have run this task less than twice since there are few new cluster unit appear after two iterations have passed. The running example of this algorithm is described as follows

Suppose previous step aligner (GIZA++) produce two alignments $a_1 = < e_1, T_{1,2} >$ and $a_2 = < e_1, T_{1,2,3} >$ CCR will find the frequency of each aligment and number of times e_i and T_i co-occurr in the bilingual corpus ($COOC\ (e_1, T_{1,2})$ and $COOC\ (e_1, T_{1,2,3})$). Then, we will have $AC(a_i)$ score for each alignment and the aligment with the highest AC will be selected. The CCR will group these cluster (e.g. $T_{1,2}$) to be a new single cluster unit.

4 Experimental Setting

4.1 Data

The bilingual corpus[1] we used in our experiment is constructed from several sources and consists of multiple domains (e.g news, travel, article, entertainment, computer, etc.). We divided this corpus into three sets plus one additional test set as shown below

Data Set	No. of sentence pairs
Train	633,589
Dev	12,568
Test #1	3,426
Test #2	500

Table 1. Information of bilingual corpus

4.2 Tools and Evaluation

We evaluate our system in term of translation quality based on phrase-based SMT. Source sentences are sequence of English words while target sentences are sequences of Thai character clusters and each cluster size depends on which approach used in the experiment.

Translation model and language model are train based on the standard phrase-based SMT. Alignments of source (English word) and target (Thai Character Cluster) are extracted using GIZA++ [8] and the phrase extraction algorithm [7] is applied using Moses SMT package. We apply SRILM [10] to train the 3-gram language model of target side. We use the default parameter settings for decoding.

In testing process, we use another two test sets difference to the training data. Then we compared the translation result with the reference in term of BLEU score instead of F-score because of two main reasons. First, it is cumbersome to construct a reliable gold standard since their annotation schemes are different. Second, there is no strong correlation with SMT translation quality in terms of BLEU score [11]. Therefore, we re-segment the reference data (manually segmented) and the translation result data based on TCC. Some may concern about using TCC will lead to over estimation (higher than actual) due to the BLEU score is design based on word and not based on character. However, we used this BLEU score only for comparing translation quality among our experiments. Comparing to other SMT system still require running BLEU score based on the same segmentation guideline.

5 Results and Discussion

We conducted all experiments on PB-SMT task and reported the performance of PB-SMT system based on the BLEU measure. First, we use a method proposed in section 3.2 followed by the approach in section 3.3 in order to the receive first translation result set (without CCR). Then, we perform a method describe in 3.4 and also follow by approach in section 3.3 in order to receive another translation result set (with CCR). Table 1 shows the number of character clusters that are decreasing over time when several different character clustering approaches are applied.

[1] Currently, the corpus we used is a proprietary of NECTEC and does not available to public yet due to the licensing issue. However, for the educational purpose, this corpus is available upon by request.

	No. of Character Clusters (or word in original data)	
Approaches	**Without CCR**	**With CCR**
TCC (baseline)	9,862,271	7,187,862
TCC with language insight (TCC-FN)	8,953,437	6,636,305
TCC with language insight and heuristic algorithm (TCC-FN-B)	6,545,617	5,448,437
Manually segmented corpus (Upper bound)	5,311,648	N/A

Table 2. Number of character clusters when different character clustering approaches are applied on the bilingual corpus

Next, we present all translation results of PB-SMT task that using different character clustering approaches. Each training set is trained with only one character clustering method which are (1) TCC (baseline), (2) TCC with CCR, (3) TCC with only orthographic insight (TCC-FN), (4) TCC-Fn with CCR, (5) TCC with language insight and heuristic algorithm (TCC-FN-B) and (6) TCC-FN-B with CCR. The results are shown in Table 3.

	Test #1 BLEU		% of BLEU Improvement	Test #2 BLEU		% of BLEU Improvement
Approaches	Without CCR	With CCR		Without CCR	With CCR	
Baseline	37.12	40.13	8.11	36.78	38.87	5.68
TCC-FN	40.23	41.90	4.15	38.36	39.09	1.90
TCC-FN-B	44.69	44.43	-0.58	40.45	40.81	0.89
Upper bound	47.04	N/A	N/A	40.73	N/A	N/A

Table 3. BLEU score of each character clustering method and the percentage of the improvement when we applied CCR to the data

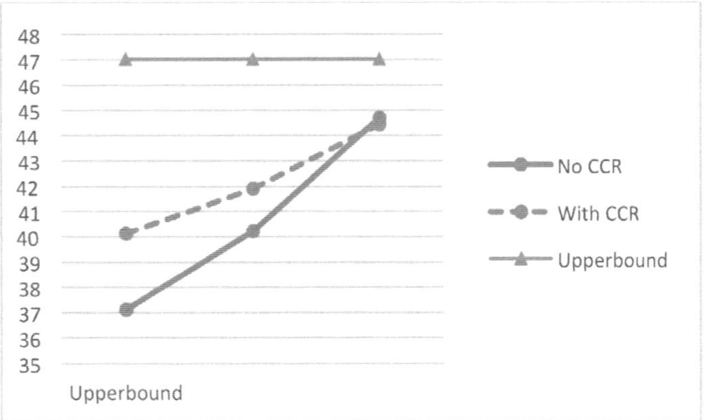

(a)

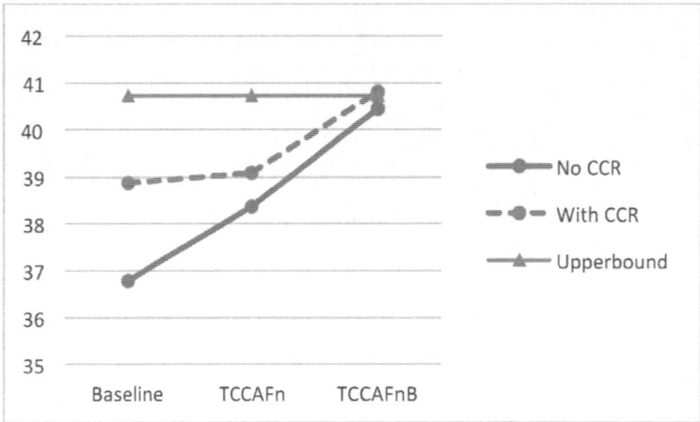

(b)

Figure 2. The BLEU score of (a) test set no.1 and (b) test set no.2

As seen from Table 3, when we apply the enhanced version of TCCs into the data with no CCR, BLEU score have gradually increased and almost reached the same level as original in test set #2. Furthermore, when CCR have been also deployed on each training dataset, the results of BLEU are also rise in the same manner with Without CCR method. There are certain significant points that should be noticed. First, CCR method is able to yield maximum of 8.1 % BLEU score increase. Second, when we apply the CCR methods and reach at some point, few improvement or minor degradation is received as shown in TCC-FN-B without and with CCR result. This is because the number of clusters produced by this character clustering algorithm is almost equal to number of words in original data as shown in Table 2 and this approach might suffer from the word boundary misplacement problem. Third, character clustering that use TCC with orthographic insight and heuristic algorithm combined with CCR approach is able to overcome the translation result from original data for the first time.

6 Conclusion

In this paper, we introduce a new approach for performing word segmentation task for SMT. Instead of starting with word level, we focus on character cluster level because this approach can perform on unsegmented corpus or multiple-guideline manually segmented corpus. First, we apply several adapted versions of TCC on unsegmented data. Next, we use a bilingual corpus to find alignment information for all $< e_i, T_i >$ pairs and then employ character cluster repacking method in order to form the large cluster of Thai characters.

We evaluate our approach on translation task on several sources and different domain corpus and report the result in BLEU metric. Our technique demonstrates that (1) we can achieve a dramatically improvement of BLUE as of 8.1% when we apply adapted TCC with CCR and (2) it is possible to overcome the manually segmented corpus by using TCC with orthographic insight and heuristic algorithm character clustering method combined with CCR. The advantage of our approach is a reduction in time and effot for construct a billinugal corpus because we are no longer required to manually segment all sentences in target side. In addition, our approach is able to cope with larger data information (e.g. 1 million sentences pairs) and adaptable to other language pairs (e.g. English-Chinese, English-Japanese or English-Lao)

7 Future Work

There are some tasks that can be added into this approaches. Firstly, we can make use of trigram (and n-gram) statistics, maximum entropy or conditional random field on heuristic algorithm in adapted version of TCC. Secondly, we might report the result from another language pair in order to confirm our approach.Thirdly, we can modify CCR process to be able to rerank the alignment confidence by using discriminative approach. Lastly, name entity recognition system can be integrated with our approach in order to improve the SMT performance.

Reference

[1] T. Teeramunkong, V. Sornlertlamvanich, T. Tanhermhong and W. Chinnan, "Character cluster based Thai information retrieval," in *IRAL '00 Proceedings of the fifth international workshop on on Information retrieval with Asian languages*, 2000.

[2] C. Kruengkrai, K. Uchimoto, J. Kazama, K. Torisawa, H. Isahara and C. Jaruskulchai, "A Word and Character-Cluster Hybrid Model for Thai Word Segmentation," in *Eighth International Symposium on Natural Lanugage Processing*, Bangkok, Thailand, 2009.

[3] Y. Liu, W. Che and T. Liu, "Enhancing Chinese Word Segmentation with Character Clustering," in *Chinese Computational Linguistics and Natural Language Processing Based on Naturally Annotated Big Data*, China, 2013.

[4] Y. Ma and A. Way, "Bilingually motivated domain-adapted word segmentation for statistical machine translation," in *Proceeding EACL '09 Proceedings of the 12th Conference of the European Chapter of the Association for Computational Linguistics, pp. 549-557*, Stroudsburg, PA, USA, 2009.

[5] J. Xu, R. Zens and H. Ney, "Do We Need Chinese Word Segmentation for Statistical Machine Translation?," *ACL SIGHAN Workshop 2004,* pp. 122-129, 2004.

[6] P. Limcharoen, C. Nattee and T. Theeramunkong, "Thai Word Segmentation based-on GLR Parsing Technique and Word N-gram Model," in *Eighth International Symposium on Natural Lanugage Processing*, Bangkok, Thailand, 2009.

[7] P. Koehn, F. J. Och and D. Marcu, "Statistical phrase-based translation," in *NAACL '03 Proceedings of the 2003 Conference of the North American Chapter of the Association for Computational Linguistics on Human Language Technology*, Stroudsburg, PA, USA, 2003.

[8] F. J. Och and H. Ney, "A systematic comparison of various statistical alignment models," *Computational Linguistics,* vol. 29, no. 1, pp. 19-51, 2003.

[9] I. D. Melamed, "Models of translational equivalence among words," *Computational Linguistics,* vol. 26, no. 2, pp. 221-249, 2000.

[10] "SRILM -- An extensible language modeling toolkit," in *Proceeding of the International Conference on Spoken Language Processing*, 2002.

[11] P.-C. Chang, M. Galley and C. D. Manning, "Optimizing Chinese word segmentation for machine translation performance," in *Proceedings of the Third Workshop on Statistical Machine Translation*, Columbus, Ohio, 2008.

A rule based approach for automatic clause boundary detection and classification in Hindi

Rahul Sharma, Soma Paul
Language Technology Research Centre, IIIT-Hyderabad, India
rahul.sharma@research.iiit.ac.in, soma@iiit.ac.in

Abstract

A complex sentence, divided into clauses, can be analyzed more easily than the complex sentence itself. We present here, the task of identification and classification of clauses in Hindi text. To the best of our knowledge, not much work has been done on clause boundary identification for Hindi, which makes this task more important. We have built a rule based system using linguistic cues such as coordinating conjunct, subordinating conjunct etc. Our system gives 91.53% and 80.63% F1-scores for identification and classification for finite clauses respectively, and 60.57% accuracy for non-finite clauses.

1 Introduction

A Clause is the minimal grammatical unit which can express a proposition. It is a sequential group of words, containing a verb or a verb group(verb and its auxiliary), and its arguments which can be explicit or implicit in nature (Ram and Devi, 2008). This makes a clause an important unit in language grammars and emphasis the need to identify and classify them as part of linguistic studies.

Analysis and processing of complex sentences is a far more challenging task as compared to a simple sentence. NLP applications often perform poorly as the complexity of the sentence increases. "It is impossible, to process a complex sentence if its clauses are not properly identified and classified according to their syntactic function in the sentence" (Leffa, 1998). The performance of many NLP systems like Machine Translation, Parallel corpora alignment, Information Extraction, Syntactic parsing, automatic summarization and speech applications etc improves by introducing clause boundaries in a sentence (e.g., Ejerhed, 1988; Abney, 1990; Leffa, 1998; Papageorgiou, 1997; Gadde et al., 2010).

We present a rule based method to automatically determine *'clause'* boundaries (beginnings and ends) in complex or compound sentences, and further categorize the identified clauses according to their types. Thus our system is made up of two parts, the first determines the boundaries of the clauses (clause identification) and the second part determines the type of the clause (Clause Classification). Rules for the system were framed by thoroughly analyzing the Hindi-Urdu treebank (Palmer et al., 2009). This provides significant insights for the task as clause boundaries can be inferred from the dependency relations marked in dependency trees. The rules devised for our system have minimum dependency on linguistic resources, only part of speech (POS) and chunk information of lexical items is used with a fair performance of the system. As far as we know, not much work has been done on clause boundary identification for Hindi and this makes this task more significant.

This paper is structured as follows: In Section 2, we talk about clause and its types. In Section 3, we discuss the related works that has been done earlier on clause identification and classification. Section 4 describes the data flow of our system and rules for identifying and classification of a clause. Section 5 outlines the system performance. In section 6, some issues related clause identification are discussed. In Section 7, we conclude and talk about future works in this area.

Proceedings of the 5th Workshop on South and Southeast Asian NLP, 25th International Conference on Computational Linguistics, pages 102–111, Dublin, Ireland, August 23-29 2014.

2 Clause and its Types

As defined in introduction, a clause is a group of words consisting of a verb (or a verb group) and its arguments(explicit and implicit), and forms part of a sentence. Depending on the type of the verb, a clause is classified as a finite clause that contains a finite verb and non-finite clause that contains a non-finite verb. For example:

(1) raam khaanaa khaakar soyaa
Ram food having+eaten sleep+past
'Having eaten food, Ram slept.'

In example (1), 'raam soyaa' is a finite clause; contains 'soyaa' finite verb, and 'khaanaa khaakar' is a non-finite clause; contains 'khaakar' non-finite verb.
We come across two types of clauses in a complex sentence:

1. Main clause, which is an independent clause, is also called Superordinate clause. It is always a finite clause in a sentence.
2. Subordinate clause, which is dependent on the main clause. It can be both finite and non-finite in a sentence.

For our task we have divided subordinate clause into five different types, which are complement clause, adverbial clause, relative clause, coordinate clause and non-finite clause (discussed shortly). Subordinate clauses can be nested or non-nested depending on a sentence. Nested here means one clause is embedded in another clause. For example,

(2) raam jo khela , ghar gayaa
Ram who play+past , home go+past
'Ram who played , went home.'

In example (2) the two clauses are: 1) raam ghar gayaa 2) jo khela. The second clause is embedded in 'raam ghar gayaa'.
Various kinds of subordinate clauses are discussed below:

(a) **Complement Clause**: These clauses are introduced by the subordinator 'ki' (that) and generally follow the verb of main clause (Koul, 2009) and occur as a finite clause in a sentence. For example:

(3) yaha sach hai ki mohan bimaara hai
It true is that Mohan sick is
'It is true that Mohan is sick'

'ki mohan bimaar hai' is a Complement Clause and 'ki' is a complementizer in example (3). It must be noted that 'complement clause' is also an argument of the main clause verb. So, in example (3), the main clause is 'yaha sach hai ki mohan bimaara hai', which contains the complement clause 'ki mohan bimaara hai', in it. This is considered to be a special case where a clause comes as an argument of a verb and becomes a part of that verb clause. We have handled this type of construction separately (discussed in section 4).

(b) **Relative Clause**: Relative clauses which are also finite in nature occur as a modifier of verb's argument and contain a relative pronoun (Koul, 2009). Such clause can be either nested or non-nested.

(4) vaha ladkaa jo khel rahaa thaa ghar gayaa
that boy who play+past+conti. home go+past
'That boy who was playing went home'

In example (4), the nested relative clause is 'jo khel rahaa thaa' (who was playing) with 'jo' as a relative marker. 'jo' modifies 'vo', the argument of the verb 'gayaa'.
Another example of this, is:

(5) raam ghar gayaa jo khel rahaa thaa
Ram home go+past who play+past+conti
'Raam who was playing went home'

In example (5) relative clause 'jo khel rahaa thaa' is a non-nested one.

(c) **Adverbial Clause**: These clauses are determined based on their adverbial markers/function in a sentence (Koul, 2009). Manner, purpose, cause, condition etc. form the types of adverbial clauses. We take this type of clauses as the modifier of the verb's modifier. These clauses are present as a finite clause in sentence. For example:

(6) jaise vaha jaaegaa waise main jaaungaa
the way he go+fut. that way I go+fut
'I will go the way he will go'

In example (6) 'jaise vaha jaaegaa' is an Adverbial Clause with 'jaise' as the (manner) Adverbial Marker. Here 'waise' is the modifier of the verb 'jaaungaa' and 'jaise vaha jaaegaa' modifies it.
It may be noted that we consider clauses that are modifiers of verb's modifiers as adverbial clauses and clauses that are modify arguments of verbs as relative clauses.

(d) **Coordinate Clause**: It is one of the independent finite clauses in a sentence that has the same status as the other clauses, and is introduced by a coordinating conjunction (Koul, 2009). For example:

(7) main ghar jaaungaa aur raam dillii jaayegaa
I home go+fut. and Ram delhi go+fut
'I will go home and Raam will go to Delhi'

'mai ghar jaaungaa' and 'raam dillii jaayegaa' are two independent clauses with the same status in example (7). And for our work we consider both clause as coordinate clauses, and the coordinating conjunct is not taken to be part of any of the two clauses. There is thus no hierarchy in these clauses. When there are more than one coordinating conjunct in a sentence, clause boundary identification becomes more complex because of nesting of the coordinate clause. This is illustrated using example (8).

(8) raam ne kaam kiyaa aur khaanaa khaayaa lekin siitaa khelii
Ram+erg work do+past and food eat+past but Sita play+past
'Ram did the work and ate food but Sita played'

In such examples there is more than one way to mark the coordinate clauses:

- ((raam ne kaam kiyaa) aur (khaanaa khaayaa)) lekin (siitaa khelii)
- (raam ne kaam kiyaa) aur ((khaanaa khaayaa) lekin (siitaa khelii))
- ((raam ne kaam kiyaa) aur (khaanaa khaayaa) lekin (siitaa khelii))

'(' and ')' are symbols to denote the start and end of the clause. As we can see there is more than one output possible for the given example. Our system only marks the linear boundary of the clause in a sentence. Nesting in more than two coordinate clauses is not handled by it. So for the example (8), our output is: (raam ne kaam kiyaa) aur (khaanaa khaayaa) lekin (siitaa khelii)
--It must be noted that we do not take coordinating conjuncts as part of any of the clauses, it is conjoining. However subordinate marker are taken to be part of clause.

(e) **Non-finite Clause**: These clauses are dependent clause in a sentence which contain non-finite verb.

(9) raam khaanaa khaakar aur paani peekar ghar gayaaa
Ram food eat and water drink home go+past
'Raam after eating food and drinking water, went home'

In above example (9), two clauses, 'khaanaa khaakar' and 'paani peekar' are non-finite as they contain non-finite verbs.

--In Hindi, We come across some complex cases where one type of clause is embedded in another type clause. For example:

(10) raam jisne khaanaa khaayaa aur paani piyaa, ghar gayaaa
Ram who food eat+past and water drink+past home go+past
'Raam who ate food and drank water, went home'

In example (10) relative clause and coordinate clause overlap with each other. The coordinate clauses are: (jisne khaanaa khaayaa) and (paani piyaa), and relative clause is : (jisne khaanaa khaayaa aur paani piyaa). So our system will mark the clause boundaries as: (raam *((jisne khaanaa khaayaa) aur (paani piyaa))* ghar gayaaa).

3 Related works

Studies in identifying clauses date back to (Ejerhed, 1988) work, where they showed how automatic clause boundary identification in discourse can benefit a parser's performance. However her experiments could detect only basic clauses. Later (Abney, 1990) used clause filter as part of his CASS parser. Papageorgiou (1997) used hand crafted rules to identify clause boundaries in a text. (Leffa, 1998) is another rule based method which was implemented in an English-Portuguese MT system.
Some more recent works in this area are: (Puscasu, 2004), in which she proposed a multilingual method of combining language independent ML techniques with language specific rules to detect clause boundaries in unrestricted texts. The rules identify the finite verbs and clause boundaries not included in learning process. Ram and Devi (2008) proposed a hybrid based approach for detecting clause boundaries in a sentence. They have used a CRF based system which uses different linguistic cues. After identifying the clause boundaries they run an error analyzer module to find false boundary markings, which are then corrected by the rule based system, built using linguistic clues. (Ghosh et al., 2010) is another rule based system for clause boundary identification for Bengali, where they use machine learning approach for clause classification and dependency relations between verb and its argument to find clause boundaries. Dhivya et al. (2012) use dependency trees from maltparser and the dependency tag-set with 11 tags to identify clause boundaries. Similar to (Dhivya et al., 2012), Sharma et al. (2013) showed how implicit clause information present in dependency trees can be used to extract clauses in sentences. Their system have reported 94.44% accuracy for Hindi.Gadde et al. (2010) reported improvement in parser performance by introducing automatic clause information in a sentence for Hindi in 'Improving data driven dependency parsing using clausal information'. However their approach for identifying clause information has not been discussed. Thus a comparison is not possible here.
Our work is similar to that of (Leffa, 1998) in that both first mark clause boundaries and then classify the clauses into various types. Both use linguistic cues such as coordinating conjuncts, subordinating conjunction, surrounding context, however , while (Leffa, 1998) use POS information and valency of the verbs , we use POS tags and chunks as the only linguistic information.

4 Methodology

We propose a rule based system which first identifies the clause(s) in the input sentence and marks the *'clause start position'* (**CSP**) and *'clause end position'* (**CEP**) with brackets and then it classifies the identified clauses into one of the proposed types mentioned in section 2. Hindi usually follows the SOV word order, so ends of the clauses can be found by just using verb information, in most of the cases. The language also has explicit relative pronouns, subordinating conjuncts, coordinate conjunctions etc. which serve as cues that help to identify clause boundaries and the type of the clauses. Thus our system uses lists of coordinate conjunctions, relative markers and adverbial clause markers (see Appendix A and Appendix B for the lists). These lists were created using (Kachru, 2006). Further, the rules for our system have been framed based on our in depth analysis of a section of the Hindi treebank (Palmer et al., 2009). Apart from the lexical cues we have also used POS tag and chunk information to frame these rules.

4.1 Algorithm

Our system consists of two parts, the first part determines the boundaries of the clauses (clause identification) and the second part determines the type of the clause (clause classification). Identification of clause boundaries is further divided into two tasks, i.e. to find the beginnings and the ends of clauses. Then, the sentences with the clause boundaries marked are processed by the clause classification component, and are assigned to one of the clause types--main clause, complement clause, adverbial clause, relative clause, coordinate clause and non-finite clause. Figures 1 shows the data flow of our system, components of which have been discussed in detail, further in this section.

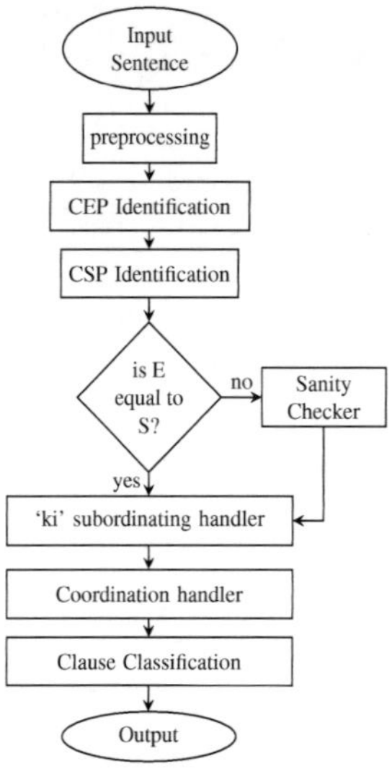

In this Data flow of our system, E represents number of *'clause end position'* and S represents number of *'clause start position'* marked by our system.

Figure 1: Data Flow

4.1.1 Preprocessing

In this module, input sentences are processed and each lexical item is assigned a POS tag, and chunk information . For example:
Input sentence:

(11) raam soyaa.
Ram sleep+past
'Ram slept.'

Output:

```
1     ((    NP
1.1   raam NNP
      ))
2     ((    VGF
2.1   soyaa VM
2.2   .     SYM
      ))
```

--Here 'NP' and 'VGF' are the chunk tags, and POS tags 'NNP' and 'VM' stand for Noun and Verb respectively (Bharati et al., 2007; Bharati et al., 2009) .

4.1.2 CEP Identification

The unmarked word order of Hindi mainly being SOV, the verb is taken to be the end of the clause. In cases where a sentence does not end with a verb , the end of sentence is taken as end of the clause. This helps to handle instances of scrambling and ellipses. For example:

(12) siitaa ghar jaa rahii hai aur giitaa bhii.
Sita home go+present+cont and Gita also
'Sita is going home and so does Gita.'

In example (12), there is an ellipses of the verb 'jaa rahii hai' in the second clause 'giitaa bhii'. In cases like this, our system marks the verb as end of the first clause and sentence end as end of the second clause. The marked boundaries in the sentence after this module will be: 'siitaa ghar jaa rahii hai) aur gitaa bhi)'.

4.1.3 CSP Identification

We have made two modules to find the start of the clauses; one identifies the start of finite clauses and the other identifies the start of non-finite clauses. As we have mentioned a clause is a finite or non-finite, depending on the verb in that clause. So we have used chunk information which gives the verb type (finite or non-finite). Both these modules are independent of each other, so running them parallel will not affect the system, and this helps to speed up the system processing.

4.1.3.1 CSP for finite clause

This module uses linguistic cues such as relative markers (*jo* 'that/who', *jisane* 'who'), coordinating conjuncts (*aur* 'and', *lekin* 'but') and so on, to identify the start of clauses. It may be noted that the immediate context of cues is also taken into account at times. For instance, a coordinating conjunct 'aur' (and) in a sentence marks the start of the clause only if it is preceded by a verb, whereas the subordinating conjunct 'ki' (that) always marks the start of a clause. After the start/s of clause/s in a sentence are identified, the module checks whether the beginning of the sentence is marked as a clause start, and marks it as clause beginning if it is not already marked. For example:

(13) raam jo khel rahaa tha nahii aayaa.
Ram who play+past+conti. not come+present
'Ram who was playing did not come.'

In example (13), first our module identifies 'jo' relative marker and marks it as a start of the clause 'jo khel rahaa tha', and then, marks the beginning of the sentence as the start of the other clause 'raam nahii aayaa'. After this, the boundaries marked in example (12) will be : (raam (**jo** khel rahaa tha) nahii aayaa.)

It needs a mention here that the boundaries marked in the previous module are also included in the current module's output.

4.1.3.2 CSP for non-finite clause

Non-finite verbs do not have Tense-Aspect-Mood(TAM) information, they take optional arguments which are not specific in number. In Hindi, we don't find any cues to detect where a non-finite clause starts. So to identify the start of a non-finite clause, we have built templates/regular expressions on chunks in a sentence, and whenever a pattern in a sentence matches the template, we mark that as a start of the clause. Following example shows the working of this module:

(14) raam ghar para jaakar khaanaa khaayega.
Ram home to after going food eat+future
'After going to home, Ram will eat food.'

In the example (14), 'ghar para' and 'raam' are two separate chunks that precede the non-finite verb 'jaakar'. As per the template, if a 'para' marked NP chunk follows the nominative NP and immediately precedes the 'jaakar' type non-finite verb, the NP chunk marks the start of the 'jaakar' non-finite clause.

4.1.4 Sanity Checker

In case the number of CSPs is not equal to the number of CEPs in a sentence, the Sanity Checker module comes into play. It iterates through the CSP identifier's output for the sentence and marks the omitted CSPs. For example:

(15) raam ghar gayaa, shyaam nahii gayaa.
Ram home go+past, Shyam not go+past.
'Ram went home, Shyam did not go.'

The absence of a coordinator between the two clauses 'raam ghar gayaa' and 'shyaam nahii gayaa', in Example (15) can lead to potential error of ommision of the CSP for the second clause 'shyaam nahii gayaa'. The output of such a sentence would be:

'(raam ghar gayaa) shyaam nahii gayaa.)'

As we can see here, the CSP for the clause 'shyaam nahii gayaa' is omitted. On detecting such an error, the sanity checker would iterate the sentence and mark the omitted CSP, and the output would then be:

'(raam ghar gayaa) (shyaam nahii gayaa.)'

4.1.5 'ki' complementizer handler

As mentioned earlier, 'ki' complement clause is an argument of the main verb and part of its main verb clause. Thus this modules executes, and identifies 'ki' complementizer and its clause in the sentence, and modifies the CEP of its parent clause. Example (16) explains this further.

(16) raam ne kahaa ki tum ghar jaao
ram+erg say+past that you home go
'Ram said that you go home.'

The input for the sentence 'raam ne kahaa ki tum ghar jaao' that this module receives would be:
'(raam ne kahaa) (ki tum ghar jaao)'
The 'ki' complementizer module iterates this input and identifies the 'ki' complement clause and its CEP. It then modifies this input by moving the CEP, immediate before 'ki' complementizer to the position immediate after the CEP of 'ki' complement clause. The modified sentence will be:
'(raam ne kahaa (ki tum ghar jaao))'

4.1.6 Coordination handler

This module handles embedded coordinated clauses in complex sentence where they fall within the scope of a complementizer, a relative marker or an adverbial marker. It makes a new CSP for these clauses immediately before the complementizer, relative marker or adverbial marker and a new CEP after the CEP of the last embedded coordinate clause. For example:

(17) raam jisne khaanaa khaayaa aur khel khelaa ghar gayaa
Ram who+rel. food eat+past and game play+past home go+past
'Ram who ate food and played a game, went home.'

Given the output for the example (17), this module identifies the 'jisne' the relative marker and inserts a new CSP immediately before it. It also inserts the CEP for their coordinate clauses after the CEP of the last embedded coordinate clause 'khel khelaa'. The output would be:
(raam ((jisne khaanaa khaayaa) aur (khel khelaa)) ghar gayaa.)

4.1.7 Clause Classification

Once the clause boundaries are identified, the output is passed on to the clause classifier where it assign them to one of the clause classes--main clause, complement clause, adverbial clause, relative clause, coordinate clause and non-finite clause. If a sentence has only one clause, it is classified as the main clause. However given more than one clause in a sentence, it iterates the sentence and assign classes to the clauses based on cues such as relative markers, coordinating conjuncts etc. Verb type also helps to deduce whether a clause is non-finite or not. It then checks for potential omission and marks the omitted clauses as main clause, since they fail to fall under any of the other five classes.
In example (17) ,conjunction 'aur' helps to mark the two adjacent clauses--'jisne khaanaa khaayaa' and 'khel khelaa' as coordinate clauses. Relative marker 'jisne' helps to identify 'jisne khaanaa khaayaa aur khel khelaa' as a relative clause and the clause that remained 'raam ghar gayaa' is taken as main clause.

5 Evaluation and Results

As mentioned earlier identification of clause boundary for finite and non-finite clauses are independent, we have evaluated them separately. Finite clause mainly have 5 types; Main clause, Complement Clause, Adverbial Clause, Relative Clause and Coordinate clause and evaluation has been done on them.

5.1 Results for Finite Clause

A fresh set of 100 sentences average length of 16 words is randomly selected from a section of the Hindi treebank. This section is different from the section from which the sentences were chosen for analysis. The selected sentences have 217 clauses. An analysis of the category of these clauses is presented in Table 1. This evaluation set was annotated manually at the level of clause boundary and their type, to evaluate performance of the system. As mentioned earlier, five types of tags ; Main clause, Complement Clause, Adverbial Clause, Relative Clause and Coordinate clause, were used to annotate them.

Clause Type	%
Main Clause	33.79
Coordinate Clause	31.48
Complement Cl ause	24.07
Relative Clause	9.72
Adverbial Clause	0.9

Table 1: Clause distribution table.

5.1.1 Results of Clause Boundary Identification

For the evaluation of Clause Boundary identification, a clause is taken to be marked correctly iff its CSP and CEP are marked correctly. A sentence with more than one clause may have correctly marked clauses as well as incorrectly marked clauses. We evaluate the task at clause level, not at sentence level. The precision and Recall for clause boundary identification are **91.30%** and **91.78%** respectively.

5.1.2 Results of Clause Classification

For the evaluation of Clause Classification, we take a clause to be correctly classified if its boundaries as well as type is marked correctly. So, clauses with incorrectly marked boundaries are considered wrongly classified. The precision and Recall for clause classification are **80.28%** and **81.04%** respectively. Table (2) shows the results for different clause categories.

Clause Type	Precision%	Recall%	F1 score%
Main Clause	77.90	91.78	84.27
Coordiante Clasue	80.00	70.58	74.99
Complement Clause	92.30	92.30	92.30
Relative Clause	93.33	66.66	77.77
Adverbial Clause	100	50	66.66

Table 2: Results of Clause Classification

5.2 Results for Non-finite Clause

A set of 96 sentences containing 104 non-finite clauses was taken for the evaluation. It was found that end of all non-finite clause were identified but there were 63 clauses whose start boundary were identified. The accuracy of the system in identifying non-finite clauses is 60.57%.

6 Error Analysis and Discussion

While evaluating our system, we come across some constructions which were not handled by it. which are:

1. Ellipses of verb: when a verb is omitted in a sentence then it is not possible for our system to mark boundaries correctly. For example:

    (18) raam ne kitaab <V> aur maine kavitaa padhii
    Ram+erg book <read+past> and I+erg poem read+past
    'Ram read a book and I read a poem'

    In example (18), there is an ellipses of the verb 'padhi' in the clause 'raam ne kitaab'. Thus, though the sentence has two clauses–'raam ne kitaab' and 'maine kavitaa padhii', our system incorrectly identifies the whole sentence as one clause due to the ellipses of the verb (denoted by <V>).

2. Scrambling in the usual word order, which is SOV in Hindi, is likely to induce incorrect identification of the clauses in our system. For Example:

    (19) ghar gayaa raam, vaha bolaa.
    home go+past Ram, he say+past
    'He said Ram went home'

In example (19), Our system is unable to identify the clause boundaries correctly for any of the two clauses, 'ghar gayaa raam' and 'ghar gayaa raam,vaha bolaa', due to scrambling in the word order. Its output for the sentence is '(ghar) (gayaa raam, vaha bolaa)', though the output should be '((ghar (gayaa raam,) vaha bolaa)'.

3. Missing subordinate conjunction 'ki' in a sentence also leads to incorrect identification of clause boundaries by our system. For example:

   (20) raam ne kahaa tum ghar jaao
   Ram+erg say+past you home go
   'Ram said you go home'

   The missing subordinate conjunction 'ki' in example (20) leads to incorrect marking of the clause boundaries as: '(raam ne kahaa) (tum ghar jaao)'. The correct clause boundaries for the sentence are '(raam ne kahaa (tum ghar jaao))'.

4. Templates used for identification of non-finite clauses are not much efficient. They are more specific and need to be more general.

7 Conclusion and Future Work

We have discussed our work on clause boundary identification and classification in Hindi and the issues pertaining to them, in the course of this paper. Clausal information in a sentence is known to improve the performance of many NLP systems, thus the need for this task. While a larger section of the Hindi dependency treebank from the HUTB project was analyzed to formulate the rules for the task. The system, showing a satisfactory performance for finite clauses in terms of F1 scores of 91.53% for clause boundary identification and 80.63% for clause Classification, while giving inadequate results for non-finite clauses with 60.57% accuracy. We would like to mention that at present our system doesn't handle classification of different instances of 'to' (else, then, or etc.) and of coordination where a punctuation serves as a coordinator. In the future we intend to incorporate this in our system. Further, since this task is a promising resource for NLP systems such as Machine Translation, Text-to-Speech and so on, and can contribute to their better performance, adopting an ML approach for this task seems quite a favorable prospect as a future work. (Gadde et al., 2010) report that even minimal clause boundary identification information leverages the performance of their system. We would like to test the performance of our system in terms of leveraging the performance of other NLP systems.

References

Steven Abney. 1990. Rapid incremental parsing with repair. pages 1–9.

Akshar Bharati, Rajeev Sangal, and Dipti M Sharma. 2007. Ssf: Shakti standard format guide. pages 1–25.

Akshara Bharati, Dipti Misra Sharma, Samar Husain, Lakshmi Bai, Rafiya Begam, and Rajeev Sangal. 2009. Anncorra: Treebanks for indian languages, guidelines for annotating hindi treebank.

R Dhivya, V Dhanalakshmi, M Anand Kumar, and KP Soman. 2012. Clause boundary identification for tamil language using dependency parsing. pages 195–197. Springer.

Eva I Ejerhed. 1988. Finding clauses in unrestricted text by finitary and stochastic methods. pages 219–227. Association for Computational Linguistics.

Phani Gadde, Karan Jindal, Samar Husain, Dipti Misra Sharma, and Rajeev Sangal. 2010. Improving data driven dependency parsing using clausal information. pages 657–660. Association for Computational Linguistics.

Aniruddha Ghosh, Amitava Das, and Sivaji Bandyopadhyay. 2010. Clause identification and classification in bengali. In *23rd International Conference on Computational Linguistics*, page 17.

Yamuna Kachru. 2006. *Hindi*, volume 12. John Benjamins Publishing Company.

Omkar Nath Koul. 2009. *Modern Hindi Grammar.* Indian Institute of Language Studies.

Vilson J Leffa. 1998. Clause processing in complex sentences. volume 1, pages 937–943.

Martha Palmer, Rajesh Bhatt, Bhuvana Narasimhan, Owen Rambow, Dipti Misra Sharma, and Fei Xia. 2009. Hindi syntax: Annotating dependency, lexical predicate-argument structure, and phrase structure. pages 14–17.

Harris V Papageorgiou. 1997. Clause recognition in the framework of alignment. pages 417–426.

Georgiana Puscasu. 2004. A multilingual method for clause splitting.

R Vijay Sundar Ram and Sobha Lalitha Devi. 2008. Clause boundary identification using conditional random fields. In *Computational Linguistics and Intelligent Text Processing*, pages 140–150. Springer.

Rahul Sharma, Soma Paul, Riyaz Ahmad Bhat, and Sambhav Jain. 2013. Automatic clause boundary annotation in the hindi treebank.

Appendix A : Conjuction List

aur 'and'	athwaa 'or'	yaa 'or'	evam 'and'	para 'but'	magar 'but'
lekin 'but'	kintu 'but'	parantu 'but'	tathaa 'and'	jabki 'eventhough'	va 'and'
isalie 'therfore'	kyunki 'because'				

Appendix B : List of Relative (and Coorelative) Markers

jo 'who'	jiskaa 'whose'	jiske 'whose'	jiski 'whose'	jisko 'whose'
jisse 'from which'	jise 'who'	jinse 'from whom'	jinhen 'to whom'	jinhone 'who'
jinmen 'where'	jaba 'when'	jisse 'from which'	jise 'who'	

Author Index